Violence and Crime in the Schools

Violence and Crime in the Schools

Edited by

Keith Baker
Department of Education

Robert J. Rubel
Southwest Texas State University

LexingtonBooks
D.C. Heath and Company
Lexington, Massachusetts
Toronto

Library of Congress Cataloging in Publication Data

Main entry under title:

Violence and crime in the schools.

    A selection from a series of papers commissioned by the National Institute of Education to serve as a companion vol. to its 1977 report, Violent schools, safe schools.
    Bibliography: p.
    1. School violence—United States—Case studies. I. Baker, Keith. II. Rubel, Robert J. III. National Institute of Education. Violent schools, safe schools.

LB3013.3.V56   371.5'8   79-5325
ISBN 0-669-03389-8

Copyright ©1980 by D.C. Heath and Company

All rights reserved. No part of this publication may be reproduced or transmitted in any form or by any means, electronic or mechanical, including photocopy, recording, or any information storage or retrieval system, without permission in writing from the publisher.

Published simultaneously in Canada

Printed in the United States of America

International Standard Book Number: 0-669-03389-8

Library of Congress Catalog Card Number: 79-5325

Contents

	Foreword	vii
Part I	*Setting the Stage*	1
Chapter 1	Crime and Punishment in the Schooling Process: A Historical Analysis *Joan Newman* and *Graeme Newman*	3
Chapter 2	Extent, Perspectives, and Consequences of Violence and Vandalism in Public Schools *Robert J. Rubel*	17
Part II	*Schools as Victims*	29
Chapter 3	Student Behavior, the Depersonalization of Blame, and the Society of Victims *Daniel L. Duke*	31
Chapter 4	A Person-Environment Fit Model of School Crime and Disruption *Richard A. Kulka, David W. Mann,* and *David M. Klingel*	49
Chapter 5	School-Community Relations Network Strategies *Jacqueline R. Scherer*	61
Chapter 6	Reflections on the Rights of Students and the Rise of School Violence *Robert J. Rubel* and *Arthur H. Goldsmith*	71
Chapter 7	Teachers—A New Endangered Species? *Alfred M. Bloch, M.D.* and *Ruth Reinhardt Bloch*	81
Chapter 8	Crime and Disruption Among Appalachian Students: A Personal Response *Sarah J. Snider*	91
Part III	*Schools as Contributors*	99
Chapter 9	Disciplinary Roles in American Schools *Daniel L. Duke* and *Adrienne M. Meckel*	101
Chapter 10	The Creation of Deviant Behavior in American High Schools *John C. Phillips*	115

	Chapter 11	School Crime and Conduct Disorder *Herbert C. Quay*	129
	Chapter 12	Deviant Subcultures and the Schools *James William Coleman*	139
	Chapter 13	The Social Patterning of Deviant Behaviors in School *Vincent Tinto*	151
	Chapter 14	Perspectives on Absenteeism in High Schools: Multiple Explanations for an Epidemic *Beatrice F. Birman* and *Gary Natriello*	167
	Part IV	*Vandalism: A Special Case*	179
	Chapter 15	Intrinsic Rewards in School Crime *Mihaly Csikszentmihalyi* and *Reed Larson*	181
	Chapter 16	Aesthetic Theory, Perceived Control, and Social Identity: Toward an Understanding of Vandalism *Vernon L. Allen* and *David B. Greenberger*	193
	Chapter 17	Preventable Property Damage: Vandalism and Beyond *Richard F. Thaw II*	209
	Chapter 18	Understanding Vandalism *S.D. Vestermark, Jr.* and *Peter D. Blauvelt*	219
	Chapter 19	Vandalism in High Schools: An Exploratory Discussion *Michael H. Ducey*	229
	Chapter 20	A Preparadigmatic Field: A Review of Research on School Vandalism *April Zweig* and *Michael H. Ducey*	243
		Bibliography	253
		Index	285
		About the Contributors	289
		About the Editors	295

Foreword

During the last decade, public opinion polls have found that the problem of order and personal safety within our nation's schools consistently leads the list of concerns about education. It is also a serious concern for teachers and school administrators; recent studies show that such individuals are frequently victims of a wide range of violent and criminal acts occurring in schools.

Editorials have been written and congressional hearings held on the problem of maintaining discipline and order in our schools. In 1974 Congress required the Deparment of Health, Education and Welfare (HEW) to study the extent of crime and disruption in our schools. The study was performed by the National Institute of Education and resulted in the 1977 report *Violent Schools —Safe Schools: The Safe School Study Report to Congress (Safe School Study)*, which documented the nature and extent of crime in schools.

While the *Safe School Study* provided massive documentation of the problem, it did not give much information that could expand our understanding of the root causes of student misbehavior. For that, it will not suffice to have data on different kinds of school crime, or even on how in-school crime rates may have changed over time. We will be able to plan rational and effective strategies to combat such crimes only when we understand *why* they occur.

In order to supply a companion volume to the *Safe School Study* effort— a companion that would set forth the basis for the understanding noted above— the Office of the Deputy Assistant Secretary for Planning and Evaluation/ Education in HEW commissioned a series of papers that would explore a wide variety of possible causes of school crime. This book contains material from that series.

The most striking feature of these papers is their diversity, for this suggests that complete understanding of school crime—and therefore of its solution—is multifaceted. Indeed, school crime itself may well not be a simple, singular phenomenon. For example, preventing criminal or disruptive acts motivated by a desire to change the physical appearance of the school (discussed in the chapter by Allen and Greenberger) is a problem that differs greatly from preventing disruption that arises from misinterpreting the symbolic meaning of the behavior of subcultural groups (discussed in the chapter by Snider).

Moreover, the diversity of these theories of school-based crime will surely challenge readers' preconceived ideas, for regardless of the point of view an individual may bring to this book, one or more of the authors will shed new light on the problem. The theories also differ considerably in the extent to which they are concerned with the practical matter of immediately reducing crime in schools. Some provide almost a step-by-step course in crime reduction, while the abstract nature of others is far removed from direct application.

Since the ultimate test of any theory of a social problem is the practical benefit derived from it, we are pleased to note that this first effort has produced some ideas of immediate practical value. However, we should not be too concerned that some of the theories are not yet capable of such implementation. We are at a very early stage in developing our understanding of school crime. It would certainly be premature to decide now which particular concept will ultimately prove most fruitful in increasing our sense of the problem and how to solve it.

It is said that nothing is as practical as good theory. In the past, the problem in this area has been finding a good theory. We hope that the wide-ranging ideas contained in this book will constitute part of a solid theoretical foundation for the study of school-based crime.

Michael O'Keefe,
Deputy Assistant Secretary
for Planning and Evaluation/
Education

**Part I
Setting the Stage**

1 Crime and Punishment in the Schooling Process: A Historical Analysis

Joan Newman and
Graeme Newman

Introduction

It is popularly believed today that the "crisis of discipline" in our schools is something special to this turbulent age. Michael Berger (1974) suggests that school violence is simply one manifestation of the modern violent urban society. Yet we must be aware that American society has been urbanized at least since the beginning of the eighteenth century. Furthermore, it is not at all clear that the present time is generally any more characterized by turbulence than were other historical periods. In fact, our age is quite possibly less violent (Sagan 1974) or at least no more violent than yesterday (Kirkham, Levy, and Grotty 1970). Certainly, as far as our treatment of children is concerned, there is little doubt that they are subject to far less violence today than they were 100 years ago (DeMause 1974; Sanders 1970).

Berger (1974) advances another popular theory of the cause of school violence. According to him, in general, violence originates among those who have no stake in society, and students are therefore particularly prone to it; for school systems typically punish them by fiat and deny their civil rights. Underlying this theory is the assumption that some kind of inherent relationship exists between the violent behavior of pupils and the disciplinary practices of the school.

It is our aim to shed light on both these assumptions from a historical point of view. We recognize that such an investigation is fraught with difficulties, mainly because of the paucity of data. Indeed, it is possible to gather some facts about violence in contemporary schools. For example, in 1974-1975 the New York City school budget allocated $8.4 million for security systems because between 1971 and 1972 reported attacks on teachers increased from 285 to 541 (National Schools Public Relations Association 1973). According to today's standards for crime statistics, such data are limited, but even the equivalents of these are simply not available in the historical materials we have investigated; those include school district reports, circulars, reports of special commissions, and so on. As recently as twenty years ago, this type of statistic was not systematically collected; schools or teachers (or students) were simply not asked to report assaults, attacks, or crimes. Thus, we were able only to search the existing collection of anecdotal material on school violence through history. Although the incidence of violence in the past may therefore appear low, the incidence of violence today is not necessarily higher. Rather, that violence may simply be observed and reported more today than it was in earlier times.

Another difficulty inherent in our endeavor involves the fact that over a long stretch of history the very definition of "school" has changed. Our original intention was to study crime and punishment in elementary and secondary schools, not in institutions of higher learning; for we did not wish to deal with student movements and protests, about which much has recently been written. However, 100 years ago (and certainly before then) the age range of students at universities was so broad that many younger adolescents attended them. We have, therefore, included appropriate material on institutions of higher learning in the earlier periods of history. Moreover, as we survey crime and punishment in the schooling process, we will consider European schools as well as those in the United States, since the latter existed long before their American counterparts were begun.

Early School Crimes and Their Punishments

It is important to begin by noting that the way children are treated in school is closely tied to the way they are treated in the family. Since the teacher obtains his right to punish a student on the basis of the common law doctrine, in loco parentis, we may safely assume that parental attitudes and behaviors tend to devolve upon school personnel.

In what is probably the most influential and controversial work in the area of the evolution of childhood, Aries (1962) argues that through the sixteenth century, children were treated, at best, as little adults: "In medieval society, the idea of childhood did not exist," says Aries (p. 128). In work, play, and dress, there was no clear distinction between children and adults. To support his theory, Aries uses such evidence as iconographic material (for instance, the form of a child was always portrayed in adult proportions), and the diary of Louis XIII's doctor, Heroard, who recorded the minute details of little Louis' life. While one can accept much of his evidence, Aries nevertheless overdraws his case. For, in fact, Louis was most often whipped for such common domestic offenses as refusing to eat.

However, DeMause (1974) does bring up another interesting point about Louis; he was subject to sexual abuse by adults. As this indicates, before the seventeenth century children were ultimately regarded as objects—either of pleasure or of ownership. "Little ones" did "not count," as Molière observed (Aries 1962, p. 128), because they could be sold off, abandoned, or killed; or simply because so many babies died from neglect or illness—easily leading parents to consider very young children as temporary family members. In addition, a child was easily replaceable. John Marshall gave up his son to King Stephen, saying he "cared little if William were hanged, for he had the anvils and hammers with which to forge still better sons" (Painter 1933, p. 14).

Even though during this period there was no distinction between the activities of children and those of adults, a significant gap still existed between the two groups, for adults were able to subject their children to severe punishment. While they were not being whipped by actual slaves as in Roman times, youngsters were being whipped by parents who were figurative "slaves" of current punishing systems of religion or law. The sickest—and most telling—behavior of all, which clearly demonstrates the intricate interrelationship between the two punishment systems, was the widespread practice of taking children to see hangings and gibbetted corpses and whipping them soundly on the site (Dunn 1920, p. 300; DeMause 1974, p. 561).

By the seventeenth century, attitudes toward children had changed. Religious doctrines of both Catholicism and Protestantism helped promote two apparently conflicting images of the child: the child as innocent, but also as the product of sin. Simply because they lived, innocent children became sinful; they were the product of sex, which itself, in the last analysis, was sinful. Thus, complete and tireless supervision and discipline became necessary. "I would rather have a dead son than a disobedient one," said Luther (DeMause 1974, p. 533).

The principle of total supervision was introduced in Jesuit schools and soon spread to other schools. Early on, serious offenders in Jesuit schools were "stripped in front of the whole community and beaten until they bled" (Aries 1962, p. 260). But as the idea of modesty developed later in the seventeenth century, adolescents were no longer completely stripped for whipping.

The medieval school initially did not teach reading and writing. These skills were either taught at home or, more likely, during apprenticeship. Since their primary aim was ecclesiastical recruitment, these schools started with the teaching of Latin. And since it became the central means of discipline in them, schools (including colleges and universities) were organized around whipping.

The Jesuits were quick to develop a highly formalized system of education, obsessed with supervising the details of each student's daily life. They laid out a system of punishments, according to which an older student was selected to administer beatings. In 1598 these punishments were more or less copied into the code of conduct for the University of Paris (Aries 1962). In the seventeenth century a system of informing was also developed which was to be used both in school and outside of it and which extended the doctrine of eternal vigilance; an informer who failed to report an offense was punished as though he had been the perpetrator. The fathers also introduced the monitor system, shrewdly deciding that the elected monitor, or the excitor, would now administer the whippings.

We should note that until the sixteenth and seventeenth centuries whipping was administered only for acts of violence; that is, it was not an "academic punishment." But by the seventeenth century whipping became a basic teaching aid. Thomas Platter complained, "My master used to beat me horribly; he used to seize me by the ears and lift me off the ground" (Aries 1962, p. 190). It was well established that the child should be beaten harder if he screamed. Later, with the rise of Napoleon, the schools easily adapted to a militaristic model. Discipline, uniforms, toughness, drill routines, "captains," and "corporals" were all infused into the school systems of France and, in parallel fashion, of England, where the concept stuck fast. But while in France corporal punishment of school children was abolished in 1882, at that time in England, it had just reached its zenith and is still widespread there to this day (Newell 1972).

But students were not merely the innocent and passive victims of school personnel; at least since the Middle Ages, students have periodically been turbulent, chaotic, violent, and rebellious. If the masters kept the upper hand, they sometimes paid for doing so; it was with some cause, then, that they insisted (as they do today) upon using corporal punishment to maintain order and to protect themselves.

Aries (1962) reports that in seventeenth-century France a large number of students carried arms, which they commonly had to check upon going into the school. Since revolts were common, masters literally feared for their lives; other people were afraid to walk past schools because they might be attacked there.

In England, even in the selective and prestigious public schools, conditions were poor and the behavior of the students was nothing short of mutinous. Between 1775 and 1836 mutinies, strikes, and violence were so frequent—and sometimes so severe—that the masters had to call upon the military for assistance. According to Archer (1921), the moral atmosphere of the schools was terrible: "... there was neither influence to encourage good nor supervision to check evil" (p. 23). At Winchester the most serious of several mutinies occurring between 1775 and 1793 broke out because the boys were not allowed to attend a military band performance. For two days the students held the college under a red flag, and the episode was only terminated by numerous expulsions (Archer 1921). At the same school in 1818 two companies of soldiers armed with bayonets were called in to control another mutiny.

In 1797 some boys at Rugby responded with extreme violence to being ordered to pay for damages they had done to a tradesman; they blew up the door of the headmaster's office, set fire to his books and to school desks, and then withdrew to an island in a nearby lake. When the school called in special constables, they read the riot act and finally took the island through force (Archer 1921). Rugby also experienced disciplinary problems with regard to drinking, gambling, and profanity.

Eton suffered similarly violent episodes. In fact, George III routinely asked Eton boys, "Have you had a rebellion lately, eh, eh?" (Archer 1921, p. 60). According to one authority (Rogers, cited in Newell 1972, p. 15), at the end of the eighteenth century at Eton "the discipline...became very lax in spite of the use of the birch, and under Dr. Foster... there was a revolt, the boys throwing their books into the Thames and walking away." Later rotten eggs were on occasion thrown at Headmaster Keate (1809-1834), who responded to this with expulsions and with floggings of some forty or fifty of the culprits. And while Dr. Keate was in charge, there was an even larger revolt at Eton with the whole school, led by the prefects, walking out for two days.

Similarly at Shrewsbury between 1798 and 1836 the headmaster had his windows broken on several occasions. The last serious rebellion at a public school occurred at Marlborough in 1851. In ending his description of this whole period, Archer (1921) concludes that discipline was non existent and that the "external disorders were indicative of worse evils which rarely came to the knowledge of the staff" (p. 61).

Delinquency and Discipline in Colonial Schools

To the Puritan settlers, the education of their children was a vital responsibility. For children had to learn to read the laws of God and the community's rules of conduct—so that they might be rescued from evil and gain salvation. In New England schools were established soon after the founding of each colony (Cubberley 1934). By 1647 Massachusetts required communities of a certain number of householders to establish some schooling (Drury and Ray 1972), and other New England colonies and Pennsylvania soon followed suit.

Because of their stern religious convictions, the Puritans were forthright in their attempts to educate, and their principles of punishment were clear:

> He that spareth his rod hateth his son; but he that loveth him chastiseth him betimes. [Proverbs, xiii, 24]
>
> Foolishness is bound up in the heart of a child; but the rod of correction shall drive it far from him. [Proverbs, xxii, 15]

John Calvin's catechism of 1556 required children to know that, should they be disobedient, "God will not only punish them with everlasting payne in the day of judgement, but he will execute also punishment on their bodies here in thys worlde; eyther by shortnyng their life, eyther by procuring them a shameful death, eyther at the least a life most miserable" (Calvin 1556). Within a decade of their founding, all colonies in fact passed laws demanding that children obey their parents. Indeed, in Connecticut and Massachusetts, capital punishment was the penalty for filial disobedience (Bailyn 1960).

Because they were so dominant in all aspects of children's upbringing, it was logical that coercion and repression characterized the colonial schools (Falk 1941). Corporal punishment was routinely used, both for purposes of control and character regeneration. While textbooks inculcated terror of a stern God, repetitive drill was the method of instruction. Teachers were chosen for impeccable characters, rather than for any talent or enthusiasm for the position. Tenure was brief and salaries low (Cubberley 1934).

We can see, then, that here, as well as in Europe, schools became reflections of the general status accorded to children and, in this instance, demonstrated the Puritan importance of unquestioned compliance to God-given authority and laws. There is little evidence of serious pupil misbehavior or violence during this early period. Apparently, those children who did attend the schools essentially accepted the moral and social authority imposed upon them; they were subdued by the austere regime.

Histories of early Harvard College (established in 1636) do reveal occasional misdemeanors and even violent incidents (Moore 1972). These are, however, most notable for their lack of seriousness, their rarity, and the insight they provide into the effectiveness of Puritan authority and reformatory discipline.

In 1645, Harvard students Ward and Welde were corporally punished for burglary. In 1672, student Thomas Sargeant was publicly whipped, suspended, and made to sit uncovered and alone at meals. His crime had been blasphemy. During the presidency of Chauncy in 1655 the entire student body "walked out" to protest the extension of the bachelor's degree residence requirement to four years. A second walkout occurred in November of 1674 in protest of Leonard Hoar's presidency (Moore 1972).

Toward the end of the seventeenth century greater prosperity in Massachusetts resulted in an increase in Harvard's enrollment; these new students importantly included ones "who came to be made gentlemen, not to study" (Morison 1937, p. 191). As of this time, the number of student disturbances began to rise; debauchery increased, as did riots, petty thefts, burglary, and window breaking. Students were also disciplined for lack of piety, sexual indiscretion, and long hair.

By the end of the revolutionary period, all states had established some form of public school education. (Despite the initiation of charity schools in the South, though, schooling was still far less widespread there than in the North.) Private English schools now catered to the new middle classes, supplementing the Latin schools and common schools established in the colonial period.

Teaching methods continued to emphasize learning by rote. Moreover, the process of schooling was apparently as aversive for some teachers as it was for the students, since between 1750 and 1770 numerous advertisements appeared offering rewards for "run away teachers" (Cubberley 1934, p. 70).

School buildings were inadequate, with little heating or ventilation, and few textbooks and blackboards were available (Cubberley 1934).

Delinquency and Discipline in the Nineteenth-Century School

With the coming of the nineteenth century there was in both America and England a growing public concern about increased community vice, particularly among juveniles. In 1791, 1821, and 1822, for instance, concerned citizens of Philadelphia met to discuss the problem of teenage gangs. In 1805 the New York Society emphasized the schools' importance in efforts to overcome delinquency, saying:

> Children thus brought up in ignorance and amidst the contagion of bad example, are in imminent danger of ruin; and too many of them, it is to be feared, instead of being useful members of the community will become the burden and pests of society. Early instruction and fixed habits of industry, decency, and order are the surest safeguards of virtuous conduct. [Bourne 1870]

This great concern over juvenile delinquency coincided with an increasingly widespread provision of education for the masses in both England and the United States. New techniques made it possible for educators to cope with many more pupils; for example, the monitorial Lancaster system, popular in the United States between 1805 and 1830, enabled one teacher to deal with many children at the same time. Thus for the first time a sizable proportion of school-age children could gain at least nominal schooling; and by 1840, it was no longer the exception for children to have formal schooling in New England. In America compulsory education laws were enacted in various states between 1865 and 1918 (and in 1870 in England). In Boston the first high schools for boys were opened in 1821, and for girls in 1825. By 1870, in this country 57 percent of the children between five and eighteen years of age were in school (Butts and Cremin 1953).

By the end of the nineteenth century a changing pattern of immigration brought into the school system increasing numbers of children of southern and eastern European (rather than British and northern European) settlers. Education thus underwent related changes; far more children attended school, their schooling extended over a greater period of time, and they constituted a much more heterogeneous group than the American schools had seen before.

Indeed, during the nineteenth century disciplinary problems in the schools became common. Foreign observers of American schools concluded that American youths were particularly difficult to discipline because they were influenced by the society's egalitarian character. For instance, Francis Grund, writing in 1837, complained that "There is little disposition on the part of the American children to obey the uncontrollable will of their masters as on the part of their fathers to submit to the mandates of kings" (p. 133). Because schools were woefully inadequate with regard to physical conditions, teaching methods, and disciplinary practices, they were in fact wild and unruly places. A Mr. Draper (Falk 1941) described his nineteenth-century Massachusetts elementary school as consisting of four recitation rooms, each of which measured 14 x 10½ feet without proper ventilation and which contained more than thirty pupils.

Teachers were at this time poorly trained and paid, most of them considering teaching to be a stopgap occupation. At the same time, though, as Cubberley (1934) writes, "in these earlier days of 1830-1860, the ability to impose discipline on a poorly taught and in consequence an unruly school was an important part of the qualifications of a teacher" (p. 411). For dealing with the very large classes, the usual teaching method was still rote drill. Attendance was poor and truancy rife; there was no real curriculum, and at any given time three-quarters of the children were not profitably employed; Thus, there was considerable misbehavior, and teachers had to be excessively vigilant (Philbrick 1874). As a consequence of these factors, "... the school was of course something like the despotic government of a military camp. Infringements of the law and order were visited with quick retribution, and there was of necessity both harshness and security in the governance of a school (McKeen 1851, p. 124). According to Horace Mann (1843), schools were characterized by "idleness and disorder... excepting in cases where the debasing motive of fear puts the children in irons" (p. 84).

Fear was cultivated by an assortment of methods of corporal punishment. "A boy has a back; when you hit it he understands" was a favorite pedagogical maxim of the time according to Cubberley (1920, p. 455). In 1830, a schoolmaster, Hauberle (1830), published a list of the punishments he had given in 51½ years as a teacher. Included were 911,527 blows with a cane; 124,010 blows with a rod; 20,989 blows with a ruler; 136,715 blows with the hand; 12,235 blows on the mouth; 7,905 boxed ears; 1,115,800 raps on the head; 22,763 nota benes with Bible, grammar, or other books; 777 kneelings on peas; 1,707 instances of holding up the rod; 613 kneelings on a triangular block of wood.

Other writers mentioned dungeoning in windowless closets, tying children to chairs, ear twisting, and so forth. Girls were usually not exempt. Since teachers were often paid according to the progress of their pupils, they tended to inflict punishments for failure to learn as well as for misbehavior.

Despite controversy and many social reforms, education lagged behind other institutions with regard to protecting children from violence inflicted by those who supervised them. Whereas an act of Congress abolished corporal punishment in the United States Navy in 1853, it is still legal in American schools except in a handful of localities.

The prevalence of inordinate corporal punishment did not provide a panacea for school problems; American schools remained generally disorderly. Horace Mann reported that nearly 400 schools in Massachusetts were broken up in 1837 because of disciplinary problems (Falk 1941). On another occasion Mann stated that in one school with 250 pupils he saw 328 separate floggings in one week of five school days, an average of over 65 floggings a day (Mann and Smith 1847).

As more teachers became suitably qualified, the amount of corporal punishment may have decreased somewhat. In 1845, a New York report proudly claimed, "during the last year, no teacher has been arrested, dismissed or even reproved, for contusively lacerating or maiming his pupils, circumstances formerly of frequent occurrence; and it is affirmed with the utmost pleasure, that in this country, there is not one insubordinate school now" (Stevens 1845, p. 172). It would appear that educators, in this country at least, perceived a direct relationship between teachers' violent behavior toward students and the students' subsequent insubordination. Moreover, this perception implies a theory which was gradually to become explicit during the twentieth century; that less punishment (especially corporal punishment), not more, would bring about better and more obedient behavior in the schools. However, during most of the nineteenth century, schools in the United States were chaotic and violent places where teachers unsuccessfully attempted to maintain control over unmotivated, bored, unruly, and unmanageable children through disciplinary methods which were often novel, and more often brutal.

At the same time in England the gradual extension of schools to serve a wider group of children was resulting in a similar increase in school misbehavior and disorder—and in a similar controversy over the use of corporal punishment to deal with such misconduct. As early as 1669, a group of children had marched to Parliament and presented the Children's Petition, describing the sufferings (including physical ones) of English schoolchildren. This had little effect, and 200 years later, in 1870, when compulsory school attendance became law, teachers and the public were still debating the merits of corporal punishment (Newell 1972) to help educate the previously uneducated masses.

The seventh Earl of Shaftesbury (Ashley-Cooper 1847) described the new Ragged Schools:

> They are open to receive all those who are excluded from superior schools by the rules and regulations indispensable to their discipline. The decent apparel, the washed face, the orderly behavior, the attendance by day, the penny a week, amount to an interdict on their admission, were they even so disposed to the National and British Schools. [p. 127]

He then described the "tumultuous conduct" in most Ragged Schools in the large towns:

> The floors were sprinkled with blood, benches broken down, lesson boards torn asunder, the scholars tumbling over each other in wild confusion, the master with his clothes torn, teachers obliged to escape for their lives out of the windows, and over the roofs of houses—all these things have but afforded a type of moral chaos. . . . [p. 41]

Although in the 1870s the London School Board took measures to limit the use of corporal punishment in its jurisdiction, teachers (and many parents) strongly opposed the new notions. These groups believed that physical deterrents were necessary because of the prevalence of lying, truancy, stealing, foul language, and insubordination among schoolchildren (newly admitted into the schools because of the Elementary Education Act) (Newell 1972). On October 6, 1889, the children entered the debate when a crowd of militant schoolboys from Kennington and Lambeth walked out of their schools and resolved not to return unless, among other demands, corporal punishment was abolished (Newell 1972); nothing came of this demonstration. Newell (1972) writes that, nearly 100 years later, there is still widespread violence among children in school, and that teachers still use this fact as a reason for opposing the abolition of the ultimate deterrent, corporal punishment—itself a violent remedy.

During the nineteenth century in America universities were also places of considerable turbulence. It is interesting to note that the majority of disturbances arose over dissatisfaction with such elements of the quality of education as teaching methods and the curriculum. Between 1800 and 1830, for example, Princeton had six major campus rebellions (Wallerstein 1969), and in 1823 explosions and riots triggered by students resulted in the expulsion of half of a class. While in the 1802 riots at Princeton students set fire to Nassau Hall, completely destroying the library, in 1914 they set ablaze a number of outbuildings in protest against the system of instruction (Rosenthal 1971). Many strikes, riots, and assaults also occurred on non-Ivy League campuses right up until 1900. At the University of Virginia, for instance, violence "reached a crescendo during the 1830s and 1840s, and before [it] died down, a professor had been killed and armed constables had to be brought on to the campus" (Rosenthal 1971, p. 5).

Some writers on the history of student protest have argued that the student violence in the nineteenth century was distinctly different from that in the twentieth century in that the former was nonideological (for instance, Rosenthal 1971; Feuer 1969). It was instead motivated by increasingly outmoded, inappropriate educational systems and methods of instruction. Our review of nineteenth-century elementary and high schools indicates that this explanation holds true for those levels; poor educational methods and student misbehavior were directly related. Was the twentieth century to be any different?

Early Twentieth Century

The early twentieth century in America was characterized by tremendous increases in immigration, in society's heterogeneity, and in the prevalence and length of schooling. Falk (1941) states that high-school enrollment increased eightfold, and college enrollment fivefold. As secondary schooling (often prolonged) was no longer for the select few who were academically interested and able, school populations became more or less cross sections of American society. In 1918, for example, 75 percent of American children aged five to eighteen were attending school, including 20 percent of black children (Butts and Cremin 1953). Moreover, these dramatic changes in the population served by secondary schools led to changes in the problems faced by those schools. According to the NEA 1928 yearbook, "these problems relate not only to curriculums and courses of study, but also to discipline, manners and morals" (Cubberley 1934, p. 466).

New York City witnessed one such confrontation between educational innovation and the traditional social order. In 1914, the Gary, Indiana, platoon system was introduced into New York City schools as a means of dealing with increased school enrollments and better utilizing educational facilities at no extra cost (Mohl 1975). However, this was evidently too radical a change for the citizens (many of them immigrants), producing in them anxieties on which political candidates came to capitalize. Then by 1917, the New York schools became the sites of a series of violent demonstrations against the Gary Plan. Between 1,000 and 3,000 schoolchildren (mostly Jewish) gathered on the Upper East Side around P.S. 171 (Madison Avenue and 103rd Street), picketed and stoned the school, beat those students who did not join the strike, and burned their schoolbooks. Although police broke up the demonstration, the crowds reassembled later and disorder spread to nearby schools. Stones were thrown, windows were broken, and fourteen child ringleaders were arrested (*The New York Times*, October 17, 1917). When the rioting spread to the Bronx and to the Brownsville and Williamsburg sections of Brooklyn on the following day, at each location mobs of more than 5,000 student demonstrators engaged in pitched battles with police. Police guards were posted around all Bronx schools and sixteen Brooklyn schools.

This disorder, insubordination, and violence in New York and in other American cities necessitated debate about the form of education best suited to imposing order and simultaneously meeting the changed needs of both pupils and society. Dewey (1933), for instance, wrote that the role of education was to free minds and enable people to cope with an emergent society.

Nevertheless, adult violence (albeit controlled) has remained the preferred method of dealing with violence on the part of children in American schools. Only a handful of states and localities have banned corporal punishment (by far the earliest to ban it was New Jersey, in 1866), and, in April 1977, the U.S.

Supreme Court reaffirmed its legality. While teachers gain their authority in loco parentis, American society condones the physical assertion of authority by parents (Gil 1970). The right of teachers to use corporal punishment in loco parentis has been consistently upheld in the courts. In defending a ruling it made in 1923, one court even implied that a teacher's authority should be as unquestioned as a king's:

> A teacher must be in authority, and have control in a school. If not, there would be no school. Many years ago, a learned and judicious school master said to Charles II in the plentitude of his power; "Sire, pull off thy hat in my school, for if my scholars discover that the king is above me in authority, they will no longer respect me." And the king pulled off his hat, to demonstrate by example that the school master's authority should be respected even by a king. [*People* v. *Petrie*, 1923 in Faulkner 1967, p. 81]

Conclusions

Although we are faced with the disturbing statistics on current school violence, the evidence available to us suggests that this phenomenon is not much more serious today than it was in previous centuries when teachers were commonly attacked and, in one case, killed. The considerable violence that occurred in nineteenth-century universities was perpetrated by students who were probably about the same age as present-day high-school juniors and seniors. It is significant that student protests in the nineteenth century revolved around "bread and butter" issues, such as instructional methods and the curriculum; unlike the protests characterizing the university student movements of the 1930s and 1960s (Rosenthal 1971), those were not responses to social or ideological issues.

It would seem, moreover, that the rigidity, sternness, and violence of various educational systems have not averted student insubordination. On the contrary, as they rebelled, students bitterly protested this very issue.

Although caning is now undoubtedly used much less than it was in the past, corporal punishment remains widespread. Most school districts have rules governing its application, so that we no longer have the unmitigated use of corporal punishment that occurred in earlier centuries. But since student violence does not seem to have decreased correspondingly, we must look elsewhere for an explanation of this phenomenon. Apparently there is not a direct relationship between pupils' violent and unruly behavior and violence on the part of school authorities.

Our general conclusion is, then, that a "crisis of discipline" has always existed in schools—or has existed at least since the Middle Ages, when the concept of childhood emerged and society came to regard children as constituting a group which was distinct from adults. This view prevailed over the centuries, intensifying to a point where teachers resorted to ingenious physical humiliations and punishments to assert their own status. The most visible and serious crises in the schools occurred side by side with massive use of corporal punishment, insistence upon immediate obedience, maintenance of rigid rules, and the learning of endless material by rote. Since the nineteenth century, we have slowly limited the use of corporal punishment and loosened rules governing behavior in school. But we have simultaneously moved to keep children as children for a much longer period than ever before—for many, for at least a third of their lives. It seems predictable that the crises of authority—adult versus child, parent versus child, teacher versus pupil—will become even more accentuated.

Thus, despite liberalization of school discipline, school violence continued: in street gangs after school; in organized strikes in school; in massive, sullen resistance to learning; and in individual children using arson or vandalism as revenge for the school's dealing with them as children, forcing them to obey and to learn. Yet if one considers the terrible manner in which children were exploited when they were treated as adults, today's form of "oppression" surely seems reasonable.

Our historical analysis has shown that violence has been a recurrent theme in the schooling process. Like crime and other social problems it is unlikely to be eliminated. We must therefore learn to live with this "crisis." Nevertheless, this does not mean that progress is impossible. In fact, one is forced to conclude that considerable progress has already been made since a marked decrease in the use of abusive corporal punishment has not been accompanied by a serious increase in juvenile violence. To this extent, then, schools are less violent places.

2
Extent, Perspectives and Consequences of Violence and Vandalism in Public Schools

Robert J. Rubel

> We have a goodly number of assaults on teachers, students and security agents. In one school, an intruder made the teacher disrobe in front of her class. He said he only wanted to take her money when we caught him. He took her keys—so we had to stake out her house until we caught him. Assaults such as this result in a loss of class time, it instills fear in the teachers, creates undue anxiety, and in the end it diminishes the teacher's capacity to teach. Valuable instructional time is lost, and in the long run the students suffer. That is why people protection has to be our priority. [*Safe School Study* 1977, p. 177]

This chapter contains three small but vital overview essays. The topics are separable but interrelated, and they all help provide an understanding and orientation to the field of crime and violence in schools.

The first discussion relates some of the most current facts known about the nature and extent of student violence and crime in schools. The second discussion focuses on relevant federal perspectives and actions in this area. The final section highlights the more salient consequences obtaining from violence and vandalism in public schools.

Nature and Extent of Violence and Vandalism: Historical Perspectives

Violence and vandalism in our nation's schools began to come to the public's attention in the early to mid-1970s as the Senate Subcommittee to Investigate Juvenile Delinquency began paying extensive attention to that phenomenon. Much of the material collected by that Subcommittee seemed to show dramatic increases in overt acts of criminal and aggressive behavior on the part of students. In the same period of time—and then throughout the whole of the 1970s—the "Gallup Poll of Public Attitudes Toward Education" consistently indicated that the population's primary concern in the education arena was the lack of discipline in schools.

By the late 1970s, a number of studies had been conducted carefully to analyze and interpret perceived increases in the nature and extent of school-based violence. These studies began to paint a picture of violence in American schools somewhat different from those presented by earlier journalistic articles;

many of the journalistic articles merely parroted findings from the Senate hearings, descrying recent "massive increases" in public school violence. The new picture showed that the epidemic which came to the public's attention in the 1970s had really taken place in the late 1960s, but could only be attributed to the 1960s after sufficient time had passed to permit interpretation of a wide range of seemingly unrelated factors.

Among the factors that these later studies mentioned as contributors to the perceived increases in public school violence are these:

1. Increases throughout the 1960s of the schools' use of high-technology equipment such as electric typewriters, closed-circuit television studios, extensive physics and chemistry laboratories, and so forth, caused larger loss-figures to appear in school districts than had been the case during earlier years when this type of equipment was unknown.
2. Dramatic increases between 1950 and 1970 in the physical size of schools (and the numbers of students in them) provided a greater opportunity for violence, and therefore greater crime risk for students.
3. Increases in the complexity of due process compliance procedures required by wide-ranging Supreme Court cases slowed down the schools' administering of some areas of discipline to students—forcing schools to increase tolerance levels for unruly and unwanted behavior.
4. Increases in the Bureau of Labor Statistics' Consumer Price Index reflected the increased costs of replacement and repair as a function of nationwide inflation in the 1960s. As inflation rose sharply, the attention of school districts had to turn with increased force toward the costs of crimes in schools, which were appearing to skyrocket.
5. Formation of offices of school security in cities throughout this country caused for the first time the collection and national aggregation of data about the nature and extent of violence in schools, producing the impression that there had been a strong upturn in criminal behavior in schools.

As these factors came increasingly to the public's attention, the public became rightfully alarmed. Demands were made repeatedly of Congress and of the executive branch of government to "do something." Exactly what should be done was never very clear—for it was never very clear what, exactly, was wrong.

And during this period, a problem hovered over this field of study; a confusion lingered. Because school districts from different cities did not use the same definitions of criminal acts (When is a fight an assault? Is a trash-can fire "vandalism" or "arson"?), and because incident reporting forms were (and are) nonuniform between school districts, it was not clear whether the problem—as presented in national magazines for public consumption—was increasing, decreasing, stabilized, real, illusory, or even significant. Some argued, for example, that what news sources put forward as an "objective portrayal of vandalism and violence in schools" in general was actually a presentation of rare and bizarre incidents and/or schools: proponents of this viewpoint contended that the popular press is primarily interested in showing us unusual and/or spectacular events to the peril of the mundane.

In an attempt to clarify all such uncertainties, Congress mandated the Department of Health, Education and Welfare to prepare a definitive report on the status of crime, violence, and vandalism in the nation's schools. That report took three years to complete; it cost $2.4 million. In brief, a few of the findings are these:

1. Concerning attacks: 1.3 percent of all secondary-school pupils are attacked each month; 42 percent of those have some injury, while only 4 percent of the 1.3 percent require medical attention (0.052 percent of the total population). These attacks are 42 percent interracial; are reported to police about 30 percent of the time; and in 75 percent of the cases, offenders are known by name to the victims.
2. Still concerning attacks: although only 1.3 percent of all secondary-school pupils are attacked in one month, 36 percent of all assaults on twelve to nineteen year olds occur in schools, while fully 50 percent of all assaulted twelve to fifteen year olds are attacked in schools.
3. Concerning thefts: 2 percent of all secondary-school pupils report theft of items valued over $10 in one month. About 54 percent of this theft occurs in classrooms.
4. Concerning robberies: 0.05 percent secondary-school students are robbed by force or threat in one month; 47 percent of those robbed know their offenders by name; 9 percent of those robbed receive minor injury; 2 percent of those robbed (0.01 percent of all secondary-school students in one month) require medical attention. In most robberies the victims are the same age, sex, and race as the perpetrators.
5. Concerning crime costs: 57 percent of all crime costs occur in suburban schools—which comprise only 38 percent of all schools. Total crime costs equal about $200 million per year—66 percent ($132 million) for replacement and repair of the physical plant; 24 percent ($48 million) for replacement of lost equipment; and 10 percent ($20 million) for replacement of supplies and books.
6. Concerning location of violence: 13 percent of all violent acts occur in the classroom; 16 percent occur in restrooms; 43 percent in hallways and stairs; and 9 percent in the cafeteria.
7. Concerning status of offenders: between 74-98 percent of all offenders (except trespassers and burglars) are currently students.
8. Concerning vandalism: 28 percent of all schools experience vandalism in one month, with the average loss being $81 per incident.

Concerning the national trend toward school violence, the *Safe School Study* is cautious. According to it, overall about 8 percent of school administrators say that in their schools violence is a "serious or very serious" problem. In terms of geographical distribution, however, there is a hidden truth; because there are numerically so many more rural than large-city schools, the 8 percent figure used by the *Safe School Study* disguises the fact that 15 percent of large-city schools, but only 6 percent of rural ones, are saying that their problems are serious.

In the *Safe School Study* some particularly important information surfaced for the first time. One such bit of new information concerns the extent to which fear on the part of students affects their school behavior. Although this is discussed in greater detail in the "consequences" section below, it is useful to note that the *Safe School Study* found that 16 percent of all secondary-school students in the country avoid three or more places in school—while a staggering 33 percent of all large-city junior-high-school students report avoiding three or more places. Bathrooms, of course, head the list of avoided places, with fully 44 percent of all previously attacked youth avoiding them. A second important finding is indicated in these few statistics, namely that the bulk of disruptive and violent behavior occurs at the junior- rather than at the senior-high-school level. A third major finding from the *Safe School Study* was that the local building administrator is not as powerless as was previously imagined to control the school's social climate; indeed, the principal is now seen as *the* deciding factor regarding the relative safety or violence of any given school.

In general, there is agreement that schools are currently experiencing more violence than can be tolerated, and that the quality of American education is clearly suffering—particularly in large cities—because of this fact. There is also general agreement that it is easier to affix blame than to develop solutions. Studies (and their resulting reanalyses throughout the 1970s) have provided ample basis for action. Some action has taken place. Much, much more remains; for students of this field are often left with the gnawing feeling that actions of sufficient scope to alter the continuing trend toward lawlessness in schools are impossible in the context of education as it is conceived in this country at this time.

Legislative, Executive, and Judicial Perspectives
About Violence in Public Schools

Throughout the 1960s and 1970s all branches of the federal government took actions which in some way affected either the understanding of or response to violence in schools. Although an exhaustive accounting of these would be inappropriate here, a brief one will add a useful perspective to an understanding of current affairs in this arena.

Legislative Perspective

Apart from a few tangential discussions relating to discipline problems in schools in the 1950s and early 1960s, the first real congressional concern over violence in schools was evidenced by the House Subcommittee on General Education commissioning of a national survey of schools to determine the extent to which riots, walkouts, and student strikes were a problem in secondary schools. Interestingly, this survey—released in 1970—pointed out that the vast majority of school-based disturbances were over school-related issues such as dress codes, curriculum policies, general rules and regulations, and so forth; and, counter to what many had feared, that they usually did not involve political protests. The survey did not give rise to any legislation, nor was there any sense that the federal government ought to play a role in riot prevention in public schools.

The next major action taken by Congress was initiated in the early 1970s by the Senate Subcommittee to Investigate Juvenile Delinquency. Having sensed that schools were becoming violent, this group asked the Library of Congress to survey 757 school districts to determine changes in some categories of serious crimes between the 1970 and 1972 school years. Partially as a result of this study's findings, public hearings were called in 1975 so that the growing public concern over violence in schools might be aired. The information gained during these hearings was widely publicized: the nation was made aware that high levels of violence and fear in schools posed serious threats to a stable educational system. No legislation was developed from these hearings.

Concurrent with the efforts of the Senate subcommittee, and about six months before the public hearings, the Elementary and Secondary Education Act (ESEA) amendments of 1974 had attached to them a provision mandating that the Department of Health, Education and Welfare carry out a major study of the nature and extent of violence in schools—and also document violence-prevention approaches then in use. The results of this study—released in 1978—are published as: *Violent Schools—Safe Schools: The Safe School Study Report to Congress* (previously cited).

Within two weeks of the release of the *Safe School Study*, the House Subcommittee on Economic Opportunity held public hearings to gather recommendations to Congress respecting possible federal-level interventions. Later in 1978 Representative Mario Biaggi (who had presented the opening remarks at these hearings) introduced a significant amendment to the 1978 ESEA reauthorization bill; this specifically addressed violence and vandalism in public schools.

According to the version of the ESEA bill that passed Congress, $15 million would be made available to a total of fifteen school districts for the purpose of addressing problems of crime, violence, and vandalism. A maximum of 10 percent of that money may be spent on security-related hardware. The project is administered by the U.S. commissioner of education, with guidance provided by the Office of Juvenile Justice; but Congress did not appropriate any money. There was no $15 million; indeed, there was not one dollar. The legislation stands as a statement of "congressional intent," not as a funded, operating program. This is likely to be the last congressional action in the area of school-based violence prevention for the foreseeable future.

Executive Perspective

Until the formation of the Office of Juvenile Justice and Delinquency Prevention in 1974, most of the government's activity in the area of in-school delinquency was carried out within HEW's Youth Development and Delinquency Prevention Administration (YDDPA). That office had only tangential contact with schools, however, for the Youth Services System concept adopted by YDDPA to reduce delinquency emphasized coordinating services to youth on a communitywide basis: schools represented only one aspect of the larger society's impact on youth.

When the 1974 Juvenile Justice and Delinquency Prevention Act was passed, virtually all authority for delinquency prevention was shifted from HEW to the Justice Department. With the 1977 amendments to the 1974 act, a U.S. law for the first time contained specific wording which mandated programs to help reduce crime and violence in public schools. In the early years of its existence, the Justice Department's Office of Juvenile Justice and Delinquency Prevention (OJJDP) operationalized this mandate by forming an interagency agreement with HEW that allowed the Office of Education's Drug Abuse Prevention Education division to carry out the crime and violence initiative in schools. In 1979 that interagency agreement was not renewed, and OJDDP let a $2.4 million fifteen-month grant to a Washington, D.C.-based consulting firm to conduct training and technical assistance to help school districts cope with problems related to criminal activity in their schools.

It is important to note that there are vast differences between the perspectives of any HEW- managed effort and any Justice-managed effort, even if the purported purpose of each is to reduce violence in schools. Specifically, the educational community will be interested in fine-tuning the mechanics of schooling (curriculum, counseling, scheduling) on the grounds that when schools successfully accomplish what they are traditionally expected to, they are free from violence and vandalism, for then the whole educational process is under control. In contrast, the Justice community will be inclined to direct its efforts toward two quite specific matters: first, toward developing a capacity to reduce crime and violence in schools which are in serious trouble; and second, through alternative programs and advocacy, toward strengthening the ability of schools to cope with youth who would otherwise be forced to enter the juvenile-justice system. The Office of Juvenile Justice, then, is really concerned with making the schools more capable of breaking a vicious circle in which some youngsters are caught—being repeatedly bounced back and forth between the educational and judicial systems, with each system expecting the other to accept the responsibility for "adjusting" these youngsters back to "normalcy."

It is clear that both the federal government and society must, in fact, work toward destroying this cycle.

Judicial Perspective

In the past few decades certain court decisions have strongly influenced American education with regard to what schools may and may not do concerning discipline, suspension, and expulsion. A brief history of these cases is outlined below in order to demonstrate the courts' intent respecting policies and procedures that must be implemented, supported, and enforced in any program or policy supported by the executive branch of government.

Dixon v. *Alabama State Board of Education* (1961): found that "due process requires notice and some opportunity for hearing before a student ... is expelled for misconduct." While this constituted the first imposition of procedural guidelines on schools, those were restricted to expulsion cases.

Gault v. *Arizona* (1967): found that under the Constitution juveniles have rights relative to procedural due process.

Tinker v. *Des Moines Independent Community School District* (1969): found that a student could not be suspended or expelled from a school unless the action of which he is accused interferes "with appropriate discipline in the operation of the school (or collides) with the rights of others." In other words, before a youth is suspended or expelled, it must be established that he presents a "clear and present danger"—a threat to the school, other students, or himself. This ruling sounded a warning to school administrators that suspensions and expulsions could no longer be used in an arbitrary and uncontrolled manner.

Goss v. *Lopez* and *Wood* v. *Strickland* (1975): found that even in suspension cases of up to ten days, procedural due process had to be followed at least to the extent of providing the accused student with formal notification of suspension and the right to a hearing, unless such actions could not be taken due to the extreme emergency of the situation. Further, if school administrators did not comply with these procedures, they could be subject to suit.

Baker v. *Owen* (1976): found that corporal punishment could be administered in schools, even when parents specifically objected, as long as school rules indicate that this punishment is to be the discipline administered for specific acts, and as long as certain procedures are followed concerning the delivery of the punishment. This ruling is important because it stipulates a number of due process procedures. Moreover, the same line of argument was further explicated in *Ingraham* v. *Wright* (1977); this ruling carefully presented the due process procedures concerning the administration of corporal punishment.

In summary, through court rulings the schools have been proscribed from arbitrarily excluding youth from the educational process; have been instructed to provide accused youth with some basic procedural guarantees concerning evidence, notification, and hearings; and—in the case of such controversial practices as corporal punishment—actually have been given specific and detailed procedural guidelines which each and every school administrator must follow.

It is clear, then, that the legislative, executive, and judicial branches of the federal government have all been significantly involved in activities related to the problem of violence and vandalism in public schools. Also, to greater or lesser extents, each of these branches has had an impact on both the public's perception of the problem and federal responses to it. Any effort undertaken at federal, state, or local levels clearly must build upon a thorough understanding of the strong influences discussed in this section. And it must be remembered that these influences are not ones that have existed only in the historical sense, having an effect at one particular point in time; rather, through the existence of executive office mandates, and through legislative and/or judicial intent, they continue to bear on problems of violence and vandalism.

Consequences of Violence and Vandalism in Public Schools

There are a number of consequences of violence and vandalism that people immediately realize. Clearly, the specter of vandalism carries with it the idea of purposeless waste and loss of resources. So, too, violence in schools carries with it a connotation of the loss of that childhood and adolescent innocence naturally associated with such institutions. Indeed, serious questions about national priorities arise from recognizing the obvious facts that youths attending schools are now heavily victimized and that little is being done about it.

Loss of Personal Freedom from Fear

The *Safe School Study* discussed student victimization and fear from many angles, the broadest of which concerns generalized fear resulting from the threat of harm. The *Safe School Study* found that 8 percent of all large-city junior-high-school youths reported actually staying home at least one day in the previous month out of fear. (This 8 percent figure is quite likely conservative, for those youngsters who no longer go to school—in part out of fear—and those who were not in school—out of fear—on the day the survey was administered are not accounted for.) More important than this discovery, though, are the findings that of junior-high-school pupils in large cities (the most severely affected areas in terms of violent incidents), fully 33 percent of the youths reported fear of three or more places in school. It is worthwhile to add, moreover, that fear levels accelerate dramatically after a student has been victimized in some way; indeed, the individual's fear of specific locations appears to increase two- and three-fold after he has been assaulted or robbed.

Fear of School Locations and of Persons

The short-term consequences of this sort of fear were easily seen in the 1975 hearings on school violence held by the Senate Subcommittee to Investigate Juvenile Delinquency. In those hearings, students related that they had to be cautious of certain parts of the school or of certain groups of fellow students within the school. Indeed, the consequences of the fear levels just discussed are specifically translatable into fear of other pupils, loss of openness and trust of other youth. This cautiousness arises from a youngster's perception that violence exists in school, and that he, as an individual, may be a target.

It is useful to point out that the fear of violence appears to exist independently from actual physical attacks and robberies. For example, although 22 percent of all junior-high-school youths report avoiding three or more places out of fear in one month, only 2.1 percent report being attacked, and only 1 percent report being robbed. Further, the chance of attack or robbery resulting in harm is quite small; about 4 percent of attacks and about 2 percent of robberies require student victims to seek medical attention. From this we may conclude that fear of crime and violence is more crippling educationally and socially than are the actual acts themselves.

Lowering of Educational Quality

Longer term consequences are commonly related in news articles and in commentary on the state of education in America. As fear of crime and violence builds in schools, the quality of education decreases: time-on-task is reduced; teachers become less open and outgoing; staff do not want to stay after school to work with pupils; staff demand greater assurances of physical safety; and so forth. Of course the cycle begins to attract a great deal of public attention as standardized test scores begin to show differentiated rates based on the social climate of schools—but such correlational analysis is seldom performed by a school district (and were it performed, it would probably not be released to the public).

Internalization of Violence

Violent crimes in schools create an invidious problem: because of increasingly violent acts, a continuing stream of unruly behavior tends to remain relatively unnoticed by students, staff, and the public. That is, as violence and vandalism take the spotlight, carelessness, thoughtlessness, minor rule infractions, impoliteness, and so forth, are allowed to become redefined as the new status quo of American public school education. This process can be viewed as the institutionalization of violence and unwanted behavior. For in the absence of active interventions, acts of a noncultural nature tend, over time, to become accepted. Extortion of small amounts of money, or smoking of cigarettes, or smoking of marijuana (in many cities) are all examples of behaviors that are fully tolerated in today's schools. It is important to reemphasize that these are only tolerated because of the potential for really violent acts to which the school must be prepared to address itself.

Loss of Respect for Authority

The last link in this "chain of consequences" relates to both the short- and long-term losses of respect for authority on the part of youth. To the extent that violence and vandalism remain untreated by the adults in a school—to the extent that the adults are seen as powerless to address these problems—students will likely determine that "might makes right" and that corrective action must, by default, occur through them (the students) rather than through traditionally approved channels. As this point of view is allowed to develop, youth will tend to generalize it further, to society as a whole; when youngsters discover that adults in schools are unable to control events, they can conclude that by extension this inability also exists throughout the community-at-large. In a very real sense, then, unchecked violence and vandalism in schools leak out to the surrounding community, so that the community becomes infected with youth-perpetrated crime.

In summary, compelling evidence shows that in schools where students and staff feel unsafe, where some locations and people instill fear, where the quality of education is affected, and where violence has become part of the normal climate, youths are being emotionally damaged at the same time that crime and violence are being communicated to the environment immediately surrounding the school. The obvious conclusion is that unsafe schools are intolerable and must be corrected.

Part II
Schools as Victims

3

Student Behavior, the Depersonalization of Blame, and the Society of Victims

Daniel L. Duke

Finding someone or something to blame for social problems has emerged as a full-time occupation for a host of social scientists, journalists, clerics, and politicians. In a different era such activity might have been called scapegoating or buck-passing, but today it is dignified by such labels as "the determination of causation" and "the investigation of environmental influences." Political, economic, and social considerations make the matter complex. For example, accounting for the origins of social problems can be potentially rewarding for some groups and damaging for others. While scientific attempts to explain phenomena are rarely designed with the intent to vindicate (at least, so the public is led to believe), it is true that certain interest groups do support researchers who can demonstrate their own innocence or the culpability of others. The political poll is a classic example of such presentations. Likewise, teacher organizations like to "prove" that declining student achievement is not attributable to low-quality instruction; and oil companies like to use statistics to demonstrate that high profits are not the result of price-fixing or other monopolistic practices. The politics of apology, as I refer to these exercises, is big business. A by-product of this enterprise is a process called the depersonalization of blame.

The thesis of this chapter is that the recent history of research in the social sciences has witnessed the unrelenting depersonalization of blame. No longer do scholars hold an individual responsible for his triumphs or his transgressions. What an individual *does* instead becomes the product of various external factors. At the risk of anticipating my conclusion for a moment, I question whether the shifting of responsibility for personal behavior from the individual to external factors (the process of depersonalization) is ultimately in the best interests of society or the individual. Particularly where inappropriate or antisocial behavior is concerned, the depersonalization of blame appears to exonerate misbehaving individuals of any responsibility for their actions. The looter is excused because of his impoverished background. The unproductive assembly-line worker draws sympathy because of the tedium of his occupation. Everyone becomes a victim of forces outside of himself. The question inevitably arises, "Can a society of victims survive?"

Portions of this chapter appeared in *The Journal of Educational Thought* 12(1978). Reprinted with permission.

The following discussion does not directly address this perplexing question. Instead, it concentrates on the process by which the blame for school discipline problems has been shifted from individual students to other factors. Although school discipline problems have not lured researchers as much as have several related subjects such as school dropouts, juvenile delinquency, and adolescent drug use, much has in fact been written on student misbehavior and schools' efforts to deal with it.

It is likely that how students behave in school has long been a prime concern of educators and laymen alike, but I doubt if past attention equals that devoted to the matter today. As in other recent years, the 1975 "Gallup Poll of Public Attitude Toward Education" indicated that the public's number one concern regarding schools was their "lack of discipline" (p. 226). That same survey also showed that there has been a great deal of interest in related areas; "use of drugs" ranked sixth, while "crime/vandalism/stealing" was eighth on the list. Americans seem to be more worried about student behavior than about busing, budgets, and plummeting test scores.

In a 1971 study of teachers' concerns, the National Education Association's research division found that over 21 percent of the teachers sampled viewed classroom management and discipline as a "major problem" (p. 101). The figure represents a 6 percent jump over 1968, and anyone keeping abreast of the literature on school discipline since 1971 would not hesitate to predict that the percentage would continue to climb. Educators regretfully report that discipline problems are even becoming more prevalent in lower grades. These and other indicators leave little doubt that the behavior of American students constitutes a serious national problem.

Who or What Is to Blame?

Once upon a time in American education individual students were apparently held accountable for their behavior in school. The authors of a popular textbook on school discipline write,

> The Colonial schoolmaster was not too troubled with the causes of misbehavior. He had been taught that there was only one real cause—the presence of Satan in the child.... Later and more moderate interpretations were that there was a good deal of "natural mischief" in any child, particularly a boy, and a practical approach to discipline in school need not concern itself too much with the *why* of misbehavior. [Larson and Karpas 1964, p. 7]

It is difficult to isolate a precise date when educators began to be as concerned with why students misbehaved as they were with how to correct the misbehavior. Some note that Freud's attack on the psychology of such men as William James gave rise to the notion that an individual's behavior was "rooted in the past and in the unconscious" (Winter et al. 1970, p. 458). More to the point, Gordon Allport concludes that twentieth-century psychological theories stress the ways in which "men respond reactively to external stimuli" and ignore "man's proactive, self-directing capacities" (in Winter et al.).

In the last half century two movements in particular have abetted the politics of apology and the depersonalization of blame. Behaviorism, one of the theories to which Allport alludes, demonstrated for many persons that human beings were shaped by stimuli in their environment rather than by their own self-determination. Alongside behaviorism came the "prevention movement," which pushed concern with curing existent problems to the back burner in an effort to get at the "root causes" of physiological, psychological, and social problems. Presumably, knowledge of "root causes" would lead to eliminating the factors that gave rise to the problem in the first place.

On the surface, those who press for prevention seem to enjoy a logically unchallengeable position. Unfortunately for the individuals charged with implementing preventive programs, consensus regarding the "root causes" of problems such as crime, economic disadvantage, and poor school performance is elusive. Writing about crime in society and in schools, James Q. Wilson (1976) notes that scholars have identified "the structure of the family, peer group relationships, and poverty as factors contributing to many problems in our society including crime generally and particularly crime in schools" (p. 4). David Bordua (1966) goes even further when he contends that deviance "occurs in the absence of effective devices for producing conformity" (p. 85). Apparently, for Bordua the "root causes" of misbehavior are societywide in nature; the society is failing sufficiently to reward behavior it publicly deems appropriate. If society is the culprit, though, how does one go about transforming such an amorphous, almost chimerical entity?

Once again I have raised a question I cannot answer. What I intend to do in the pages that follow is to offer a systematic review of various attempts at reaching beyond the individual student to account for school behavior problems. For ease of analysis, the review will divide these efforts into those that concentrate on family background, peer group influence, the quality of teaching, the school system, and society in general. It should be remembered, however, that many researchers find more than one cause for discipline problems. While indications of multiple causes are frequent in the literature, rarely are there references to factors such as individual free will or initiative (Allport's so-called "proactive, self-directing capacities"). It is this critical omission that prompts this chapter and my use of the term depersonalization of blame to describe contemporary efforts to explain student misbehavior.

Blaming Family Background

Few influences on the behavior of the young are more vulnerable to criticism than the family, especially the parents. In this regard, we would do well to set aside for a moment all the arguments that student misbehavior results from low intelligence, low socioeconomic status, or both—factors that many trace directly to a student's parents—and to consider the matter of inept or inappropriate parenting. In a concise review of research on school discipline, William Gnagey (1970) cites the results of a study by Thurston, Feldhusen, and Benning (pp. 17-18). The three researchers found that the following factors commonly appear in home situations of children who are identified as "constant classroom deviants":

1. The discipline of the father is either lax, overly strict, or erratic.
2. The supervision by the mother is at best only fair, or it is downright inadequate.
3. The parents are either indifferent or even hostile toward the child.
4. The family members are scattered in diverse activities and operate only somewhat as a unit or perhaps not at all.
5. The parents find it difficult to talk things over regarding the child.
6. The husband-wife relationship lacks closeness and equality or partnership.
7. The parents find many things to disapprove of in their child.
8. The mothers are not happy with the communities in which they live.
9. The parents resort to angry physical punishment when the child does wrong. Temper control is a difficult problem for them at this time.
10. The parents believe they have little influence on the development of their child.
11. The parents believe that other children exert bad influences upon their child.
12. The parents' leisure time activities lack much of a constructive element.
13. The parents, particularly the father, report no church membership.
[Gnagey 1970, pp. 17-18]

Several studies plus considerable conventional wisdom support the research just cited. Herschel Rader (1975), in a review of research, observes that the "importance of the mother in the etiology of delinquent behavior has long been axiomatic" (p. 31). W.P. Robinson (1975) who conducted a large-scale study of adolescents in England and Wales, reports that misconduct in school is influenced by student boredom, which, in turn, is correlated with "the values, interests and behavior of parents" (p. 150). Interestingly, Robinson finds little relationship between student boredom and "the material and financial conditions of the home."

Rudolf Dreikurs, the late psychiatrist and expert on student misbehavior, attributed much of the problem to poor family climate. He estimated that three out of four American families start the day with a fight (Westin 1973, p. 14). Rising rates of separation, divorce, and unwanted pregnancy, as well as combative domestic environments, are indeed bound to exact a heavy toll on the development of the children involved.

That family climate is a critical factor in the rearing of the young is demonstrated by the findings of a study of 10,000 high-school graduates conducted by Berkeley's Center for the Study of Higher Education. This study concludes that a positive family climate, as indicated by parents who are loving, energetic, and ambitious, is directly related to a student's academic motivation, which is itself connected with such other attributes as persistence and behavior (Trent et al. 1965, p. 97).

Further support for the critical value of the home environment comes from a comparison of high-school dropouts and graduates admitted to college. As early as the first grade, the two groups differed significantly from each other with regard to such things as academic performance, behavior ratings, absenteeism, and IQ (Yudin et al. 1973). Family background is the likely cause of much of the variance.

Children from broken homes have long been associated with low achievement and adjustment problems in school. In an unusual study, three British researchers compared the characteristics of fifty delinquent boys of high intelligence (IQ above 115). Unlike many delinquents, these youngsters' problems obviously did not derive from lack of ability. The researchers found, however, that many of their sample did have an important point in common: coming from single-parent homes or having parents who were receiving psychiatric treatment (Gath et al. 1970).

Exactly how parents and family climate influence the behavior of the young is subject to debate. Some researchers feel that parents of "problem children" have been poor models or selfish (Ahlstrom and Havighurst 1971). Roy Menninger is quoted as saying, "Young people are rebellious largely because their uptight, self-righteous, and hypocritical parents are not giving them a meaningful piece of the action" (in McKenney 1969, p. 5).

Others impugn Benjamin Spock and permissive parenting for school discipline problems. An attitudinal study of Missouri state leaders reveals that many believe that misconduct in school is rooted in the combination of parental pressure for more permissive schooling and teaching liability laws that discourage teachers from actively disciplining students (Lambert 1975). Emery Stoops and Joyce King-Stoops present the standard, if somewhat exaggerated and simplistic, indictment of permissive parenting:

> Through the last four decades, parents have been in the gradual process of abdication. The head of the household gave way to joint husband-and-wife powers which encouraged children's playing one head against

the other. When a spank-the-bottom parent was cancelled out by a permissive mate, the kids ran wild through the home and right into the classroom. [1972, p. 12]

It is one thing to indict the quality of parenting and quite another to say that parents are to blame for discipline problems in school because they do not endow their offspring with sufficient intelligence to succeed in school, or because they fail to achieve a standard of living high enough to provide the middle-class amenities associated so directly with positive school experiences. While the issue of inherited intelligence is still hotly contested, there is agreement among many that students from lower socioeconomic statuses are more likely to become "behavior problems" (Powell and Bergem 1962). To what extent parents have control over their own socioeconomic status is also open to question though.

Perhaps the last word on the quality of parenting in the United States was provided by Urie Bronfenbrenner in 1970. Comparing childrearing in the United States and the Soviet Union, he concludes that American families are not as child-centered as Russian families. American parents spend less time with their children and, in effect, have abandoned them to the questionable influences of television and peer group. As James Coleman (1961) demonstrates in his large-scale study of adolescent culture,

> The adolescent lives more and more in a society of his own, he finds the family a less and less satisfying psychological home. As a consequence, the home has less and less ability to mold him. [p. 312]

Blaming the Peer Group

Assuming that Coleman and Bronfenbrenner are correct when they maintain that some American parents do not create a satisfying environment at home, there is still no proof that misbehavior in school is the direct outgrowth of unsatisfactory domestic environments. Presumably, young people must learn to misbehave just as they learn to obey rules or to read. There is compelling evidence that the peer group is the primary instrument for "teaching" adolescents to act in ways school authorities find unacceptable. Bronfenbrenner would argue that the peer group instructs by default because parents have abdicated their roles as models of appropriate behavior. Whether through default, the natural attractiveness of age-mates, or an inherent tension between generations, the adolescent peer group is undoubtedly a critical determinant of attitudes and behavior.

As early as 1911 G. Stanley Hall, the eminent psychologist, decried the undesirable consequences of gang culture for urban youth. Hall wrote that the majority of American boys had at some point in their lives belonged to a gang, but he attributed the urge to participate in such groups more to "instinct" than "maturer influences" (p. 301). During the 1930s sociological research into the causes of delinquency revealed that deviant acts were generally committed in group situations, a fact that served to confirm the harmful potential of unsupervised collections of youth (Bordua). In the 1940s Robert Havighurst and Hilda Taba recentered the concern over deleterious peer group influence from the streets to the school. They pointed out the negative consequences of peer rejection and the destructive social pressures existing in adolescent culture. In 1966 N.M. Lorber supported their contentions with the finding that children who are socially unacceptable to their classmates often act in disruptive ways in the classroom.

James Coleman explains that one reason the adolescent peer group is so influential is demographic. With more teenagers than ever before, U.S. schools have become "adolescent cultures," complete with their own sets of values. With reference to Soviet schools, however, Bronfenbrenner observes that adolescent values need not be opposed to the best interests of the school. In the United States, though, few writers report many positive aspects of adolescent values. Presenting the findings of a participant observer study of an urban high school, Stuart Palonsky (1975) illustrates just how negative peer-directed values can be:

> The reality generated by the interaction with their age-grade peer group defined their classes as boring and not meaningful. Failing and cutting were approved by their groups as legitimate responses to boredom and irrelevance.... [pp. 98-99]

Palonsky raises the possibility that the adolescent peer group's values may possess a kind of legitimacy based on the inability of teachers to make learning exciting and meaningful. The next section extends this line of argument.

Blaming Teachers

Could it be that teachers—those who often complain the most vociferously about discipline problems—really are responsible for student misbehavior? A number of researchers reply in the affirmative.

Being criticized is nothing new to the teaching profession, of course. In the early 1960s James Bryant Conant and James Kerner, among others, spoke strongly in favor of making access to the profession more rigorous and selective in order to weed out mediocre teachers. More recently, Charles Silberman, a journalist by trade, has impugned not only teacher education—always a popular target for critics of American schools—but also the teachers themselves.

He maintains that much of what teachers do is poorly understood by them and inhumane. Indeed, research on teacher expectations suggests that student success can be influenced by what the teacher believes the student can do—a finding that brings up the disturbing possibility of the "self-fulfilling prophecy" and supports the contention that teachers can harm as well as help students (see Rosenthal and Jacobson 1968).

Researchers and journalists are not the only people who question the quality of teaching in public schools. An analysis of student perceptions of how school can be improved reveals that the young respondents place far more blame for problems on their teachers than on themselves. Among the students' recommendations for improving the quality of teaching are "greater teacher effort," "more interesting activities and classes," "less favoritism by teachers," and "more stringent controls" (Farley and Rosnow 1975). Interestingly, administrators and parents often cite these same concerns along with one additional criticism—teachers' failure consistently to enforce school rules.

While various people seem to feel that teachers contribute to the very problems about which they complain, consensus regarding how this process occurs is lacking. In one review William Gnagey finds that teachers can "cause" student misbehavior by playing roles like "the absolute director," "the matinee idol," and "the nonentity." Along rather similar lines, W. Pritchett and D.J. Willower (1975) conclude that students tend to harbor negative attitudes toward school and teachers when they perceive teachers to be acting in a rigid or custodial manner.

While the references just cited suggest that discipline problems are related to the role played by the teacher, other studies imply that problems result from the teacher's inadequate understanding of reinforcement theory. Summarizing research on the subject, W.E. Schmidt and Vernon Tyler (1975) state that teachers often unwittingly reinforce disruptive behavior. Likewise, B.F. Skinner notes,

> What appears to be punishment is sometimes reinforcing; a student misbehaves to annoy his teacher or to be admired by his peers when he takes punishment. If the teacher's attention is reinforcing, unwanted responses which attract attention are strengthened. [1968, p. 190]

Terry Huff and John Schnelle (1974) indicate that elementary students judged to be well-behaved and those judged to be poorly behaved are equally capable of detecting inappropriate classroom behaviors on video tape. The researchers conclude that a student in the latter group misbehaves "not because he lacks 'awareness' of inappropriate forms of behavior but more likely because of prevalent reinforcement systems" (p. 1252).

In the past few decades it has been popular to maintain that punishment by teachers does little to control classroom misbehavior or improve student performance in the long run (see Skinner, pp. 95-103). Merle Meacham and Allen Wiesen claim, for instance, that punishment is not just generally ineffective, but that it actually may foster misconduct:

> In controlling children through punishment, threat, and coercion, the excessively punitive teacher is, in effect, teaching the children to be aggressive by serving as a model of aggressiveness. [1974, p. 66]

Few observers feel that teachers purposely seek to be models of aggressiveness or reinforcers of disruptive behavior. If teachers are to blame for discipline problems in school, Thomas Good and Jere Brophy argue this is simply because they are unaware of what they are doing (1973). Lisa Serbin and K. Daniel O'Leary contend more specifically that teachers are unaware of the extent to which they shape their students' behavior:

> As nursery-school children busily mold clay, their teachers are molding behavior. Unwittingly, teachers foster an environment where children learn that boys are aggressive and able to solve problems, while girls are submissive and passive. [1975, p. 57]

Suggesting that "bullies are made, not born," these researchers seem to account for the fact that there are typically more boys than girls identified as school "behavior problems."

Thomas Gordon (1974), author of the Teacher Effectiveness Training program, writes that teachers often create a structured teacher-centered environment, not realizing that such a setting all but ensures "that students will remain helplessly dependent, immature, infantile." Gordon goes on to argue that, "Instead of fostering the growth of *responsibility,* teachers and administrators dictate and control students of all ages as if they were not to be trusted and could never be responsible" (p. 8).

Classroom communication is another area in which a lack of awareness on the teacher's part can give rise to student behavior problems. Both Gordon's program and his applications of transactional analysis to schools stress the critical relationship between what teachers say in class, how they say it, and how students behave (see Ernst 1975; Gordon). Don Thomas and several colleagues find that teachers who voice disapproval without periodically expressing approval or praise experience increased classroom disruptions. They cite a supporting study of first graders to demonstrate that their finding is true even of six-year-olds:

> The more often a teacher told first graders to "sit down," the more often they stood up. Only praising sitting seemed to increase sitting behavior. [Thomas et al. 1970, p. 111]

Since the depersonalization of blame is a difficult process to stop once it commences, it is only natural that those who blame teachers for discipline problems pave the way for others to indict those who teach teachers. Thus, Good and Brophy observe that "teacher-training programs have seldom equipped teachers with specific teaching techniques or provided them with specific skills for analyzing and labeling classroom behavior." My course at Stanford's School of Education on "School and Classroom Discipline" is one of the few classes offered on the subject at a teacher training institution, a disquieting fact in light of the public and professional concern over student misbehavior.

It is one thing to contend that discipline problems result because teachers are ill-trained to deal with misconduct—that they reward the wrong behavior, play favorites, enforce rules inconsistently, and punish innocent students. It is quite another matter to argue that teachers contribute to discipline problems by teaching poorly (the distinction here is between instruction and classroom management). The strong evidence showing a direct relationship between lack of school success and student discipline problems implies that good teaching is the first line of defense against misbehavior (Powell and Bergem; Duke 1976b; Mueller 1966). The work of John Dollard and others points to the close connection between frustration—often triggered by academic failure—and school aggression (see Gnagey). If teachers neglect students who need help in developing fundamental skills or fail to enlist outside assistance to help students with learning problems that cannot be handled in the regular classroom context, then they may have to accept much of the blame for the behavior problems that typically ensue.

Blaming the School System

Times have changed considerably since Edward Stulken published an article entitled "Education Prevents Delinquency" in a 1933 issue of *The Phi Delta Kappan*. At that point in time, the creation of special schools was being hailed as the key to eliminating wasted lives and juvenile misconduct. Nowadays, though, many observers believe that schools create rather than prevent discipline problems. W. Gordon West (1975) posits, for example, that "the very structure of contemporary schooling fosters 'immorality' (delinquency)."

In recent years it has become more common to shift the blame for a variety of social problems from individuals and groups to institutions; bureaucracies have been particularly hard hit (Duke 1976). These current arguments generally focus on characteristics within the very structure of institutions that compel individuals to behave or misbehave in certain ways. (A frequently heard cry among the Watergate conspirators, for instance, was that the "system" was to blame for what they did.) Schools and "the school system" have not been immune to this type of criticism.

Discipline problems have been explained through analyses of several different dimensions of contemporary schooling in the United States. West maintains that schools ensure that some students always will fail, thereby perpetuating dissatisfaction and misbehavior. Minimizing the negative influence of both family background and peer group, he argues that the reduction of adolescent deviance in school can occur only by eliminating educational environments where success cannot be obtained by all.

Lending support to West's contention are Francis Cullen and Vincent Tinto (1975), who use Mertonian analysis to indicate that a school's restriction of the opportunity to achieve academic success is a major source of discipline problems. They also claim that the tendency to respond to academic failure with deviant behavior is strongest among minority group students and students from low socioeconomic statuses.

Some researchers contend that schools create behavior problems by neglecting to deal with values or by instilling values that are antithetical to good citizenship. Among those taking the latter stance is Patricia Sexton (1967). She believes that schools stimulate student resistance, resentment, and rebellion by stressing the value of individual achievement and competition to the exclusion of more cooperative values. W.P. Robinson, in the previously cited study of boredom in English schools, agrees with Sexton:

> The association between boredom and competition is also noteworthy. Where competition between individuals is constructed and encouraged and where winning is rewarded, it is inevitable that there must be losers. But is it not absurd to construct a system of education where only a minority are viewed as winners? And what are the chronic losers to do? Very few people will persist at playing at some game in which they invariably lose, and yet we tolerate a situation in which children are consistently allowed to lose every school day, for perhaps ten years of their lives. [p. 151]

Theodore Brameld (1957) harbors a different view. He feels that, "Insofar as American education has tended to regard its chief business as that of conveying information and training in skills, it has tended to store its values ... in the educational attic ..." (p. 13). In other words, Brameld feels that schools are guilty not of inculcating the wrong values, but rather of neglecting values altogether.

An article on crime in school by James Q. Wilson presents yet a third perspective on the connection between values and student misbehavior. Wilson refers to a study by Arthur Stinchcombe in which rebelliousness appeared to originate among "young boys and girls who from the outset are aiming at ... a working class lifestyle" (p. 5). The conclusion of this line of thought is that by ignoring the values and aspirations of the non-college-bound, secondary schools encourage dissatisfaction and defiance. In a review of research on school deviance, Paul Bellaby (1974) finds corroborating evidence for Stinchcombe's conclusion. Looking at secondary schools in England, he reports that many students first manifest hostility toward school during or near their sophomore year—when schooling particularly seems irrelevant to their "concept of the future." This finding seems to contradict the research that suggests high-school "problem" students can be identified as early as the first grade. Apparently, some adolescents who intend to pursue vocations after graduation feel that positive school experiences cannot come out of the stress on acquiring academic information rather than marketable skills.

Schools have been implicated in the creation of their own discipline problems in ways other than those which involve their ensuring that some students fail and neglecting the matter of values. Charles Silberman attributes much of the school system's woes to sheer "mindlessness," the failure of teachers and administrators "to ask *why* they are doing what they are doing—to think seriously or deeply about the purposes or consequences of education" (p. 11).

A California study of violence in schools provides criticism that is more specific than Silberman's. It blames school violence in part on ineffective school administrators, inconsistent disciplinary practices, oppressive school rules, inadequate counseling, curriculum irrelevance, and staff bigotry (*Teacher* 1974). This rather blanket indictment of the school system is reflected in a longitudinal study of U.S. schools by the American Institutes for Research (AIR 1976) which identifies seven problem areas, most of which have some bearing on student misbehavior and dissatisfaction:

1. grossly inadequate vocational guidance
2. too many harmful teachers
3. lack of individualized instruction
4. inadequate curriculum
5. lack of personal support
6. too few alternative ways to learn
7. ineffective education for citizenship in a democratic society.

Along with other recent writings on education, the studies just cited call into question the quality of schooling in the United States and the viability of compulsory, universal education. But the "buck" need not stop with the schools of America. If in reality schools do little more than reflect the interest and biases of the society in which they exist, then the ultimate culprit in the school discipline "crisis" must be none other than society itself.

Blaming Society

What is it about contemporary U.S. society that prompts some observers to maintain that it is to blame for youthful misconduct? After all, other nations do not report such severe problems with disobedience and disrespect in school. Once again, no single factor is put forward to explain school discipline problems. About the only thing on which observers agree is the fact that schools do not exist in isolation—that is, that what goes on inside schools is also manifest outside.

Some explanations, such as the one which follows, are vague indictments that prove virtually useless in pinpointing the causes of student misbehavior:

> The statement that there are no delinquent children, only delinquent parents, is open to serious question. This view assumes that a parent could do better if he merely decided to do so. . . . Can we take for granted that the parent knows what is best and can apply his knowledge? The circumstances in which the parent lived as a child and as a youth have served to mold him so that his own fears and insecurities become a part of him. Actually society as a whole is responsible for delinquent behavior since both the parent and the child are its products. [Resnick 1974, p. 116]

Other accounts concerned with the fact that behavior problems are increasing among American youth, both inside and outside of school, focus on the phenomenon of adolescence. Adolescence is seen to be a creation of society, a culture-based holding operation designed to keep physically mature youth out of a saturated job market. Urie Bronfenbrenner speaks of the negative impact of an age-segregated society, one in which young people rarely interact with adults who could serve as models or children who could provide opportunities for service. James Coleman (1972) feels it is not surprising that teenagers are bored with school and life in general; they have few opportunities in contemporary society to be genuinely productive. Robert Havighurst (1974) echoes this contention when he states that since 1950 American society has denied its youth "maturity-promoting experience" (p. 6). Rudolf Dreikurs adds that "adolescents resent the willingness of the adult community to give them any part in deciding about activities and regulations regarding their own welfare" (Dreikurs and Grey 1968, p. 5). The obvious conclusion of these observations is that a society which babies its adolescents should expect adolescents who behave immaturely.

In the wake of widespread reports of government scandal and the corruption of high officials, it is also possible to argue that misbehaving youths are simply following the lead of their elders. When we realize that students from affluent backgrounds are just as capable of disobedience and disrespect as are those from impoverished homes, we must also see that upward mobility—the great American promise—is not an automatic solution to discipline problems. S.L. Halleck contends,

> We must re-examine our time-honored reverence for affluence, power,

and bigness, and face the possibility that affluence bores, that power corrupts, and that big institutions diminish the stature of man. [in McKenney, p. 5]

In an essay of this length it is impossible to touch on all the possible impetuses for student misbehavior that society either creates or tacitly sanctions. In passing, however, mention must be made of the influence on youthful aggression of television and the movies; the school disturbances attributable to the profound levels of racism found in many quarters of society; and the yet unstudied effects of overcrowding on student conduct. Does class conflict play a role in escalating discipline problems? Has society become so relativistic that young people can no longer have clear notions of right and wrong? How is the rise in crime rates linked to the increase in student misbehavior? Currently, there are more questions than answers regarding the relationship between school discipline and societal influences.

Blaming Nobody

A review of contemporary efforts to account for school discipline problems would be incomplete without reference to those who argue that much of student misbehavior is a normal, even healthy, part of growing up.

In his massive study of student movements, Lewis Feuer (1969) maintains that conflict between generations is a basic historical theme, albeit one that sometimes produces tragic results. William Kvaraceus (1966), a leading student of adolescent deviance, cautions against ignoring the positive aspects of misconduct:

> The communication channels between adolescent subculture and adult culture are seldom open and clear. Many youths unconsciously communicate to the adult society via their norm-violating behavior that "something is wrong" within the adolescent subculture or in the individual's personal make-up. A delinquent act can serve as an SOS signal which the adult community cannot afford to ignore. [p. 217]

Extending Kvaraceus's idea, R.P. McDermott (1969) contends that,

> School failure and delinquency often represent highly motivated and intelligent attempts to develop the abilities, statuses, and identities that will best equip the child to maximize his utilities in the politics of everyday life. If the teacher is going to send degrading messages of relationship regardless of how the game is played, the child's best strategy is to stop playing the game. [p. 113]

Although he takes a more moderate stance than the previous two writers,

David Ausubel likewise maintains that misbehavior is an important part of youth in many instances. Ausubel contends that breaking rules provides the young with experiences that can serve as future reference points. "Acknowledgment of wrong-doing and acceptance of punishment are part of learning moral accountability," he claims (Ausubel and Robinson 1969, p. 469). The implication is that children who grow up without having misbehaved and suffered the consequences lack a critical component of moral development.

The Depersonalization of Blame and the Depreciation of Individual Integrity

The previous pages summarize recent attempts to determine the origins of student misbehavior. Some of these accounts clearly fit into the category I term the "politics of apology." In other words, they represent deliberate efforts to vindicate or to shift the blame from one factor to another. Other accounts represent more objective investigations. Whatever the motives, the net result of these endeavors has usually been to minimize the responsibility of the individual student for his inappropriate behavior in school—or what I refer to as the depersonalization of blame. I maintain that this process is not always in the best interests of the student, the school, or the society, though in the short run it may be politically expedient.

One undesirable by-product of the depersonalization of blame is the tendency for individuals in positions of authority to give special treatment to those who misbehave. Confronted with "evidence" showing that a student's misconduct is the likely result of strife at home, association with the "wrong crowd," or too much violence on television, a compassionate teacher or administrator is compelled to display understanding and tolerance toward students who break school or classroom rules. Naturally, this kind of reaction creates a problem. Why should students conform to rules if those who disobey them receive as much or more adult attention as those who do not? Token economies and other enticing reward systems are generally used to improve the behavior of "problem" students, not to reinforce the actions of "good" students. The student who always obeys the rules and respects his teachers is expected to survive on intrinsic motivation alone. Meanwhile, his misbehaving counterpart receives not only more attention from his teachers, but often the adulation of his peers as well. While I do not mean to imply that misbehaving students should be ostracized or treated with undue harshness, I am suggesting that a second thought be given the ways in which they are handled.

This last point leads us to a second undesirable by-product of the depersonalization of blame. By consistently accounting for an individual's behavior in terms of factors external to him, researchers are actually contributing to the depreciation of individual integrity. If a student's behavior in school is, for instance, exclusively the product of family background, peer group, teachers, the school system, and societal influences, then why would he bother to obey rules or act appropriately? For that matter, why would anyone aspire to perfection, act altruistically, cooperate with his fellow human beings, or owe his allegiance to a cause greater than himself in a society where his behavior is determined or externally shaped?

While this chapter is not intended as an existential polemic against social scientists who, perhaps unwittingly, would exonerate individuals of all responsibility for their behavior, it does attempt to sound a note of caution. Are all people truly victims of forces beyond their control? What is the prognosis for a society of victims in which everyone can blame his transgressions or problems on someone or something else?

Rather than close on what appears to be a pessimistic note, I would like to argue that individuals are responsible, at least in part, for their own behavior— for both their achievements and their failings. It is well to remember that students misbehave because they forget the rules as well as because they are subconsciously striking out at an authoritarian father. The irrelevance of the curriculum and televised disrespect for authority are not the only reasons why students skip classes. At times, they simply prefer doing something else—a reaction not uncommon among adults who stay home from work for "personal" reasons. Whatever the school discipline problem, it is important to keep in mind the role played by a student's free will. To minimize or eliminate this role is to diminish the student's humanity.

Ultimately, the improvement of school discipline will depend on whether educators and parents can convince young people that they themselves are largely responsible for their own behavior. The continued depersonalization of blame, assisted by the currently popular politics of apology, will not inspire American youth to look first to themselves to correct their misbehavior. Only a reaffirmation of the individual's responsibility for acting appropriately can accomplish this function. As Jesse Jackson, one of Martin Luther King's lieutenants, wisely observes with regard to the education of black students:

> We keep saying that Johnny doesn't read because he's deprived, hungry and discriminated against.... One of the reasons Johnny does not read well is that Johnny doesn't practice reading. [in *Time* 1976, p. 6]

The Unfinished Agenda

The compulsion to identify the environmental factors that "cause" students to misbehave has led to a neglect of several important activities. There is of course a continuing need for research on school discipline; but we must have more than just that type of study which searches for correlates of misbehavior for a known population of "problem" students or which reports on the effectiveness of a teaching technique for controlling classroom disruptions. Researchers must go on to:

1. investigate the individual student's role in misbehavior and in correcting his misbehavior;
2. look at discipline problems as school, rather than purely classroom, phenomena;
3. determine what degree of student misconduct is functional or even desirable;
4. trace how concepts of appropriate and inappropriate behavior change over time and from place to place;
5. study why schools in countries other than the United States report so few discipline problems;
6. employ techniques such as stimulated recall to find out how students perceive misbehavior, both their own and other students';
7. tap the vast amount of data which most schools maintain on discipline.

To complement this expanded research on school discipline, educators must mount efforts to incorporate into the regular curriculum such subjects as student behavior, rights, and responsibilities. After all, if the public cares how its young people behave, why should not schools provide instruction on behavior and test students on such matters as school rules and the consequence of disobeying them. A step in the direction just outlined has been taken by the Kettering Foundation's Task Force '74, which actually identified a list of basic student responsibilities to accompany the plethora of lists of student rights.

If the issue of student responsibilities can be handled in a positive, nonpunitive way, rather than as a seeming backlash against declining student behavior, it is possible that the problem of school discipline can be curbed. The ultimate resolution of the problem, though, depends on the ability of young people—and adults—to stop seeing themselves as victims and to begin seeing themselves as responsible human beings able to determine a significant portion of their behavior.

4

A Person-Environment Fit Model of School Crime and Disruption

Richard A. Kulka, David W. Mann, and David M. Klingel

Because the escalation of public concern over increased violence in schools has occurred primarily during the past five to ten years, most efforts to study the problem are of recent vintage, and rigorous studies focusing specifically on the nature and causes of criminal behavior in schools are still rare. From the viewpoint of educational practice, this paucity of systematic research on school crime is indeed quite unfortunate. But it nevertheless offers an opportunity rare in the annals of social science: the opportunity to develop an adequate and systematic conceptualization of the problem prior to engaging in extensive research or in broad-scale intervention.

In this chapter we approach the conceptual task of constructing a theory of school crime via consideration of a similar problem area, that of juvenile delinquency. Delinquency in school is at least a subset of delinquent behavior in general. Thus, an adequate conceptual model of sufficient generality to account for the broadest possible range of research evidence on juvenile crime should be relevant to the study of school crime. Not incidentally, it should also be able to account for nondelinquent behavior. In our view, the type of theory required is a multilevel, interactive, behavioral model (Yinger 1965) of juvenile crime. Such a schema should characterize delinquent behavior (like any other response or behavior) as a function of the interaction between characteristics of the individual and characteristics of the environments or situations to which he or she is commonly exposed (Lewin 1935; Murray 1938).

Increasingly, social theorists have invoked the concept of "congruence" or "fit" to specify the nature of that interaction. Models of person-environment congruence or fit have now emerged in virtually every major domain of social research (Feather 1975; French, Rodgers, and Cobb 1974; Getzels 1969; Kahana 1978; Lawler 1973; Locke 1969; Moos 1974; Pervin 1968; Stern 1970; Veroff and Feld 1970); and a large number of studies conducted in diverse social settings suggest that the fit between person and social environment may be an important predictor of physical or psychological well-being and of maladaptive behavior. (For an extensive review and critique of theory and research on

---

Work on this chapter was supported in part by research grants G-77-0023 and G-78-0049 from the National Institute of Education.

person-environment fit, see Kulka 1976, 1979.) Nevertheless, to our knowledge, no theories or studies currently exist which explicitly conceptualize delinquent behavior as a function of person-environment congruence or fit.

A Model of Person-Environment Fit

Although several promising theories of person-environment (P-E) congruence are available, one particular model, a quantitative schema proposed by French, Rodgers, and Cobb (1974), seems particularly suitable for conceptualizing delinquent behavior. It appears both flexible enough to incorporate essential features of the others and sufficiently comprehensive to account for a variety of research findings. The basic assumption of the model is that adjustment may be conceived of as the goodness-of-fit between characteristics of the person and properties of his or her environment. (This view has been elaborated in a number of papers; for example, Caplan, Cobb, French, Harrison, and Pinneau 1975; French et al. 1974; Harrison 1978; Kulka 1976.)

Basic Concepts

The theory may be described in terms of a few fundamental concepts. First, the model proposes four basic elements:

1. the *objective environment*, which includes aspects of the physical and social world that exist independently of the person's perceptions of them;
2. the *subjective environment*, representing the person's perceptions and cognitions of relevant aspects of his or her objective environment;
3. the *objective person*, the person's objectively demonstrable characteristics (that is, needs, values, abilities, and other relatively enduring attributes), independent of his or her perceptions; and
4. the *subjective person*, the individual's perceptions or cognitions of his or her objective characteristics (that is, the person's self-concept or self-identity).

Employing these four elements, the model distinguishes between subjective person-environment fit and objective person-environment fit. In the former, characteristics of both the person and the environment are assessed as the person perceives and reports them, while in the latter both components are measured independently of the person's perceptions and cognitions of them.

Second, the theory proposes that for both objective and subjective P-E fit there are two basic subtypes, describable in terms of two sorts of demands and two corresponding forms of supplies to meet these demands. The motives (needs or values) of the person represent one type of demand, which may or

A Person-Environment Fit Model

may not be met by environmental supplies in the form of opportunities for gratification. The other type of demand emanates from the environment and consists of role demands or requirements; the person's skills or abilities constitute the supplies to meet such demands. The model assumes that both forms of misfit—opportunity-need and ability-demand—are indicators of poor adjustment and that they will be related to various forms of psychological strain (low self-esteem, job dissatisfaction, depression) or psychological strain, and to other symptoms of poor mental health; they will also be related to various coping and/or reactive behaviors.

Predicted Relationships Between P-E Fit and Strain

Hypothesized relationships between various dimensions of P-E fit and strains are generally represented by one of three hypothetical functions, as illustrated in figure 4-1. Curve A illustrates a monotonic curvilinear relationship between size of deficiency for a particular resource or ability and a given measure of strain; excess of either environmental or personal supplies does not influence level of strain. Thus, the curve of strain plotted against P-E fit decreases as the

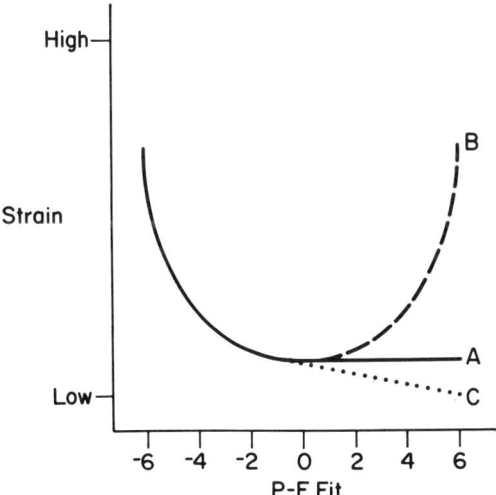

Note: The hypothesized relationship between P-E fit and psychological strain as adapted from French, Rodgers, and Cobb (1974).

Figure 4-1. Three Hypothetical Person-Environment Fit Curves

magnitude of deficiency decreases; it reaches an asymptote at perfect fit and shows no further changes with increasing excesses of supplies. For example, a thirsty man will drink until he has quenched his thirst, and additional supplies of water will not result in greater satisfaction.

In contrast, the other two curves reflect hypotheses which suggest that excess supplies or abilities will make a difference. In one instance (Curve B) the relationship between fit and strain is U-shaped, strain being lowest at the point of perfect fit, but rising with increases in either deficiency or excess of supplies. This type of relationship is proposed in situations where two or more important motives are involved and where excess supplies for one motive may result in deficient supplies for another. For example, if academic abilities are exceeded by teacher demands, strain would result as in Curve A; however, as abilities increasingly exceed demands, boredom, apathy, or resentment may result from frustration or from lack of opportunity to use a valued skill.

A similar example illustrates the hypothesis suggested by Curve C, whereby excess supplies may result in decreased levels of strain. Such relationships are posited when excess supplies for one motive can be used directly as (or exchanged for) supplies for other motives. Accordingly, students whose reading abilities exceed the difficulty of reading materials may exhibit less strain than do those whose ability matches the material, because rewards such as teacher praise and high grades may be associated with that relationship (compare Jorgenson 1977). Recent studies by Caplan and others (1975), Harrison (1978), and Kulka (1976) have reported empirical relationships approximating each of these three hypothetical functions.

A Student-School Fit Model of School Crime

Ideally, a general model of person-environment fit applied to the problem of delinquent behavior or school crime should include a description of the broad range of institutions that children and adolescents confront. However, space does not permit such comprehensiveness, so we will focus on one major social institution: the school—an institution characterized by Elliott and Voss (1974) as "*the* critical social context for the generation of delinquent behavior [emphasis added]" (p. 204). Moreover, a large body of empirical research suggests the critical importance of school experiences, involvements, and performances in the prediction of disruptive, rebellious, and delinquent behavior (for example, Erickson, Scott, and Empey 1964; Glaser 1975; Polk and Schafer 1972; Wenk 1974; West 1975).

In figure 4-2 we describe therefore a more specific model of the theoretical relationship between school crime (as a subset of delinquent behavior in general) and person-environment fit. The model treats the problem as a behavioral response to various forms of psychological strain engendered by the school

A Person-Environment Fit Model 53

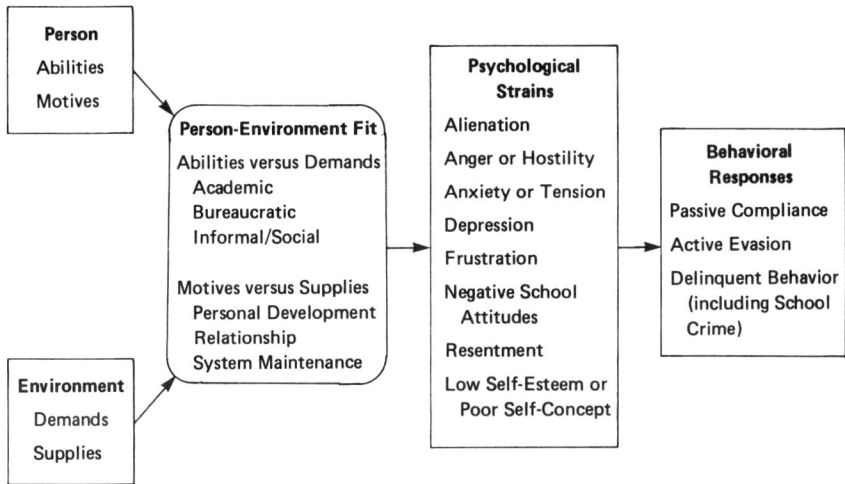

Figure 4-2. A Simplified Model of the Relationship between Person-Environment Fit and School Crime

experience. On the one hand, there are the strains of self-denigration and anxiety resulting from failure to meet school-related role demands. On the other, there are the strains of dissatisfaction and alienation which result from the persistent frustration of students' needs or values.

Given this basic distinction between two major categories of person-environment fit, the selection of salient dimensions within each type requires that we ask: what are the major tasks, dilemmas, or problems of adaptation which confront adolescents in the social environment of the school?

Ability-Demand Dimensions

Figure 4-2 illustrates the three main categories of role requirements—academic, bureaucratic, and informal/social—which seem particularly relevant to measuring person-environment fit in school. Students and their parents are keenly aware of the importance of academic achievement for future success (Gold 1963; Vinter and Sarri 1965). Perhaps the salience of innate or acquired scholastic abilities and their corresponding demands is therefore obvious. However, achievement in the role of students is not only measured in terms of skills and information. It is also measured in terms of "proper" behavior (Boocock 1972), or of the "hidden curriculum" (Jackson 1968; Silberman 1971)—a morass of rules, regulations and procedures designed to mold individual behavior to the demands of institutional living. Demands so created achieve centrality and motivational significance by virtue of being linked to the same reward system as that of the official academic curriculum; thus, they form the core of what Walberg (1972) has called the "bureaucratic student role." Nevertheless, the high school "is not only an adolescent's place of work; it is also his club" (Douvan and Gold 1966); and several investigators (for example, Boocock 1972; Coleman 1961) have emphasized the powerful impact of a dominant peer value system based on popularity, athletics, and social leadership skills.

Motive-Supply Dimensions

Most of the important dimensions relevant to the congruence between student motives and characteristics of the school environment seem to be subsumable under three broad categories of social climate dimensions described by Insel and Moos (1974): (1) personal development; (2) relationship; and (3) system maintenance or system change. Consequently, the selection of motive-supply dimensions of person-environment fit from each of these categories should provide a reasonably complete picture of congruence in this area as shown in figure 4-2.

Personal development dimensions which seem especially salient to the school context include needs and opportunities for:

1. achievement (as in Atkinson and Feather 1966);
2. recognition and social status (Coleman 1961);
3. independence and autonomy (for example, Buxton 1973; Douvan and Adelson 1966);
4. "relevance" of school activities to present and future life circumstances (Stinchcombe 1964); and
5. self-utilization or self-development (Argyris 1957; Backman, Kahn, Mednick, Davidson, and Johnston 1967).

Particularly important *relationship* dimensions in the school environment appear to involve needs and opportunities for affiliation with peers (Buxton 1973; Coleman 1961; Douvan and Adelson 1966) and for supportive relationships with teachers (for example, Brophy and Good 1974; Gold 1978). *System maintenance* and *system change* dimensions, which concern the organization and operation of the school, include the particular styles employed for establishing and maintaining control in relation to student needs and values (for example, Getzels 1969), and student opportunities and motivation for the exercise of power within school (Boocock 1972; Wittes 1970).

Psychological Strains and Behavioral Responses

Figure 4-2 also emphasizes that the stress engendered by poor fit with respect to the school environment may lead to several types of psychological strain. These may in turn induce various behavioral responses intended to alleviate such strain. Here we are unable to provide a definitive enumeration of the psychological strains which may intervene between person-environment incongruence and delinquent behavior. However, previous theory and research suggest that one or more of the types of strain indicated are probably involved in this process (see, for example, Gold and Mann 1972; Hirschi 1969; Kulka, Klingel, and Kahle 1979; Sarata 1976).

In turn, any consideration of potential behavioral responses to such strains must recognize what Yinger (1965) has called the "principle of multiple possibilities": delinquent behavior is clearly not the inevitable consequence of person-environment incongruence in general or of any form of psychological strain. Individuals react to strain in a number of ways—some of them conforming, some not. Out of a variety of possible adaptations, we have chosen to emphasize in figure 4-2 three similar to those suggested by Rhodes and Reiss (1969): (1) passive compliance (that is, resigned acceptance of the situation); (2) active evasion (truancy or dropping out); and (3) delinquent, rebellious, or disruptive behavior (including school crime).

Support for the Model

Although the person-environment fit model of school crime articulated here appears to have a number of desirable features, little direct empirical evidence relating dimensions of P-E fit to delinquent behavior is currently available. Thus, we must rely on two sorts of indirect evidence to demonstrate the potential utility of the model. First, we will attempt to illustrate the considerable conceptual overlap between the P-E fit model and a number of traditional theories of delinquent behavior. Second, we will attempt to show that a number of research findings in the delinquency literature may be interpreted in terms of the model.

Theoretical Support

In our view, one major strength of the person-environment fit model is its capacity to integrate diverse theories appearing in the extensive literature on delinquency and aggression and in the growing literature on school crime and disruption. In explaining criminal and deviant actions, some of these theories emphasize "person" or "psychological" variables, while others emphasize "environment" or "sociological" variables (compare Cortes and Gatti 1972; Martin and Fitzpatrick 1964).

For example, numerous theories emphasizing situational or social defects imply insufficient opportunities for gratifying important needs, with resultant opportunity-need incongruence. Such "insufficient opportunity" theories include:

1. those that cite poverty, unemployment, and poor educational opportunities as causes of crime (Burgess 1952; Shaw and McKay 1942);
2. those that emphasize the frustration of needs for status and success due to the unavailability of legitimate opportunities for upward mobility (Cloward and Ohlin 1960; Elliott 1962; Merton 1957);
3. those that see frustration in general as the main cause of aggressive and violent behavior (Berkowitz 1969; Dollard, Doob, Miller, Mowrer, and Sears 1939);
4. explanations of delinquency and aggression that focus on the frustration of specific needs (Bandura and Walters 1959; Jenkins 1974; Jordan 1970; Marwell 1966; Sorrentino 1975, pp. 24-26);
5. theories that argue that delinquents tend to be higher than average in the strength of particular needs (Quay 1965);
6. tracking (Schafer and Olexa 1971), labelling (Gove 1975), and school ejection or "push-out" (Edelman 1975) theories (these may all be interpreted as involving deprivation of opportunities and frustration of needs for affiliation, full participation, and respect); and
7. explanations which view delinquent behavior and school crime as resulting from the failure of schools to meet students' legitimate needs for achievement and competence, status and recognition, individual autonomy, participation in decision making, fair discipline, stimulating and relevant activities, and for warm, supportive relationships with peers and adults in school (DeCecco and Richards 1975; Fish 1970; Kvaraceus 1955).

Similarly, numerous theories emphasizing individual or psychological deficits and conflicts involve some notion of abilities being insufficient to meet role-appropriate expectations and requirements, with consequent ability-demand misfit. Examples which illustrate this include:

1. theories of delinquent behavior which focus on deficiencies in cognitive-intellectual abilities (Silberberg and Silberberg 1971; Singer 1976);
2. explanations which emphasize the consequences of deficient capacities for ego and superego control (Grossbard 1962; Redl and Wineman 1951);
3. status frustration theories which highlight an inability to meet pervasive requirements for educational and occupational achievement (Cohen 1955; Reiss and Rhodes 1963; Short and Strodtbeck 1965);

4. role inadequacy theories which emphasize an inability to fill successfully certain social roles (Gold 1970);
5. explanations involving low academic capabilities and school failure as provoking or predisposing factors in delinquency (Elliott and Vos 1974; Empey and Lubeck 1971; Hirschi 1969); and
6. theories that conclude that delinquent and disruptive behavior is due to lack of commitment to school (Hirschi 1969; Polk and Halferty 1966; Stinchcombe 1964). (Such theories imply a rejection of school expectations for performance and participation, resulting in decreased motivation and capability to meet such demands, and thereby increasing ability-demand misfit.)

In summary, we suggest that a broad range of theories of delinquent behavior and school crime are implicit person-environment fit theories. The etiological factors they emphasize—insufficient opportunity and ability—are provocations to delinquency precisely because they are incongruent with salient personal needs or pervasive social role demands.

Indirect Empirical Support

Perhaps the model's most important feature is its capacity for synthesizing a broad range of empirical results relating the school experience to delinquent, rebellious, and disruptive behavior, by interpreting such findings in terms of ability-demand or opportunity-need discrepancies on a number of salient dimensions.

The most obvious research findings which illustrate the centrality of the match between individual abilities and requirements of the school are, of course, those that emphasize the relationship between delinquent behavior and poor academic achievement (for example, Empey and Lubeck 1971; Gold 1963, 1970; Gold and Mann 1972; Hirschi 1969; Kaplan 1975; Rhodes and Reiss 1969), along with other requisite skills or abilities related to academic success, including general aptitude or intelligence (as in Palmore 1967; Short and Strodtbeck 1965; West 1969) and reading skills (such as Glueck and Glueck 1950; Liddle 1963; Silberberg and Silberberg 1971). Indirect evidence for this dimension is also available from studies which link perceived academic ability to delinquency (in Hindelang 1973; Hirschi 1969).

Although fewer and somewhat less direct, there are also empirical results which suggest a relationship between delinquent behavior and institutional or bureaucratic aspects of the student role. For example, as Schafer and Polk (1967, p. 233) assert, "there is considerable evidence that students who violate school standards pertaining to such things as smoking, truancy, tardiness, dress, classroom demeanor, relations with peers, and respect for authority are more likely to become delinquent than those who conform to such standards" (compare also Erickson, Scott, and Empey 1964; Havighurst et al. 1962; Healy and Bronner 1963; Kvaraceus 1945; Polk and Richmond 1972). One might add to this list other transgressions, including carelessness, laziness, inattentiveness, and other "irresponsible" or socially nonconforming behaviors (as in Ferracutti and Dinitz 1974; Glueck and Glueck 1950; West 1969).

Indirect empirical evidence implicating informal/social ability-demand incongruence takes one of two forms. First, a number of studies suggest that delinquent or delinquency-prone adolescents tend to be less popular and have poorer relations with classmates or peers in school (as in Ferracutti and Dinitz 1974; Glueck and Glueck 1950; Havighurst et al. 1962; Stott 1964; West 1969). Second, studies by Schafer (1969), Hirschi (1969), Kelly and Balch (1971) and others (see Polk and Schafer 1972) report a significant negative relationship between delinquent behavior and participation in extracurricular activities, including athletics. Among other things, such findings document the negative impact of failing to meet pervasive expectations for interpersonal skills and extracurricular participation (Coleman 1961; Douvan and Gold 1966).

The particular salience of fit between student needs and opportunities available within the school is highlighted by the fact that an adolescent's location or relative status within the school milieu can substantially affect the probability of opportunity-need incongruence on a variety of dimensions. Vinter and Sarri (1965, p. 358) report, for example, that students who received low grades might, as a consequence, be denied a variety of important privileges and opportunities within the school. Similar curriculum or ability tracking, solidly established as a correlate of delinquent behavior (for example, Kelly 1974, 1975; Schafer and Olexa 1971), often involves reduced opportunities for educational and occupational advancement, for quality of instruction and teacher expectations, for status and recognition among teachers and other students, and for engagement in certain prestigious and rewarding activities (Schafer and Polk 1967).

Among the studies which imply a relationship between delinquency and some of the more specific opportunity-need deficiencies described above are those reviewed by Wenk (1974). They suggest that the schools' failure to help students achieve personal growth may play a significant role in the juvenile crime problem. Other studies report that delinquents tend to perceive lower opportunities to achieve success goals than do nondelinquents (see Elliott 1962; Short 1964). Moreover, the typical school reward system (that is, the grading system) is relatively unresponsive to improvements in performance independent of one's relative standing (McPartland and McDill 1977), yet is commonly linked with access to other opportunities for successful performance within the school (Vinter and Sarri 1965). Thus opportunities for achievement outside the classroom are also likely to be more limited for delinquency-prone adolescents. If then, as some research suggests, delinquents tend to have greater needs for achievement than do nondelinquents (Cortes and Gatti 1972; Siegman 1962), a potential link between achievement opportunity-need misfit and delinquent behavior is even more evident. Finally, considerable research indicates that student perceptions of whether school is relevant to their current and future lives are related to delinquent and rebellious behavior (for example, Elliott 1962; Ferracutti and Dinitz 1974; Schafer and Polk 1967; Short 1964; Stinchcombe 1964; Thomas et al. 1977).

Perhaps the most significant research findings which appear to implicate discrepancies between opportunities and needs regarding relationship dimensions are those documenting a relationship between delinquent behavior and absence of warm, supportive relations between teachers and students (as in Cardinelli 1969; Ferracutti and Dinitz 1974; Gold 1963; Goldman 1961; Hindelang 1973; Hirschi 1969; Thomas et al. 1977; VandenBerg 1975). Regarding school vandalism, for example, Cardinelli (1969) found that schools tended to have more problems when teachers lacked genuine interest in pupils (compare Gold 1963); and Goldman (1961) reported that good relationships among administrators, teachers, students, and others (including the school custodian) were associated with low levels of school vandalism. Also relevant here is a recent study by McPartland and McDill (1977) establishing a link between school size and student offenses against persons and property; for increases in size involve not only the number of students who can find meaningful academic, athletic, or social roles within the school (Barker and Gump 1964), but also a more impersonal and uncaring environment (U.S. Senate Subcommittee to Investigate Juvenile Delinquency 1977). Moreover, despite fears to the contrary (see Moore 1964, p. 187), there has been an almost total lack of violence in alternative schools (Berger 1974), where personalization and humaneness are given a high priority (see Bowman 1959; Gold 1978).

Finally, there is some research evidence suggesting the importance of opportunity-need fit related to dimensions of system maintenance or change. The proposed benefits of smaller or reorganized educational units, as well as those of increased rule clarity (see U.S. Senate Subcommittee to Investigate Juvenile Delinquency 1977), are relevant to this dimension. However, the empirical results currently available pertain primarily to opportunities and needs for student influence or participation in decision making (for example, Hoy 1972; McPartland and McDill 1974; Strauss 1974; Thomas et al. 1977). Of particular note here are recent studies by McPartland and McDill (1974), who report significant relationships between indicators of school stability and student satisfaction with both the content and the process of school decision making, and by Thomas et al. (1977), who found feelings of student powerlessness to be directly related to involvement in delinquency.

Somewhat more direct empirical evidence consistent with a person-environment fit model of delinquent, rebellious or disruptive behavior in school is available from a recent study of adolescents at two Detroit suburban high schools (Kelly 1979). From that study, several same-time and cross-time relationships between measures of person-environment fit and indicators of aggressive and rebellious behavior were found (Klingel 1974; Kulka 1974, 1976), including significant relationships between these P-E fit measures and an explicit index of school crime (Kulka, Klingel, and Mann 1978). Moreover, several of these relationships manifested one of the nonlinear forms specified by the model.

Overall, we believe that the above research findings convincingly illustrate the potential impact of student-school incongruence on student misconduct and delinquent behavior. Likewise, we anticipate that future research will provide additional evidence implying the utility of a person-environment fit model for understanding school crime and disruption.

Conclusion

On the most general level, we conclude here that the concept of person-environment congruence or fit is a particularly appropriate paradigm for conceptualizing and understanding delinquent behavior and school crime. Not only is much existing theory and research compatible with this conception, but adoption of this paradigm also offers several other important advantages. In particular, because it defines the problem in terms of the relationship between an individual and his or her environment, the paradigm directs our attention from either the person or the environment alone and instead to their interaction. The implication of this refocusing is that successful programs to reduce delinquency and school crime may require accommodation and change by both the individual and the environment (see Sarata 1976).

A second general conclusion is that our public schools not only serve as a setting for crime and disruption, but, because of their unique assignment in society, they also play a major role in generating such behavior. Moreover, the conceptual model we have suggested speaks directly to the nature of these problems—problems of students as well as those of schools—and specifies a locus for potential intervention.

5 School-Community Relations Network Strategies

Jacqueline R. Scherer

School crime is seldom analyzed within a comprehensive framework of school-community relationships. Instead, student behavior is often viewed apart from other social phenomena, as if behavior within the school can be separated conceptually from that which takes place in other social situations. Although such a distinction may contribute to analytical simplicity, one of its unintended consequences is to prevent the development of practical models of crime prevention.

This chapter suggests that behavior can be better understood as the product of complex socialization processes operating at many different levels within the social system. Deviant behavior includes all those acts called criminal and can be understood as failure in the socialization process. One way to reduce deviance would be to improve the socialization processes at all levels; but to do this requires a more comprehensive approach to the role of all participants in socialization, including school personnel, families, welfare departments, health care organizations, recreational groups, churches, youth assistance agencies, and others who work with young people. In this view, the organizations and groups with responsibility for youthful socialization are connected, so there is little possibility that the offender can slip "through the cracks" left by the otherwise separate caretakers comprising the socialization system.

One approach to this issue would be through a socialization community (Lippitt 1969) that includes home, school, church, youth groups, and others who participate in the social processes directly affecting the life of the child.[1] However, such a conceptualization implies that the various components recognize their common interest in socialization and operate with some consensus. This is more an ideal or goal to be sought than an empirical reality, for the various organizations are most often seriously at odds with each other.

A social network constitutes a more effective conceptualization of the inner relationship between the school and other community groups. It is also a clearer representation of the social ties that youths negotiate in everyday interaction. Network analyses do not carry the normative connotations associated with community, but still direct attention to the whole. Social networks may be thought of as visual conceptualizations or representations of the linkages between individuals or groups (usually thought of on charts as "points") within a given arena (or life-space). The individual or group is represented as a point in space linked to others by lines. This provides a visual account of the structures in which transactions between individuals and organizations occur, and most importantly, the linkages between the various segments of the field.[2]

Although network language may be new and sophisticated, network methodologies may be confusing to many; the logic of this approach is a fundamental dimension of John Dewey's thinking (1897). He wrote:

> Education being a social process, the school is simply that form of community life in which all those agencies are concentrated that will be most effective in bringing the child to share in the inherited resources of the race, and to use his own powers for social ends. (Dewey 1897, (pp. 407-409)

Dewey also recognized that effective communication between educational personnel and others within the community was essential. Unfortunately, such communication often does not exist. Juveniles who come in contact with several socialization agencies encounter inconsistency more frequently than cooperation. Many times the right hand is not aware of what the left hand is doing; the distribution of resources among agencies, the scope of activities, and the goals of the different groups are more often than not uncoordinated. Such separation leads to ineffectiveness.

Most network analyses are ego-centered. The individual is the central focus and relationships are defined in terms of the person. With this in mind networks can be constructed or utilized to provide important personal supports for the individual to insure that he has linkages to important resources (Warren 1976; Speck and Attenave 1973).

More recently, network analysis has been developed at the level of the organization—that is, the agency, organization, or group is the unit of study. In the following discussion, the school is viewed as one of many community organizations operating in an interorganizational arena or community. The school's social network is described and the connections between the school and other groups in the community arena are identified. This makes it possible to develop positive suggestions toward strengthening linkages between the parts. It is assumed that in doing this, the socialization processes will become more effective and deviant behavior will be reduced.

The Social Network of Schools

From the literature it is possible to construct a model of school-community social networks which can be applied to most communities. However, it is essential to confirm by empirical research such measures as: density of contacts within the network; frequency of contacts between two points; the range of contacts over time; the intensity and psychological potency of contacts; the durability of contacts over time; and the location of contacts. Research could also ascertain the type of resources that flow across network channels. For example, Galaskiewicz (1979) has determined that three types of resource exchanges operate in a community: money, information, and moral support.

One salient feature of any school's social network is the powerful domain it monopolizes. (By domain we mean recognized scope of influence.) The school's domain includes its goals, resources, activities, and ideological strength as protected by compulsory school attendance laws. This extensiveness insures the existence of formal ties between the school and virtually every single young person in the community. In the socialization network, the school is second in power only to the family.

Because of the school's dominance, school staff are in a position to initiate most outside contacts—and to limit these, as much as possible, to formal situations within the school. Parents can be restricted to participation in such activities as PTA or student-teacher conferences. School personnel can refuse to cooperate with social service agencies on the grounds that they have a limited academic concern for the student; or they can expand their focus so that "schooling" can include recreation, health, nutrition, or safety. Furthermore, school personnel can facilitate or inhibit access to youth by other socialization agencies, justifying decisions on the basis of professional interpretation of domain activities.

A second feature of the social network of the school is formality. Because the school domain is protected and maintained by legal supports, ties are generally legalistic, formal, and rigidly structured. The child becomes a student who plays a role in the organization. Relationships are characterized by specialization, regulations, and organization, rather than by informality and personalization.

The development of powerful state and federal educational bureaucracies is reflected in the increasing number of nonlocal ties that school personnel must maintain. In addition, school financing is characterized by the growth of outside funding and kept separate from other community budgeting.

In terms of organizational exchanges, there is little interaction between the school and other socialization agencies (Warren et al. 1974; Galaskiewicz 1979). As a general rule, only the school principal or highest administrative officers are excused from the actual school building during the day to attend community social service council meetings. Moreover, many teachers would prefer not to accept responsibility for participating in the wider socialization community.

School-Community Relations

Delinquency is given low salience by school personnel for several reasons. Inadequately socialized juveniles are frequently difficult to teach, and middle-class public opinion often reacts with hostility to offender programs in the school. Most teachers and school administrators are not trained to work with this population. As a result, school dismissal is the ordinary response to troublesome behavior.

For their part, community organizations tend to encounter serious problems in their efforts to aid socialization failures. Although they spend considerable time helping individual students cope with school failure, most agencies simply do not have resources and legitimacy equal to those of the school. To make matters worse, the strategies most effective in dealing with juvenile delinquents appear to be those that bypass the law and order agencies.

Klein (1973) provides three criteria for evaluating the success of delinquency service and prevention strategies: diversion, absorption, and normalization. Essentially, Klein believes that in the offender's network there must be new linkages to provide alternate socialization paths. Existing network ties must be utilized more effectively, or particular offenses should be decriminalized so that the offender would have a better chance to become integrated into conventional social life. Each of these criteria has significant consequences for school-community linkages, and no one can be effective without ties among the multiple organizations of socialization.

Linkages

Given the reality of interorganizational contacts in which units basically operate independently, it is important to examine linkages with care. Most activities of a given organization are unevenly coordinated with those of other organizations, or enjoy "undirected cooperation." In the last two decades there has been considerable discussion of liaison programs and coordination efforts; but the rewards for undertaking a concerted approach to working with key linkage organizations have appeared to be minimal and the losses real. As a result, some communities have begun new programs, ostensibly located between the school and other community organizations, to serve as liaison agencies or facilitators. However, these have almost inevitably evolved into independent agents, operating separately and accountable to no one. There are serious discrepancies between organizational goals and actual behavior in most programs directed at delinquency.

Several important questions emerge from these observations. How can school personnel establish linkages with others involved in the socialization network? Is there any way in which the school network can be redesigned? Does the nature of the child's "involuntary" tie to the school affect his relationship with other organizations maintained through voluntary ties? Some strategies to deal with these questions can be outlined as follows:

1. increasing the number of linkages between the school and other agencies of socialization;
2. using a variety of channels for contact;
3. formally recognizing shared responsibilities for socialization;
4. extending the range of the socialization network;
5. developing more liaison staff;
6. reducing the impact of negative linkages;
7. conducting research on social networks.

Increasing the Number of Ties

An obvious strategy for improving the school's social network is to increase the number of linkages between the school and the community. School critics have argued for such a change, demanding that school walls be torn down. Some advocate the "deschooling" of society and the destruction of "hard" walls, while others simply want to "soften" the walls and reduce the isolation of the schools.[3] Specific ways to increase ties are:

1. *Utilize school space for community socialization organizations.* For example, locate youth assistance offices or city recreation department offices in school buildings, or provide space for personnel from voluntary socialization organizations, such as churches, to assist youth. (This is already done regularly for social workers and, in many large cities, counselors.)

2. *House crisis centers within school walls.* Peer counseling centers operating within regular school programs have enjoyed modest success. It is possible further to develop intervention centers which provide coordinated services to youth.

3. *Develop formal and regular linkages between the school and other community organizations.* It might be useful to view this as a process which begins with informal cooperation and moves toward formal agreements. Weinstein and Morover have developed a typology of the four patterns of organizational relationships found in health and welfare organizations that may be fruitfully applied to the socialization network (Weinstein and Morover 1977). The categories are:

a. Informal cooperation—for instance, client referrals, information exchanges, professional consultations, and service planning.
b. Formal cooperation—for instance, written agreements providing for personnel exchanges, material exchanges, patient transfers, and counseling services.
c. Formal purchase agreements—one organization agrees to purchase services from another, as recognized in a contract of specified duration, usually listing hours of service and a certain percentage of an employee's time.

The goal here is to avoid duplication of services or staff when there is a low volume of demand for such services.

d. Coordinated services—two or more organizations work together in joint programs, shared facilities, or pooled resources to provide a package of services.

4. *Encourage informal interorganizational ties at the middle level of the organization.* Teachers and agency staff can meet in community groups. The emphasis upon managerial participation in such groups as the Junior Chamber of Commerce, Kiwanis, Rotary, United Fund, and welfare planning groups is well established in both industry and commercial organizations; but school representation has generally been restricted to high-level administrators. Teachers might on occasion be relieved of classroom responsibilities so they may attend such meetings. Community involvement could become a part of the professional development of public school teachers, as it has for academic staff of universities. Agency representatives likewise can become regular participants in school activities, assisting in such areas as curricular policy development.

An examination of existing channels between the school and other community groups reveals that the most numerous, as well as the shortest, channels between the school and families are those followed by students. Underutilization of these effective linkages is wasteful. If they are used to tie the school to agencies and organizations in the community, students can become effective participants in the socialization process. Such student involvement, operating on both formal and informal levels, will facilitate the strategy of increasing the linkages.

Prominent educational critics have noted the importance of sponsoring students more actively in school and community organizations, citing the importance of developing autonomy, learning the skills of group work, and gaining self-confidence through activities. The National Commission on Resources for Youth has encouraged participatory programs for young people in both school and community programs. Other efforts to engage students in the socialization process include: the Integrated Community Education System, which enables students to become "partners in research" within the local community (Wenk 1976); the Open Partnership, which leads to shared decision making by everyone concerned with education (Ryan 1976); and a growing number of work-study vocational education programs which develop student internships outside the classroom. The Panel on Youth concluded that the best way of encouraging young people to take on more responsibilities is to encourage more interaction with others in a wide variety of nonschool settings, so that the time youngsters spend in formal educational contexts is actually decreased. It was also suggested that the federal government provide funds for host organizations in the community.

Recognizing Shared Responsibilities

Most staff do not view themselves as providing social services. Recent literature on interorganizational relationships in the social services discusses schools only marginally. Moreover, most citizens do not see the problem of welfare financing as related directly to the issues of educational funding; and to date, debates over accountability have not directly linked academic services with other specialized social services. As a result, interpretations of school domain have remained relatively unchallenged. It is unlikely that schools will voluntarily redefine existing assumptions about domain; however, it may be possible to encourage voluntary cooperation between schools and community organizations.

The lack of official recognition of the shared domain in youthful socialization has made the design of sound follow-up programs impossible. Young people (for instance, offenders, disabled learners, disruptive youth, or medically handicapped juveniles) who have experienced difficulties in particular socialization organizations generally have not received continuous services.[4] At the same time, many students are simply pushed out of school by administrative rules through expulsion or suspension.

Support and feedback are two essential ingredients in resocialization efforts, and both require strong network linkages. Self-help groups, professional crisis counseling, reference group support to encourage change, and other valuable but informally organized support systems can provide support and feedback. The goal of such efforts would be to increase the "social capital" of these poorly socialized youngsters so that they may have many sources of support. All members of the socialization network would be held accountable for follow-up and follow-through with problem-oriented young people.

Increasing the number of ties and the overlap between organizations will make socialization networks more dense, but the range of these networks also can be extended. Schools have remained aloof from important socialization activities occurring outside their immediate domain. The most blatant example of this has been television, which clearly plays a potent role in the intellectual, emotional, and character development of young people. Parent-teacher groups have become increasingly concerned about the effects of media, but school officials have been reluctant to participate in coordinating programs or supervising the development of media policies.

Another area in which the school remains uninvolved is recreation. Except with regard to formal school sports programs or officially sanctioned school activities, school staff generally do not support recreational programs. Many schools are required to provide transportation for students who engage in school-supported recreational events, yet Boards of Education seldom request funds for improved public transportation that would allow recreational programs to be developed further.

Strategies that require school staff to cooperate actively with other socialization organizations might make school personnel more aware of how important those groups really are to the tasks of education. Such strategies include placing school staff on governing boards of community groups, sponsoring community seminars on youth, planning commissions to regulate and design policies that coordinate activities, and providing official recognition of mutual responsibilities in socialization.

Expanding Liaison Staff

Another strategy for increasing school-community linkages is to develop more liaison staff and to design more creative roles for such personnel. The growing attention to youth advocacy represents one such effort. Youth advocates can effectively espouse the interest of individual youth, crossing the boundary lines of many socialization organizations and refusing to accept a limiting definition of their role. Outreach workers (community aides, attendance staff, social workers) can provide a continuous flow of information across channels.

To be effective, liaison staff must be given sufficiently high status and must have enough autonomy to effect real change. If they do not, they become instruments of administrative policies without independent bases. To a large extent, this has happened to school guidance counselors, who spend most of their time testing, screening, and guiding students into school tracks rather than operating between home and school or linking various areas of the student's life.

Liaison efforts must also be accompanied by practical support in the form of resource commitment. Thus, implementing liaison strategies requires high-level involvement and attention.

Reducing Negative Linkages

It would be misleading to assume that all school-community linkages have positive results. For example, there is often unofficial collusion between police and school staff, which diminishes student trust in all official organizations. Business contacts may restrict the school's perspective in such important areas as curriculum, and many peer contact groups actually support delinquency. It is important to analyze the negative as well as the positive qualities of network contacts, and to develop strategies that reduce the number of negative contacts or increase their distance from the school.

Weak Ties

The development of a school-community socialization network has several interesting possibilities for bringing about change. First of all, such a network need not be characterized by close-knit connections that would be almost impossible to develop and sustain, given the many demands placed upon the school at the present time. Indeed, Granovetter has suggested that weak ties may be most important. According to him, the strength of ties is "a combination of the amount of time, the emotional intensity, the intimacy (mutual confiding) and the reciprocal services which characterize the tie" (Granovetter 1977, p. 348). He discovered, for example, that information about jobs came through weak network ties. The existence of weak ties permits mobility and exchanges that bring about social cohesion. Applied to schools, this suggests that even weak ties between members of the socialization network will produce some cohesive approaches to problems of offenders.

This suggestion is not at variance with the literature on helping networks. Warren and Clifford suggest that the "number of different helpers utilized, as well as the variety of helping behaviors they provide, tend to limit the negative impact of problems" (Warren and Clifford 1973, p. 155). Since the delinquent offender is most likely to be pushed out of school, he would have fewer helping ties than youths still attending school. A corollary, of course, is that the school has an important role to play in becoming more integrated into the socialization network.

Networks and Change

Another advantage of conceptualizing school-community relations in terms of networks is that some of the pressure to deal with a complex multiplicity of problems is taken away from the school (see Hollingsworth 1979). The vocabulary of networks does not emphasize "change," but "liaison" with or "ties" to other organizations. This implies diffusion of responsibility; it also suggests enlargement of the schools' activities rather than criticism of failure to do something else. Most of the educational reform literature has been directed toward changing teacher attitudes or asking school personnel to "do" more with fewer resources. However valid this may be, it is politically more attractive to discuss liaison and shared responsibilities than to insist upon radical restructuring of either individual or organizational structures.

Conclusion

Specialized professionals and distinctive organizational missions have contributed to the need for liaison programs and more contact between all participants in the socialization process. Because the school has a protected domain, it has more control over interorganizational contacts than other community organizations. This chapter has suggested that viewing the school as part of a community interorganizational arena and utilizing social network analyses to describe interaction is a feasible approach to these concerns. Network analyses also suggest new possibilities for introducing change into school-community relationships.

Notes

1. Lippitt (1969) defines the "key elements in this total process of raising the young" as both institutions and individuals who "frequently interact with the young" (p. 339). He notes that socialization leaders share the view that the least-liked socialization outcome is lack of respect for authority; the best liked is active commitment to work. This important article concludes with a research agenda that has interesting points of convergence with delinquency research agendas.

2. The literature of network analyses has grown considerably in the last decade. One of the most comprehensive collections of readings is Leinhardt (1977).

3. An example of one who wants to break down formal barriers would be Illich (1971); a less extreme position would be that of Oliver (1976).

4. Rothman and Walker (1976) discovered that 75 percent of all psychiatric professionals never follow up a client when he or she returns to school.

6

Reflections on the Rights of Students and the Rise of School Violence

Robert J. Rubel and
Arthur H. Goldsmith

The last fifteen years have seen major changes in our social institutions. In two such institutions—the courts and the schools—the changes seem to correlate with each other. This chapter examines the relationship between judicial decisions guaranteeing student rights and the noticeable rise in school-based violence and tolerance of unruly student behavior. The thesis presented here is that while school violence has increased during the period of peak judicial activity in the areas of student rights and due process, the relationship is not causal but contributory. School administrators feel threatened by judicial rulings, and this litigious intimidation has led to an increased tolerance of the unruly student.

While the absence of constitutional protections will not reduce school crime, the court rulings, properly read and understood, have not unduly handcuffed school authorities in their efforts to administer discipline. But for a variety of reasons school officials have become reluctant to act forcefully and firmly when confronted with actual student misconduct. Their threshold of tolerance has risen to the point where school administrators are willing to accept increases in student misbehavior. And the court rulings have caused school officials such confusion and consternation about their rightful disciplinary authority as to have unwittingly contributed to the increasing violence in the schools.

Background

There are two principal sources of authority for the control of students by schools: in loco parentis and state enabling statutes (Goldstein 1969). As summarized by Reutter,

> The common-law measure of the rights and duties of school authorities

---

An earlier version of this chapter appeared as "The Relationship Between Student Victories in the Courts and Student Violence in the Schools, *Contemporary Education* (Summer 1979). Reprinted with the permission of Indiana State University.

relative to pupils attending school is the *in loco parentis* concept. This doctrine holds that school authorities stand in the place of the parent while the child is at school. Thus, school personnel may establish rules for the educational welfare of the child and may inflict punishments for disobedience. The legal test is whether a reasonably knowledgeable and careful parent might so act. The doctrine is used not only to support rights of school authorities, . . . but to establish their responsibilities concerning such matters as injuries that may befall students. (Reutter 1970, pp. 2-3)

Similarly, state enabling statutes authorize local school boards to establish reasonable rules and regulations for operating and keeping order in schools; these do not necessarily have to be put into written form (*Hasson* v. *Boothby*, 318 F. Supp. 1183 [D. Mass., 1970]).

The classic statement of this type of authority is made in the 1966 case of *Burnside* v. *Byars*, 363 F.2d 744 (5th Cir. 1966):

The establishment of an educational program requires the formulation of rules and regulations necessary for the maintenance of an orderly program of classroom learning. In formulating regulations, including those pertaining to the discipline of school children, school officials have a wide latitude of discretion. But the school is always bound by the requirement that the rules and regulations must be reasonable. It is not for us to consider whether such rules are wise or expedient but merely whether they are a reasonable exercise of the power and discretion of the school authorities.

In determining the constitutionality of a given school punishment which has no specific prior promulgated rule, the courts will consider the following factors: the offending student's prior knowledge of the wrongfulness of his conduct; the clarity of the public purpose served by the punishment; and that act's inherent potential for having a chilling effect on constitutionally protected activity (*Hasson* v. *Boothby*, 1970). To be valid, any rule—whether explicit or implicit—not only must meet the test of reasonableness, but must as well serve a legitimate school-related function; the latter may involve education, promotion of health or safety, maintenance of order and discipline, or other housekeeping duties (Goldstein 1969).

Because the school's legal jurisdiction can be expanded to cover acts not occurring directly on school property or during school hours, its disciplinary authority may also extend beyond the confines of the school yard and school day. The legal basis for these forms of rule development and discipline resides not so much in the dying doctrine of in loco parentis as it does in the direct and detrimental effect that such off-campus acts have on the school's functioning, efficiency, and morale (*O'Rourke* v. *Walleer*, 102 Conn. 130, 128A 25, [1925]; Annotation, "Right to Discipline Pupils for Conduct Away from

School Grounds or Not Immediately Connected with School Activities," by Daniel F. Feld, 53 A.L.R. 3d 1124).

Since the onslaught of judicial activity in the field of student rights has put to rest the common law concept of in loco parentis, today that doctrine is no longer a viable or valid legal or educational justification for the exercise of school power. In loco parentis has been replaced by the school's constitutional relationship with its students.

Procedural Due Process

Over the past decade, a series of important court decisions has changed the state's relationship with its young people. The major breakthrough occurred in 1961 with *Dixon* v. *Alabama State Board of Education*, when the appeals court held for the first time that due process requires notice and some opportunity for hearing before a student is expelled for misconduct (*Dixon* v. *Alabama State Board of Education,* 294 F.2d 150, 158 [5th Gr., 1961] ,*cert. den.,* 368 U.S. 930). Then in 1967, in *In re Gault* (387 U.S.1), the U.S. Supreme Court declared that juveniles facing serious criminal charges and loss of freedom are entitled to the same due process rights as adults under the Fourteenth Amendment of the Constitution. The Court specified that juveniles arrested by police must be accorded at least the (1) right to notice of the charges in time to prepare for trial; (2) right to counsel; (3) right to confrontation and cross-examination; and (4) privilege against self-incrimination.

The *Dixon* and *Gault* cases had several important consequences. By the early 1970s the legal principles and procedures spelled out in them had successfully been applied to public high school expulsions (see *Voight* v. *Van Buren Public Schools,* 306 F. Supp. 1388 [E.D.Mich. 1969] and to suspensions (see *Williams* v. *Dade County School Board,* 1971).

In 1969, the U.S. Supreme Court issued its now famous and far-reaching decision in *Tinker* v. *Des Moines Independent School District* (393 U.S. 503). This decision declared that students do not shed their constitutional rights to freedom of speech at the schoolhouse gate. The age of student rights was fully upon us.

In the years that followed, lower federal and state courts had to wrestle with the myriad procedural and substantive issues involved with student discipline—inundating the courts with cases challenging the school's authority to restrict student speech (*Tinker*), solicitations (*Katz* v. *MacAulay*, 438 F.2d 1058 [2nd Cw, 1971] , *cert. den.* 405 U.S. 933 [1970]), and smoking (*Anderson* v. *Independent School District No. 281,* 287 Minn. 515, 176 N.W. 2d 640 [1970]). It was not until the mid-1970s, however, that the U.S. Supreme Court took up the problem of due process in the schools. In January 1975, in *Goss* v. *Lopez* (419 U.S. 565), the Court stated that students may not be summarily suspended, even for one day, without following fundamentally fair and fact-finding procedures. According to this due process requirement, in short-term suspensions of up to ten days, a student is entitled to oral or written notice of the charges, an explanation of the evidence, and an opportunity to be heard. Dictated by the Constitution, these procedures were considered "rudimentary" and certainly no more than what a fair-minded administrator would do on his own. And, if school administrators did not comply with these requirements, *Wood* v. *Strickland* (420 U.S. 308), decided a month after Goss, ruled that school officials could be subject to suit and held financially liable for damages were they deliberately to deprive a student of his clearly established constitutional rights.

Closely connected with issues of due process and discipline, the problem of corporal punishment came before the High Court in *Baker* v. *Owen* and *Ingraham* v. *Wright*. Although *Baker* v. *Owen* only affirmed a lower court ruling (423 U.S. 907, affirming 395 F. Supp. 294 [1975], *Ingraham* v. *Wright* (430 U.S. 651 [1977]) was a full-fledged opinion that reasonable corporal punishment is not cruel and unusual punishment under the Eighth Amendment to the U.S. Constitution. In Justice Powell's view, the imposition of burdensome due process protections upon the administration of corporal punishment would have destroyed the efficacy of corporal punishment as a disciplinary device. The common law provides a sufficient legal remedy for students who suffer from excessive corporal punishment.

Two decisions in March of 1978 lend additional support to the proposition that the Supreme Court is trying to extricate the judiciary from the thicket of educational decision making. In *Board of Curators of the University of Missouri* v. *Horowitz* (435 U.S. 78 [1975]), when a medical student was dismissed for academic deficiencies, the Supreme Court held that academic dismissals—as opposed to disciplinary ones—do not require a hearing before the school's decision-making body. The Court said that so long as the school "fully informs" the student of the faculty's dissatisfaction with his progress and of the danger that such dissatisfaction poses to continued enrollment and timely graduation, then such procedures satisfied due process.

In *Cary* v. *Piphus* 435 U.S. 247 (1978), two students were given the usual twenty-day suspension for allegedly smoking or possessing marijuana. Because they did not receive a due process hearing, the students sued for $5,000 damages resulting from the deprivation of their constitutional rights. While the court rejected the notion that monetary or pecuniary damages for constitutional violations can be presumed without proof of actual injury, it did hold that mental and emotional distress and reputational injury caused by denial of due process are compensable upon sufficient proof that the injury actually was caused.

These recent decisions of the Supreme Court can and should be interpreted to mean a judicial pulling back from the student rights front and a correlative affirming of the school administrator's discretion. Such discretion has never been more firmly established and will not be judicially invalidated so long as it is deliberately and carefully carried out.

Freedoms of Expression

Court cases defining students' rights to freedoms of religion and expression in schools have been numerous. As early as 1943, in *West Virginia State Board of Education* v. *Barnette* (319 U.S. 624), the Supreme Court held that students could not be compelled to salute the flag if that action violated their religious rights of freedom of conscience and belief. In *Tinker*, the wearing of black arm bands was declared to be symbolic speech and so within the protection of the First Amendment. As a consequence, school officials could no longer prohibit or suppress speech in the absence of a factually based forecast of substantial disruption or material interference with school discipline; staff members have no right to interfere with or prohibit students' free expression, even if that is offensive, unpleasant, controversial, or discomforting.

Hair and Dress Codes

Court cases testing the power of school administrators to suspend pupils for violations of hair and dress codes were prevalent in the late 1960s and early 1970s. Early court cases on hair length (*Leonard* v. *School Committee in Attleboro*, 349 Mass. 704, 212 N.E.2d 468 [1969]) and cleanliness (*Davis* v. *Firment*, 269 F. Supp. 524 [E.D.La., 1967]), ruled in favor of the schools' power to determine such regulations (Annotation, "Validity of Regulation by Public School Authorities as to Clothes or Personal Appearance of Pupils," 14 A.L.R., 3d 1201). Later decisions held that students have a right to privacy and personal liberty regarding their hair length and dress style.

In *Yoo* v. *Moynihan* (20 Conn. Supp. 375 [1969]), a student's right to style his hair came under the definition of his constitutional right to privacy. School officials had no legal grounds for proscribing long hair when there was no evidence that such hair posed a disciplinary problem, caused a disruption during school hours, interfered with his or others' school work, or involved a health or sanitary risk to himself or others. Then, in *Richards* v. *Thurston* (424 F. 2d 1281 [1st Cir. 1970]), the Court reasoned that a student's right to wear long hair derived from his interest in personal liberty.

In *Crossen* v. *Fatsi* (309 F. Supp. 114 [1970]), a dress code prohibiting "extreme style and fashion" was ruled unconstitutionally vague, unenforceable, and an invasion of the pupil's right to privacy. On the grounds of the code's being insufficiently clear and specific—and too ambiguous and subjective—the Court stated that it was too elastic; for it left decisions on what constituted "extreme" style or fashion solely to the principal's discretion. The Court said that a dress code would be permissible if it furnished adequate guidelines and clearly informed students as to what kinds of dress were unacceptable. Were dress to cause any disruption, distraction, or disturbance, then discipline would be proper. It is now the case that dress and grooming codes must be drawn and drafted as narrowly and as specifically as possible, they must directly relate to a purpose involving health, hygiene, sanitation, safety, damage to property or disruption of the education process, and they must avoid sexual stereotypes (Title IX, 45 C.F.R. sec. 86.31[b]).

Although there is no clear consensus among the courts across the country as to whether and to what precise extent hair and dress codes implicate constitutional interest, those same courts have indicated that schools cannot prohibit the wearing of slacks (*Scott* v. *Board of Education, U.F. School District #17, Hicksville*, 61 Misc. 2d 333, 305 N.Y.S. 2d 601 [1969]), or dungarees (*Bannister* v. *Paradis*, 316 F.Supp. 185 [1970]), or hair "falling loosely about the shoulders" (*Richards* v. *Thurston*, 424 F. 2d 1281 [1970]) and cannot set simplistic standards against sloppy, casual, or extreme styles (*Crossen* v. *Fatsi*, 390 F. Supp. 114 (D. Conn., 1970]). It is permissible for school boards to prohibit "transparent hosiery, low necked dresses" (*Pugsley* v. *Sellmeyer*, 250 S.W. 538 [1923]), or short skirts (*Tardif* v. *Quinn*, 545 F. 2d 761 [1st Cir., 1976]), or opened, unbuttoned clothes that overexpose a person's legs, thighs, cleavage, or chest. Likewise, to protect school floors, metal heelplates may be prohibited (*Stromberg* v. *French*, 236 N.W. 477 [1931]). While schools may censure students who are unsanitarily, obscenely, or scantily clad (*Bannister* v. *Paradis*), they are also allowed to require students to keep their hair "out of their eyes" (*Roger* v. *Board of Education of C.R. Coblentz School*, 365 N.E. 2d 889 [1977]) and to wear hair nets in laboratory or swimming class for reasons of safety or sanitariness. In an effort to uphold specific grooming rules in a vocational school (because that institution's purpose is immediately related to employment), *Bishop* v. *Cermenaro* (355 F. Supp. 1269 [D. Mass., 1973]) ruled that long hair, mustaches, sideburns, beards, and goatees may be regulated to an extent consistent with enhancing a school's image. But such regulation must not interfere with a student's privacy and personal-liberty interests.

There is no clear answer to the question of how to draft a constitutional dress code. Whereas a policy merely prohibiting "extremes" will not pass constitutional scrutiny, dress that is distracting or dirty, that impairs the safety of its wearer and others, or that interferes with the educational process may be prohibited. Ultimately, at the heart of this whole matter is the issue of whether enforcing the rules which govern appearance or attire will serve a sound educational purpose. This is an educational policy problem—not a legal one.

Changes in Levels of Violence in Public Schools

The most detailed analysis of changes in the nature and extent of crime and violence in public schools over the period under discussion (early 1960s to present) was conducted for the Justice Department's Office of Juvenile Justice and Delinquency Prevention by Rubel (1976). In the introduction to that study's report, Rubel warns that tremendous confusion over definitions of offense types, changes in reporting methods, and the general unfamiliarity of educators with law-enforcement issues together constitute an almost prohibitive block to close scrutiny of this area. After discussing these obstacles, Rubel goes on to demonstrate that analysis can be conducted on certain types of offenses that occur in schools. Among his conclusions are: (1) that offenses against school property increased dramatically throughout the 1960s and were brought under control only by the formation of security offices in school districts beginning in the early 1970s; (2) that by the mid- to late 1970s, offenses against property had become a major concern of suburban districts, while offenses against persons had become a major problem for large-city jurisdictions; and (3) that riots and group disruptions were limited to the late 1960s and early 1970s.

Since the majority of important court cases under discussion occurred in the late 1960s to early 1970s—the same period in which Rubel discovers in-school disruptions to the most frequent—it is useful to examine other researchers' findings on riots and disruptions in about the same period.

First, Havighurst (1970, p. 105), finds that group disruptions seem to be more frequent in high-status schools than in other types of schools. This is consistent with the view that the more sophisticated and legalistically oriented students attending such schools were those most often involved in group disruptions (for instance, riots, walkouts, sit-ins) meant to draw attention to violations of students' personal rights. In this context, we ought to remember that the 1960s were a period of massive college riots which culminated in the early 1970s with challenges to U.S. policy on the Vietnam war; for it is likely that high socioeconomic-status (SES) schools experienced more disruptive behavior than others in large part as a result of influences that older siblings attending the disrupted colleges had on these younger students. However, in closely examining reasons for high-school disruptions, other researchers have discovered an unexpected trend.

Pucinski (1970) and Larson (1972), who are responsible for the second group of studies of interest here, find that the vast majority of high-school disruptions are nonpolitical. Indeed, when both Pucinski and Larson polled secondary schools, seven out of eight schools reporting disruptive activity stated that the focus of that activity was on school rules and regulations (such as dress codes, freedom to distribute newspapers, or suspension practices): only one out of eight of the riots was politically motivated.

Third, Meyer et al. (1971) discovered that by 1971, group disruptions had been replaced with the twin plagues of apathy and/or crime on the part of students. Meyer's work is interesting because his findings that disruptions had largely ceased by the early 1970s coincide with evidence presented here that most of the court resolutions of issues prompting such disruptions had also been made by that time.

In summary, then, unlike college disruptions which focused on national issues not easily resolved, secondary-school disruptions were almost always prompted by local school rules and institutional policies which could be satisfactorily altered. The very short duration (about three years) of riotous behavior as a national problem in secondary schools clearly indicates that school administrators were in fact able to resolve rapidly the types of problems which the younger students were reaching.

Tentative Conclusion—The Logical Link

To this point, this chapter has discussed: (1) the authority of school officials to enact and enforce rules and regulations; (2) court rulings which have subjected school disciplinary authority to constitutional standards and safeguards; and (3) trends concerning various forms of unlawful activity in public schools. Now we must find the logical link between the court rulings and increases in unwanted and unlawful behavior in schools.

Courts and Crime—A Theoretical Construct

As juvenile criminals were given rights under the Constitution (*Gault*); as constitutional limits were placed on the types of school rules under which youth could be disciplined (*Tinker* and progeny); and as the requirements for procedural due process were imposed upon school administrators taking disciplinary action (*Goss, Ingraham,* among others), local school authorities grew increasingly wary of being tough in the ways they disciplined students. Specifically, principals became overly cautious of suspending youths for acts (such as insubordination, wearing of outlandish clothing, classroom disturbances, loitering in halls, and so forth) which only a few decades previous would have immediately caused them to put pupils out of school. This reluctance on the part of principals to suspend youths exhibiting "borderline" behavior has forced school authorities to increase their tolerance of boisterous or bad behavior throughout the school.

Increased judicial activism in the academic arena has contributed to, but has not caused, an increase in unruly behavior. Because school officials have come to tolerate increased disruptive behavior, school violence has, in turn, increased. But it is not the court rulings, per se, that have brought about these changes; rather, the key factor has been the attitudes of school administrators. That is, violent and unruly behavior is more likely to increase in schools whose administrators have come to fear *Wood*-like litigation than in schools whose administrators are familiar with the actual court rulings and know the limits of their rightful authority. Administrators have been unduly influenced by sensational media portrayal of the seemingly unlimited rights these rulings appear to give students (VonBrock 1977, p. 69).

Unschooled and unsure of their authority, school administrators perceive themselves as hobbled, handicapped and handcuffed by recent court actions. Unchecked by previously available sanctions, this sea of fearful and unruly behavior thus created forms the breeding ground for truly serious criminal acts in schools—acts which threaten the continued viability of many schools in our country.

Freeing school officials from the court-imposed constitutional requirements of fair and due process will not simply fail to solve the problem of school violence—this might even further exacerbate it. Only by becoming informed about the law and about the environmental and personal causes of antischool behavior can school officials overcome their fears of litigious disputes and of student disruptiveness. Then, free of such apprehension, they will be able to take firm and forceful action.

Wood imposes upon school officials a duty to remain informed about constitutional developments in the field of school discipline. Whereas no official is expected to predict at his peril the course of constitutional law, it is legally imperative that all officials be aware of local precedents, controlling decisions, and settled, indisputable and clearly established constitutional rights (*Wood* v. *Strickland*, and *Procunier* v. *Navarette*, 434 U.S. 555 [1978]).

The courts are not in the business of second-guessing school administrators' efforts at disciplining disruptive students. If the decision to discipline is deliberate, careful, and not capricious, school officials have no cause for worry over constitutional sanctions.

In the end, the Constitution only requires that a school official who must act swiftly do so sincerely and with the good faith that what he is doing is right and reasonable. That is all the courts have required or can compel.

7

Teachers—A New Endangered Species?

Alfred M. Bloch, M.D. and
Ruth Reinhardt Bloch

John K., a 42-year-old Caucasian, was a high-school teacher in the inner city of Los Angeles, California, from 1965 to 1977. He watched school morale and discipline progressively deteriorate with a commensurate increase in school violence and vandalism. Vagrants and truants roamed the campus, disrupting classes, threatening and sometimes attacking teachers. Combat between opposing gangs was almost a daily occurrence. Participants used fists, knives, chains, lead pipes, and guns. The school's administrators seemed either powerless or indifferent to the teachers' concern for their personal safety. They were unable to keep nonstudents off campus or to control their activities.

Despite the obvious danger to his own safety, John K. was a conscientious teacher who believed it was his responsibility to intervene when gang fights occurred on campus; most other teachers had "learned to look the other way." As a consequence, John was repeatedly threatened and sometimes beaten. Although he recovered from the beatings, he noticed that insidious pain in his right leg increased until it caused him difficulty in climbing stairs and, ultimately, in walking even short distances. Physicians who examined him dismissed the symptom as "psychological." Despite the pain, John continued to teach; he believed he was a good teacher, a tough teacher, who could handle any situation. He continued to value his ideals of education and discipline more than his own safety.

Just before Christmas vacation, John entered the audiovisual control booth of the school auditorium. As he closed the door, he confronted two male students cutting power lines and smashing electrical equipment. One student fled; the other began beating John with his fists. The student who had fled returned; he held John while the other grabbed a chair and began battering the teacher's head and shoulders. John's screams and calls for help were either not heard or ignored. The battering continued, and he finally lost consciousness.

After John's wounds were sutured and dressed, he tried to discuss the incident with the school principal. The principal (apparently uncomfortable with the poor safety record of his school) informed him, "This incident is *your* fault, and reflects your inability to relate to the minorities." The results of the students' physical attack on John were immediately obvious. The results of the sustained psychic stress combined with an especially severe physical attack, and the final blow—criticism from his principal—ultimately resulted in John's psychological decompensation. He was unable to continue teaching.

Shortly after John quit, his symptoms of leg pain increased and atherosclerosis (a stress-aggravated condition) was diagnosed. Doctors performed a surgical bypass procedure, using bilateral Teflon replacements for the now obliterated arteries to his legs. He has not been able to return to teaching.

John K. is one of 575 teachers comprising this study; all have succumbed emotionally and/or physically because of the extraordinary and continued stress that occurs, with or without actual physical trauma, while teaching in an inner-city school. Between 1972 and 1979 all patients were referred to me for psychiatric evaluation, and in some cases, treatment and hospitalization (Bloch 1978).

Teachers in this study are black, white, Hispanic, and Asian-American and have taught in inner-city schools for periods ranging from two months to eighteen years. That is, they have functioned in a stressful environment, one that is too often dangerous and even life-threatening. Indeed, these teachers have reported seeing weapons, guns and knives, for instance, on campus, as well as students taking, holding, and selling drugs.

While campus violence and vandalism are rampant, teachers are on the front line, being threatened with assault, murder, or rape. If they are unlucky, the threat becomes an assault. According to the National Education Association, assaults on some 70,000 teachers occurred in 1978. But most still go unreported.

In my experience treating teachers, certain aspects of working in inner-city schools appeared constant. Each teacher reported his environment was extremely stressful, and each believed that violence and vandalism were out of control on campus. Teachers indicted some school administrators for poor leadership, indifference, and reluctance to discipline or expel disruptive or violent students. Apparently, these same administrators have also been reluctant to allow official reports of student assaults on teachers. In such an environment, school morale is poor; teachers are fearful and anxious about their physical survival. They often referred to their schools as "combat zones."

Most have repeatedly petitioned their administration to transfer them to a less violent school. Their petitions have either been "discouraged" (ignored), sometimes for several years, or denied directly. In an attempt to get themselves off the hook, administrators too often refer to those who have complained as "unsuccessful teachers." Interestingly, 92 percent of the teachers reported their attackers were not their own students, but rather, individuals they never saw before or since—such individuals as other students in the same school, vagrants, students suspended from other schools, youths belonging to the gang of a student they had disciplined. And when the teacher has no exit, compensatory mechanisms break down and symptoms develop.

When these teachers underwent psychiatric evaluation, a distinct pattern became evident. Most had unconsciously expected students to see them as wise, parental figures. When they were assaulted, teachers were therefore unable to accept the fact that violence had been directed toward them, that they were indeed the target.

Factors causing such teachers to seek psychiatric help bore striking and consistent resemblance to the psychiatric casualties of World War II, described by Grinker and Speigel as "combat neurosis" (Grinker 1945). They observed that the soldiers' ability to maintain the physical and psychological health necessary for functioning within the life-threatening environment of combat depended primarily on one factor: morale. With rare exception, the number of combat soldiers reporting to "sick bay" was directly correlated to the morale of their units. Companies with poor morale usually had a high incidence of soldiers reporting with a variety of specific physical complaints, for instance, nausea, diarrhea, flu, cardiac palpitations, migraine, dermatitis, as well as such complaints of psychic stress as nightmares, memory loss, anxiety, weight loss, and fatigue.

Among teachers from schools with low morale there was a high incidence of similar physical and psychological complaints with consequent high absenteeism. In the absence of administrative support, teachers who sustained unrelenting psychic stress became symptomatic—usually with the psychophysiologic sequelae of sustained psychic stress as well.

Teachers in this study presented symptoms of neurosis; they were fearful, anxious and depressed, and chronically fatigued; they exhibited excessive startle response and had nightmares and difficulty sleeping. Conversion symptoms and cognitive impairment developed and impeded their ability to function as teachers; they were unable to concentrate and had become forgetful. Understandably, vicious circles developed. Diminished self-esteem was a constant.

Each teacher was given routine psychological tests: the Bender-Gestalt Perceptual Motor Test; Minnesota Multiphasic Personality Inventory (MMPI); Beck Depression Inventory; and Sentence Completion Test. If there were symptoms of psychosis or organic brain dysfunction, extended neuropsychological assessment was also performed: Graham-Kendall Memory for Designs; Draw-a-Person; Wechsler Adult Intelligence Scale (WAIS); Rorschach Psychodiagnostics; and Thematic Apperception Tests.

Predisposing factors were observed. More than 75 percent of the evaluated teachers had an impaired ability to deal effectively with fear or danger. (In this regard, character structure differed from that of police officers who were also studied.) The MMPI and projective tests revealed passive, obsessional character structure with relatively rigid superegos. These same individuals were also idealistic and dedicated.

Unconsciously, the teachers under consideration perceived their authority as being that of idealized parental figures; in relation to children, their attributes and duties included wisdom, justice, love, and protection. Thus they were not only unable to understand when they became targets of hostility or violence; but they were also actually unable to strike back. Moreover, teachers from schools where administrative support and morale were poor were significantly less able than others to cope with stress. These internalized their rage and fear so that anxiety, depression, and somatic symptoms developed in them.

School administrators generally try to present a low profile. They seem to be reluctant or unable to support and protect these teachers in crisis because of continuing budget cuts and the enormous pressures placed on them by school district officials and by the community. This may explain why, in exasperation, principals may criticize the assaulted teacher who tries to report the incident. Indeed, assaulted teachers often report that the principal confronts them with such questions as, "Why did you let your class get out of control?"

During evaluation the teachers also described their work-day world in the inner city. They reported that violence directed toward them included direct threats of murder, rape, actual physical assault and injury by students with and without weapons, as well as theft, arson, and various other forms of vandalism of their personal property. Violence on campus not specifically directed at them included such acts of vandalism as smashing windows and doors, arson and bombing of school buildings, stealing and destroying campus equipment, fighting between students and gang members, murder, and rape. Some even reported that open-locker searches on their campuses revealed drugs, dynamite, knives, stilettoes, ammunition, rifles, and handguns. Making matters particularly complex, the presence of nonstudents, gang members, truants, and vagrants on campus is still a major factor contributing to violence in inner-city schools. For teachers report that neither the administration, security personnel, nor security seemed able to keep these persons off campus or to restrict their activities.

During class teachers were required to lock all the windows and doors in their rooms to prevent intruders from entering. But their own classes often contained violence-prone students who had police records; and many teachers reported overcrowding by as much as 75 percent. Teachers were not to remain in the classroom alone. However, those coming from schools with intercom systems reported that those systems were frequently either stolen or in disrepair.

The combination of gang warfare and the presence of weapons on campus is volatile. One teacher told of a gang member who, upon being transferred from another school and assigned to his metal shop, felt obliged to "wipe out" a student of an opposing gang whom he spotted in the same class. When the intended victim failed to attend school on the day his rival planned to attack, the latter was exasperated; so he took out a handgun and fired two clips of ammunition into the classroom and school office before staff members subdued him. Security personnel were not available because they had been investigating a stabbing that had occurred concurrently in another area of the same campus.

As a result of sustained exposure to this type of environment, in most of the evaluated teachers hitherto-effective psychological defenses had collapsed;

and this reaction was accompanied by the consequent risk of overwhelming anxiety and resulting symptoms, both psychological and psychophysiological. Thus most of the teachers had extensive medical records which predated psychiatric referral, documenting a full range of stress-related diseases including dermatitis and migraine headaches; gastrointestinal disorders including nausea, diarrhea, colitis, anorexia, and peptic ulcer; such cardiovascular symptoms as heart palpitations, hypertension, and coronary (artery) disease; and such respiratory illnesses as repeated infections (flu, bronchial asthma, and so forth) and hyperventilation. Although psychogenic in origin, these symptoms result in obvious physical disability.

Unless massive denial is used, the common response to danger is fear, the most potent source of arousal of the autonomic nervous system—and somatopsychic effects occur. That is, internal and external factors conspire to produce conflict which culminates in sympathetic arousal; there are changes in respiration, blood concentrations, and urinary steroid excretions. Sustained arousal of hypothalamic action systems finally affects target organs such as the skin, heart, lungs, and gastrointestinal tract. Of these processes, William Kiely, M.D., writes that response to stress

> induced by the demand of the work situation ... activates biochemical and physiological mechanisms to such a degree ... as to exceed functions of structured tolerance at the organ of tissue level. Hence, many develop vascular hypertension of sustained variety, active peptic ulceration or persistent glucose load intolerance. [Kiely 1973, p. 521]

Indeed, certain diseases (such as diabetes mellitus) may be direct consequences of physiological changes arising from repeated and sustained arousal of hypothalamic action systems under the modulating influence of limbic system and midbrain reticular activating system controls. The specific target organs which are affected depend on genetic or constitutional predisposition.

As for psychiatric treatment for teachers under such stress, that has had to be pragmatically oriented, short-term, and supportive, with the primary objective of returning a healthier, more resilent instructor to the classroom. When a teacher is decompensating, crisis intervention is instituted. In these instances, patients are encouraged to ventilate their fears, agonies, and anger at being "let down." They are helped to understand that they are not "unsuccessful teachers" just because they have developed symptoms. They simply could not function in a violent situation when they were the targets, especially without support from or protection by their leaders. Gradually, with treatment, symptom reduction has occurred, and the teachers' self-esteem and confidence have returned. Patients have "graduated" to group therapy, shortly thereafter to return to the classroom or to seek another profession.

The importance of administrative support in reducing the sufferings of such teachers cannot be overemphasized. The number of threats directed at a given teacher greatly exceeded the incidents of actual physical violence. However, student effort at threatening, harassing, or intimidating a teacher is usually not considered reportable. When teachers attempted to report an incident, school administrators too often communicated the implicit message that "It would not be in your best interest to pursue the matter" and "It won't look good on your record." Indeed, teachers claim that they are made to feel responsible for eliciting the attack, much as the rape victim is, and that they are chastised for not "rechanneling the student's negative energy into more acceptable productive outlets." As a consequence of such attitudes, a significant number of the teachers described multiple prior unreported assaults.

Susan M., for instance, is an exceptionally bright and dedicated 42-year-old woman. She reported to a Los Angeles inner-city school seeking employment and was proud of her successful record of seven years of experience in another district. Two years before, during a serious rape attempt, she was forced to disrobe at knifepoint in front of her class. Following the incident, the school administration could not have been more supportive. The student (not one of hers) was arrested. She did not lose a day of teaching and gradually recovered from the episode with the help of outpatient psychotherapy.

Susan M. moved to Los Angeles, where she was assigned to teach an overcrowded class of "problem" high-school students, many of whom were on probation for juvenile offenses. Her classroom was a small bungalow located on the periphery of the campus. The census was high, the class was in chaos, and there was little more she could do than "baby sit" these students. Morale was extremely low. Susan asked for assistance or class-size reduction to no avail. The intercom had long been broken, the result of vandalism. After suffering a minor assault by a gang member on school grounds, Susan, frightened and trembling, attempted to report the incident to the principal. The latter informed her that the incident was her fault and that he should not be burdened with it—adding that nothing could really be done after the fact, anyway. A description of this principal as nonsupportive would be an understatement. So Susan became extremely anxious and tremulous and began hyperventilating. The incident became the focus about which she decompensated. She was ultimately hospitalized following a suicide attempt. Susan M. has never returned to teaching.

Some teachers in this study are indeed totally disabled. They have retired early, forfeiting benefits; some were lucky to find other employment. Most, however, are indeed dedicated to teaching. They have returned to their original schools to function under a Damoclean sword: the threat to their job security if they are "unsuccessful teachers" and the continued ordeal of facing violence in their classrooms and on campus.

Conclusions

This series of teachers presented symptoms of psychophysiologic disorders and neurosis, best described as traumatic in origin. The relationship between stress, physiological response, and physical illness has been well documented in certain diseases; the relationship between stress and psychological depletion has been studied extensively. The psychiatric needs of teachers who collapse under stress is varied and depends on many factors; but because of the similarities cited earlier, we feel that analyses of the responses to stress by survivors of war are applicable to teachers in this series.

The consensus of military studies of morbidity following periods of stress was based primarily on these factors; (1) severity of the event; (2) chronicity of the stimulus; (3) unexpectedness of the event; (4) lack of counterbalance to unpleasant stimuli; and (5) impaired morale. Patients in this series have shown the same correlation between the incidence of their symptomatology and these factors of stress.

Careful investigation of etiological factors of patients in this series, based on guidelines from previous studies of psychiatric casualties of war, indicates that certain preventive measures can be taken to diminish or avoid the psychological or psychophysiological breakdowns we have observed in these teachers.

A general assistance center for teachers, independent of the school district, should be developed in each community. The troubled teacher should be able to go there for mental health assistance, referrals, support, crisis intervention, legal assistance, and so forth. These services all ought to be confidential—not part of the given teacher's "record."

Teachers who will be assigned to particularly stressful schools must be specially trained. To minimize the impact of psychic or physical trauma, such teachers need to be rehearsed and familiarized with the consequences of the potential event. This would decrease the intense psychophysiological response of fear during dangerous situations. Didactic group training would be especially beneficial.

Adequate training would develop (1) a qualified (rather than total) belief in personal invulnerability; and (2) methods to cope with and diminish the anger of violence-prone, acting-out students—methods such as learning the language of the streets, as well as the "games students play."

Crisis intervention is another vital aspect of the general assistance center. Personnel would consist of two teachers with mental health training who would be supervised by a psychiatrist or a clinical psychologist. Their functions would be (1) to defuse crises by implementing open forum discussions at schools where teachers and students are involved in conflict; and (2) to offer immediate and subsequent psychiatric care needed to decathect trauma if the stress response syndrome is not worked through and mastered.

To effect a strong morale in teachers, especially those assigned to the inner city, the following areas are important:

1. *Sharing.* There should be an ongoing opportunity for sharing or working through the events and consequences of campus situations. This would reduce psychic load and facilitate the development of good morale through constructive attitudes and efforts. In this capacity, "rap groups" led by teachers with mental health experience could be useful. Leaders with greater expertise might come in should assault or breakdown occur.

2. *Leadership.* The teaching staff, especially in schools with high profiles of violence, must be able to believe in the absolute integrity and support of their leaders, the school and district administrators, as a constant.

3. *Rotation.* Unless teachers specifically wish to continue in schools with high profiles of violence, they ought to be rotated to less stressful schools after a specified (two or three year) period. In World War II combat pilots had to fly only fifty missions, and no more. Year after year many teachers in these schools apply unsuccessfully for transfer out of the "combat zone." The only other way out of their situation is illness or early retirement. If a teacher is unable to continue in his profession even with the assistance noted above, then vocational rehabilitation counseling should be made available.

4. *Implementation of Effective Student Discipline.* Students should not be allowed to return to the same school after attacking a teacher or staff member. Punishment must be fair, firm, and consistent. After a one- or two-day suspension, students too often return as "campus heroes." Moreover, most teachers report that the greater majority of their students could be motivated to learn. Instead, the teachers' valuable energy is siphoned off in dealing with a small minority of "troublemakers." Special schools and classes geared to these students' special needs could also permit their former classmates to receive a serious education. Simply transferring troubled students from one regular classroom or school to another is not the answer; they continue to wreak havoc in their new environments, as long as those are basically similar.

5. *System of Reporting.* Classroom teachers should have an opportunity to report directly to the school board concerning adverse school conditions, unfair administrators, overcrowding, violence, and other problems. This is most important, for it would enable the individual to sustain a hope that someone will be made aware, that some change for the better may occur (Bloch 1977).

Nationwide, each school year thousands of teachers are refusing to teach in inner-city schools, or resigning from their profession. They cannot continue teaching where they face threats of physical violence each day, witness violence to other teachers as well as to students, experience theft and vandalism of their personal property as well as the school's, and know only that "it'll get worse!" Because of the need for marked changes in the system, especially in the support systems available, teachers are becoming "an endangered species." As this occurs, we all lose.

8
Crime and Disruption Among Appalachian Students: A Personal Response

Sarah J. Snider

A tenth-grade girl handed the principal a quarter at the door. The movie cost only a dime, but he had no nickels for change. He gave her two dimes, she gave him a nickel and entered the gym. Later, he called her into his office and asked if she had given him the nickel. She said yes, and he said, "I'm short a nickel. Did you give me the nickel?" She simply stared at him while he demanded that she look him in the face and tell him that she gave him a nickel. After a long silence during which the two were locked into a mutual stare, she was dismissed. Six days later, strange odors and smoke began to appear in the hallway and lighted cigars were found in ten lockers.

An eleventh-grade boy approached a defaced door, and moments later a teacher rounded the corner. "I knew sooner or later you would do just what your brother did when he was here," she said. She then took him to the principal's office and explained that he had defaced the door. The student was paddled and suspended for three days. Eight days later, the front door of the school was blown off with black powder. A fourth-grade student was walking behind another girl who fell down. An instant later a teacher appeared and asked, "Do you want me to whip you or do you want your own teacher to whip you?" The student flippantly replied, "Why don't you both do it?" The teacher did whip the student with a switch. When the student was released, she found the girl who had fallen down and hit her until she cried. After recess, the first student's teacher went back to the child's seat, told her to bend over, and paddled her. When the bell rang for lunch, the fourth grader found the girl who had fallen and hit her until she cried. After lunch, the principal called the former into his office and spanked her. As she was going home on the school bus, she again looked for the girl who had fallen, but that child had decided to walk the three miles to her home.

These episodes have in common the fact that a child was falsely accused,

---

This material was originally prepared under a contract to the National Council on Crime and Delinquency as part of a collection of papers turned over to the Office of the Assistant Secretary of HEW for Planning and Evaluation. A slightly modified version of that original article appeared in *Clearinghouse* 53 No. 4 (December 1979) under the title "Cultural Characteristics and Their Relationship to Disruptive Behavior among Appalachian Students." This chapter is a further refinement of the second paper, but is still based upon the original document as submitted to HEW.

and responded in what appears to be an extreme and unusual manner. The responses are not extreme or unusual, however, in the culture in which they occurred. To the Appalachian child, cowardice is so odious that he will accept the punishment for a crime he did not commit rather than defend himself verbally and risk having others think he is afraid of that punishment. But, according to this philosophy, unjust punishment must be avenged. Although on the surface the child appears to remain passive, in reality he does no such thing; he will avenge the unjust punishment—often in such a way that the vengeance is not necessarily associated with the punishment, so that it may appear to be malicious, sometimes senseless destruction. Persons unaware of this code of conduct frequently believe that the refusal to offer a defense is a sign of guilt; and they are unable to comprehend the whole series of events that is stimulated by an accusation or even by simple questioning which may be interpreted as an accusation.

While it would seem logical for the child to defend himself by simply explaining the circumstances of an incident so as to avoid punishment altogether, the Appalachian child is bound by a cultural code which denies him that possibility if he is to retain what he considers to be his personal dignity. The Appalachian child measures himself more according to the unique values of his subculture than according to the more general values of American society. Whereas he is sometimes able to compromise his behavior enough to function as a social being in the general society, he is not able to compromise values regarding personal being without great duress and an almost certain diminishing of self-concept. The crime and/or disruption which result when the child is faced with what he interprets as a loss of personal dignity or compromise in values are not simple unlawful behaviors arising out of poverty; they are, rather, personal responses to needs or stimuli. The former may range from a yearning to be touched to a need for food, and the latter may range from casual remarks about the family name to false accusations of wrongdoing. Whatever misbehavior or crime a child thus engages in, he will almost never give so straightforward a reason for it as, "I am hungry; therefore, I will steal someone's lunch."

It is not unusual for crime or misbehavior among the poor to be attributed to poverty. However, the very terms *the poor* and *poverty* may hold one of the keys to understanding more accurately the factors underlying the criminal or disruptive act. First it is necessary to realize that *the poor* implies that all poor people can be clumped into a single group. But the label *poor* may in fact very well be the only commonality which exists among poor people. So an observer who regards this one commonality as the causal element in deviance is being too naive to explain behavior. It is essential to look beyond that obvious element to discover the specific nature of the specific person who is poor; for the nature of the Appalachian person who may, coincidentally, be poor is different from that of members of other societies and is the source of different behaviors.

One characteristic of the Appalachian which is often misunderstood, even by Appalachians, is the attitude toward physical contact. In many rather large families, physical touching, especially cuddling, is reserved for the youngest child; all family members cuddle the baby until a new one arrives. At a very early age, then, the child ceases to receive displays of physical affection and comes to believe that such displays are properly given only to the baby. That is, the Appalachian youngster soon regards a former source of pleasure with mixed feelings: the desire to be touched affectionately and the fear that such touching is condescending since it is generally reserved for "baby" people. It is not unusual for such ambivalence to lead to disruptive behavior designed to elicit physical interaction even though that interaction will be negative. For instance, in one Appalachian school where students tended to require increasing numbers of paddlings as they progressed from one class to the next, a group of second graders were asked the significance of the teacher's paddling them. One little girl instantly responded, "It means she loves us"—and all the others agreed.

Another little-understood behavior characteristic involves the meaning attached to eye contact. The lowering of the head and looking down which is so often associated with guilt has a somewhat different significance in Appalachia. There, this physical attitude usually means "You are an authority figure," or perhaps, "You are my elder." Thus people frequently assume that the Appalachian child living outside of Appalachia—for example, in the "hillbilly ghettos" of Ohio and Michigan—is admitting guilt when he simultaneously lowers his eyes (to communicate respect for an authority figure) and does not attempt any verbal defense (intended to communicate strength of character). To one outside the subculture, these gestures actually say, "He can't defend himself and he can't look me in the eye because he is guilty." An Appalachian high-school student living in a manufacturing city verbalized a reaction typical of such displaced children when she said, "If that's the kind of person she thinks I am, I'll just show her"; and she proceeded to steal the teacher's purse and throw it into a river. Because a teacher may be interpreting according to his own background what the Appalachian is saying by means of behaviors learned in his own background, the two may make no contact when they communicate; therefore, the teacher may unwittingly stimulate acts, like the theft described in the example, which may then be termed malicious. Again, such theft has been motivated not by the child's possible poverty, but rather by his feeling that his personal integrity has been questioned. A theft by an Appalachian student is, then, more likely to be an attempted statement of protest than an attempted effort to obtain a possession. It is particularly important that this concept be understood, since theft is the crime most often explained by its relation to poverty.

An understanding of the Appalachian system of values can help communication and personal growth; that is, it can do much more than merely suppress misbehavior and crime. Even though they are often so described, Appalachians are not necessarily culturally deprived. Rather, they have a culture that is their own—that differs from the mythical middle-America culture. Even in Appalachia, however, teachers often expect their students to possess specific qualities characteristic of the middle-America culture and, upon not finding them, assume that there is a void which should be filled. Such teachers then initiate a frustrating process in which they attempt to instill in students those values which the general society considers proper and to elicit behaviors which it deems appropriate. This process is often imposed upon the most promising children, according to a notion that these are diamonds in the rough which a degree of polishing will bring out. But to the great surprise of those who make such efforts, these students, who are usually highly intelligent, often respond by committing some violent act. For example, when the supervisor told one girl that she would sound better if she said "potatoes" more clearly while serving in the cafeteria line, the girl dumped the contents of a large pan on the supervisor's feed and exclaimed, "Looks like I spilled the taters—I'm sorry, potatoes." The student interpreted what was probably an altruistic act as a statement that she would not be acceptable until she rejected her own background.

Rather than being empty vessels to be filled, Appalachian children have acquired the aspects of their culture that enable them to survive or operate successfully within that culture. When attempts are made to supplant their culture with another, the students quite naturally resist, for practice of the new culture would lead to their being rejected by their own society. Jeers received from acquaintances or strangers who can be avoided are preferable to jeers from family and neighbors who are always present and who will continuously taunt at the slightest hint that an individual is trying to escape his background. This attitude is perhaps best exemplified by the behavior of a young girl who went away to a northern city and discovered irregular verbs. Sitting among her old friends back home at the grocery store, she was asked about the weather up north and replied, "Oh, it just blew and blew and snew and snew," to which a boy across the room responded, "Aw, shat!" This interchange brought on such jeers and taunting that the girl subsequently refused to frequent the store, even though it was the local gathering place and belonged to her parents. Likewise, another student was given a home economics assignment to cook salmon croquettes as part of a family meal to be prepared at home. Being unusual, the croquettes provoked commentary, and the family laughingly referred to them as "little turds." Dishes were smashed during the uproarious laughter, and the girl vowed never to cook again. At school the next day she told the teacher that this kind of cooking was stupid, and she refused to participate in any more of the class's cooking activities.

Because the Appalachian child's need for belonging is usually met within the family and/or the subculture, it is necessary to discover what behaviors are expected of a person in that family or culture. The behaviors must then be viewed in terms of what they mean in the Appalachian culture and what values they reflect. It is first essential to understand that the same behaviors do not reflect the same values in all societies or cultures. Since he fears rejection by the broader society, the child clings to the subculture's values with a tenacity that often makes rejection inevitable. That is, in order to prove he is not denying his heritage and thus forgoing his place as a member of the group, the Appalachian child acts in ways which ensure rejection outside the group. For instance, when a young woman attempted to behave in ways that suited an "outside" husband who viewed her as his Pygmalion, she felt so much stress that she rebelled and assumed the most extreme aspects of her mountain culture. After surviving a divorce and completing requirements for a teaching certificate, she was unable to maintain a position as a teacher because she insisted on saying "you'ns," which she explained was no more incorrect than "you all" or "you guys," neither of which was rejected as "you'ns" was.

Another avoidable characteristic that often forces rejection is the Appalachian disdain for hypocrisy, which could very well be the one unpardonable sin in Appalachia. Hypocrisy is abhorred to the extent that upon meeting someone, Appalachians will often show their very worst side in order to demonstrate that they remain themselves in all situations. For people who feel thus about hypocrisy, diplomacy is a very fine line that divides these attitudes. As one boy put it, "I would rather be rude than hypocritical." Because outsiders often interpret this absolute honesty as reflecting rudeness or disrespect, Appalachian children frequently find themselves in verbal or physical battles that they do not understand—for they only said what they meant and what was true.

A proper understanding of their values could help Appalachian children function with less frustration in both societies. For example, sensing that a student was torn between the language of her parents and that of her school, a teacher discussed language with her in terms of formality and informality. Realizing that using the different language at school would not constitute a rejection of her parents, the student was able to employ both languages in their proper settings, moving quite readily from such sentences written at school as "He came every Thursday" to the spoken "He come ever Thursdy." In this case the problem, a typical one, was not that the student could not understand or learn formal English, but that she could not write and speak a different language at school until she was certain that she was not rejecting her parents.

Understanding the Appalachian child's pattern of responses to anger, hurt, and even joy could revolutionize society's attitudes toward those responses. It is customary to punish, or at least negatively reinforce, violent reactions. However, the Appalachian child who becomes violent when hurt or angered may have more potential as a useful citizen than the one who slumps into submission and passively accepts events as they come. This concept is demonstrated in the histories of a valedictorian and a salutatorian who were classmates in a small Appalachian school. The salutatorian engaged in physical battles every day of her elementary school career. Though she was punished every day, she continued being violent. This pattern constituted her reaction to disparaging remarks about herself and/or her family. She was known as a violent person, and even her mother predicted that she would end up in prison. On the other hand, when the valedictorian was the object of identical disparaging remarks, he dropped his head, looked at the ground, and remained passive. He was known for being able to take things in stride, and it was often said that he never let things upset him.

In the one case, violence was punished, while in the other, passivity was rewarded. However, this story's end reveals that in a crucial respect, the two individuals had been misunderstood. The personal pride which drove one to rage against frustration and the lack of it which allowed one to remain passive were major elements in their styles of survival. By working at assorted jobs and supporting herself through college, the violent student became successful in a professional field. The passive one timidly remained in his hometown and worked in a coal mine until it closed, at which time he began to receive welfare checks which have continued for years; there is no sign that his situation will change.

The schools reward passivity on the grounds that it is a "showing of proper respect," while they frequently regard as troublemakers children who attempt to shape their own destinies. It is not unusual, however, for the "troublemaker" to become highly productive in society and for the passive child to become no more than a consumer continuing to receive what is given. Often, when Appalachians reach the point of accepting what is considered a dole, their pride is shattered and they passively accept their worthlessness—or their pride is injured and they strike back violently. If he does not realize the strength of individual pride in the Appalachian, the kind-hearted outsider will find it difficult to understand why his car window was broken while he was leaving a Christmas basket of fruit on a doorstep.

Great strides could be made in equipping Appalachian children to function in society were their teachers to realize that violence and passivity in the Appalachian child are not necessarily character traits to be rewarded or punished, but responses to significant events. Rather than rewarding passivity or punishing violence, teachers need to enhance the child's self-concept and instruct him in varied problem-solving methods. When he is subject to physical punishment at home and paddling at school, the child's only model for problem solving may be violence, and, understandably, he attempts to deal with personal frustration through violence. Passivity and violence should be viewed as indicators of problems—not as problems in themselves. It is when teachers operate with this understanding that they will help bring about personal growth and not merely suppression of crime and misbehavior.

By being aware and appreciative of their students' unique values, teachers in Appalachian schools could help them develop skills necessary for functioning in both the general society and the Appalachian society. Accepting the validity of the children's values could provide a foundation for mutual respect, which could enable those children to accept suggestions about alternate behaviors for various situations. Such an approach would reduce personal conflict over the fear of rejecting the Appalachian society and of being rejected by it. Once they no longer need to fight to keep their heritage, Appalachian youth would protest less frequently by means of crime and disruption.

It is even more important that there be understanding and acceptance of the Appalachian child's culture on the part of teachers in manufacturing cities and commercial farm areas where Appalachians have migrated and formed "hillbilly ghettos." Among those displaced people, the potential for crime and disruption is increased; for they are constantly aware that they are a small island within a larger society. Because of the proximity of the two societies, the need for defending one's position is much greater and crimes against people and property occur more often.

The problem of the "ghetto hillbilly," who generally lives in an area segregated from the greater society, is compounded in the school. There, he is very quickly recognized as different, but the nature of the difference is not understood. Because of the lack of communication between teacher and pupil, immediate disruption often occurs; but more importantly, learning is impeded, so that a climate for future disruption is created. When these displaced and misunderstood children fail to learn what is routine for their age, they are labeled slow, and unfortunately, they may be largely ignored. As a result, their self-esteem is diminished, and concurrently, their involvement in crime and disruption may increase.

Since crime and disruption in the Appalachian school as well as among displaced Appalachian children in ghetto schools are often erroneously attributed to poverty, the real causes of the trouble are usually not dealt with adequately. Unacceptable behavior among Appalachians is highly complex, and it is a basic means of personally responding to needs and stimuli. There must be greater understanding, especially on the part of teachers working with the ever-increasing number of "ghetto hillbillies," of the personal nature of the child's disruptive or criminal behavior; teachers must develop this if they are ever to break away from stereotyped views and ineffective solutions and respond to the needs of an individual child in a society within a society.

**Part III
Schools as Contributors**

Disciplinary Roles in American Schools

Daniel L. Duke and
Adrienne M. Meckel

Confusion over the nature and extent of crime and violence in public schools may be rooted, in part, in a fundamental confusion over disciplinary roles played by educators. Through exposition of these roles and understanding of their consequences for students, a more thorough grasp of the conditions surrounding school-based violence may be gained. Such exposition and understanding are fundamental to informed planning, itself the precursor of responsive intervention. It is the purpose of this chapter to clearly delineate the varied disciplinary roles acted out daily in American schools. To do this, organizational and theoretical questions must precede discussions of role conflicts or of various kinds of perceived behaviors.

Organizational Background

A school, like other organizations, possesses a control structure. Etzioni (1965) defines such a structure as a "distribution of means used by an organization to elicit the performances it needs and to check whether the quantities and qualities of such performances are in accord with organizational specifications" (p. 650). Control structures prevent organizational entropy and facilitate the achievement of organizational goals.

A school, unlike some organizations such as factories, must deal directly with the behavior of clients as well as that of employees. In this regard, Ouchi (1977) contends that the two primary mechanisms available for controlling the behavior of organization members are supervision and evaluation. This chapter focuses on the former, describing the various functions associated with supervising student behavior in American schools. The use of evaluation as a control mechanism will not be discussed.

Supervisory functions related to student behavior have traditionally been subsumed under the rubric of *school discipline*; those engaged in these functions have been referred to as *disciplinarians*. At the elementary level, classroom teachers have tended to be the principal disciplinarians, while vice principals and deans of students have been responsible for dealing with most student

---

Portions of this essay appeared in the *British Journal of Teacher Education* 6(1980). Reprinted with permission.

behavior problems at the secondary level. In a recent paper Duke (1979b) suggests that educators have sought to contend with the contemporary "crisis" in school discipline in two ways: by expanding the range of disciplinary functions and by increasing the number of individuals involved in performing them. Here we will concentrate specifically on the precise nature of the changes and on the possible reasons for their failure to eliminate student behavior problems.

Theoretical Background

We are examining these issues from the point of view of the role theorist. By way of general background, Katz and Kahn (1978) provide a useful overview of role theory. Maintaining that such theory is a "major means for linking the individual and organizational levels of research and theory," they define organizations as open systems of roles. The latter consist of the "recurring actions of an individual, appropriately interrelated with the repetitive activities of others so as to yield a predictable outcome" (p. 189). Turner (1978) maintains that roles embody various kinds of expectations about how incumbents should behave. Using a theatrical metaphor, he identifies three specific types of expectations: (1) expectations from the script, (2) expectations from the other players, and (3) expectations from the audience.

Among other things, expectations pertain to specific behaviors or tasks. Katz and Kahn contend that organizational effectiveness is related to the ways in which tasks are allocated to roles and to the ways in which behavioral expectations are communicated to persons occupying roles.

Numerous efforts have been made to conceptualize role-related problems that can undermine organizational effectiveness. In summarizing some of this work, Zaleznik (1965) identifies three such problems: role conflicts, role ambiguities, and multiple roles. To this trio, we add another, one that our recent field studies have found to be of great importance—role dissociation. We will discuss each of these problems as it relates to disciplinary roles in schools.

We have gleaned the data forming the basis of our discussion of role-related problems from a general review of the literature on school discipline, previous research by the senior author, and field studies currently being conducted by both authors. For the past two years we have been conducting observations in an elementary, junior high, and senior high school in an urban California community; we have attended meetings, conducted regular interviews and debriefings, and reviewed official documents. While we do not pretend that these three schools are representative of all schools, we do feel that their discipline problems are certainly not unique.

Role Conflict

Zaleznik (1965) states that a role conflict can occur between individuals, as in the case of two or more people failing to establish a reciprocal role relationship, or within an individual, when he receives competing demands or expectations. Both types of role conflict can impede role performance.

We contend, moreover, that the likelihood of role conflict increases as (1) the number of roles increases; (2) the number of functions per role increases, or (3) the responsibility for particular functions is distributed over more roles. Field observations and reports from educators suggest that these three processes have characterized the basis of school discipline in recent years.

It is probably fair to say that, of the various roles performed by school personnel, those that are related to discipline have come to be among the most unstable and least well specified. As we suggested above, relative certainty once existed as to who would serve as disciplinarian and what his or her functions would be. Schools were smaller then; and while student behavior problems were probably less frequent and less severe, serious troublemakers could be expelled with relative ease. Courts did not use decisions based on the constitutional rights of students to undermine educators' in loco parentis authority. Nor did widespread paranoia over malpractice suits and school liability exist.

To say that times have changed is to risk understatement. Reported increases in student behavior problems, including unprecedented acts of violence and vandalism, and growing public demands for more control in schools have made school discipline a very complex and politically sensitive subject. Nowhere is this complexity more apparent than in the proliferation of new discipline-related job titles and functions. Whereas once one person may have been responsible for discipline, in many secondary schools today a dozen or more individuals are directly concerned with student behavior problems. Instead of one role—that of disciplinarian—there are a variety of disciplinary roles. In other words, the school-control structure can be characterized by increasing division of labor and task specialization: for the role of disciplinarian is no longer basically undifferentiated. While these developments obviously reflect an interest in improving the effectiveness of school-control structures, they appear to have increased the likelihood of role conflict.

With regard to how this variety of contemporary disciplinary roles is actually effected, the authors found three general categories of functions related to school discipline: (1) disciplinary functions, including the duties traditionally performed by the disciplinarian; (2) technical support functions; and (3) quasi-official functions. Sometimes individuals within the same role group (that is, deans or counselors) perform all the activities associated with a certain function, and sometimes they share functions with other role groups (that is, teachers or school social workers). An appreciation of the potential for role conflict inherent in contemporary school-control structures can be gained by briefly reviewing the functions subsumed under each of the three general categories.

Disciplinary Functions

One of the central features of control structures is a set of rules governing the behavior of organization members. Specifically, schools have rules for conduct in class and outside of class; several functions are associated with these rules. The first of them is the task of *rule development*, which may come into play in anticipation of a future problem or in response to an existing one. Once rules exist, the need arises for the *determination of sanctions*. Sanctions are applied when students do not obey school rules and they may range from parent conferences and after-school detention to suspension and expulsion.

Once they have been established, rules generally necessitate *enforcement*. This may entail patrolling parts of the school where the risk of misconduct is high, checking student absences to verify their legitimacy, or simply ensuring the maintenance of classroom order. Obviously, enforcement becomes more difficult as the number of rules increases; in fact, it has been suggested that rule development may reach a point of diminishing returns, where there are too many rules for school personnel to enforce effectively (Duke 1978b). As a result, personnel often stop trying to enforce rules altogether.

Rule adjudication is a fourth disciplinary function, one involving the determination of the guilt or innocence of individuals accused of breaking rules. While the U.S. Constitution requires guilt to be proven, rule adjudication in schools is typically characterized by the assumption that accused students must prove their innocence. If innocence cannot be established, students may be punished. This final disciplinary function is referred to as *sanctioning*.

Historically, most disciplinary functions were all performed by the same person (the classroom teacher in elementary school and the principal or vice principal in secondary school). Rule enforcement was the only function in which other school personnel might become involved. Such a situation was clearly not in keeping with the separation of judicial responsibilities specified by the U.S. Constitution, according to which the roles of lawmaker, accuser, and judge must be performed by different individuals. This requirement was originally intended to reduce the likelihood of conflicts of interest that might jeopardize the rights of the accused.

In recent years, some schools have begun to distribute responsibility for disciplinary functions among several role groups. Parents, students, and teachers are occasionally asked to participate in the development of school rules and sanctions (Duke 1978a), and student courts exist in a small percentage of schools. In California, school districts are expected to possess an official board of review to adjudicate cases in which students have been suspended for truancy. These boards typically consist of a school administrator, teacher or counselor, and probation official. But perhaps the greatest redistribution of responsibility has occurred in the area of rule enforcement. In the high school under study, for example, rule enforcement is shared by school administrators (principal, assistant principal, two deans), counselors, teachers, campus supervisors (college students serving as paraprofessionals who check on questionable out-of-class activities), and off-duty police personnel (who monitor nonstudents on campus and report students who are supposed to be in class). In addition, district security personnel and private security guards are sometimes called in for emergencies or special occasions (such as dances and athletic events).

When so many people are involved in the execution of school discipline, there is an increase in the possibility of differing interpretations of school rules and definitions of rule-breaking behavior. This constitutes a kind of problem which comes under the general heading of *coordination problems*. Coordination is defined as "those activities that are used to facilitate interaction and integration among persons in various roles" (Deal, Intili, Rosaler, and Stackhouse undated, p. 57). It is when these activities are impeded or inhibited that coordination problems arise in technical support functions as well as in disciplinary ones.

Technical Support Functions

The development of technical support functions has been indicative of the growing division of labor in school discipline. Some of these functions are designed to reduce the number of student behavior problems, while others are intended to increase the school's capacity for dealing with greater numbers of such problems. Eight relatively distinct functions have been identified— sanction supervision, crisis teaching, problem diagnosis, counseling, troubleshooting, problem monitoring, notification, and recordkeeping. While these are sometimes performed by specially trained personnel, at other times they are included in the general responsibilities of teachers and school administrators. However, administrators have frequently not received the special training necessary in technical support functions.

Sanction supervision encompasses any follow-up activities that result from the sanctioning of student rule-breakers. Functions may range from operating an after-school detention hall or in-school suspension center to meeting periodically with students to determine whether they are honoring their behavior contracts. These activities are typically performed by administrators, teachers, and counselors.

Another technical support function—one that has received considerable attention lately—is *crisis teaching*. For this, students are referred to special teachers because they have been unable to function for short periods of time in conventional classroom settings. Unlike sanction supervision, crisis teaching involves a concerted attempt to provide direct instruction. When even this kind of short-term intervention proves inadequate, alternative programs or schools may be necessary. Teachers in these generally less restrictive environments display many of the skills of crisis teachers, though they work under somewhat more stable conditions. Indications are that alternative programs can be effective for many students with histories of behavior problems (Duke and Perry 1978).

Problem diagnosis and *counseling* are often part of the general school guidance program. Unfortunately, though, these activities often do not take place until a student has already had considerable contact with the school-control structure. While counselors or school psychologists may engage in diagnosis and counseling, many urban schools employ social workers to maintain ongoing counseling relationships with students outside of school. Moreover, several recent programs, including Individual Guided Education (IGE), have attempted also to utilize classroom teachers as counselors and advisors.

Because problem diagnosis and counseling may not occur until after students have had serious trouble, school personnel have been urged to devote more time and energy to *troubleshooting* (Duke 1977)—trying to anticipate which students are beginning to experience difficulties that, if not confronted, could lead to major problems. Team teaching can be used to facilitate troubleshooting, since it brings together on a regular basis teachers who work with the same groups of students.

Problem monitoring is similar to troubleshooting, except insofar as it involves decision making or planning and more participation on the parts of students and parents. Though it has not yet been widely adopted, a highly publicized problem monitoring role is that of the school ombudsman. The primary function of an ombudsman is to receive concerns and complaints from anyone associated with the school and report them to the appropriate individuals. This activity is directly in line with a key assumption underlying problem monitoring: that many student behavior problems occur because youngsters with legitimate concerns do not have easy access to school personnel who will listen.

Another technical support function entails the *notification* of people associated with or affected by student behavior problems; the need for this has increased in recent years as school discipline has come under closer scrutiny by courts and civil liberties advocates. Parents, for example, may be notified when their children have been accused of certain infractions. If the infraction also is a violation of statutory law, probationary authorities may have to be contacted. Notification functions often are performed by school secretaries and volunteers, and community liaisons are sometimes hired to keep parents informed concerning their children's progress in school.

Disciplinary *recordkeeping* has grown in importance for the same reasons as notification; that is, recordkeeping is often necessary because of the increasing possibility that school disciplinary decisions will be subject to judicial review (Duke, Donmoyer, and Farman 1978). For instance, because of the complaint that minority students are suspended from school in proportionately greater numbers than white students, the federal government has required schools to maintain accurate records on all suspended students (Neill 1975). Along similar lines, records on truancy must be kept because state funds to local schools are based on attendance figures. It has been suggested (Duke 1977), though, that keeping accurate, up-to-date records on student behavior problems is necessary for reasons other than these legal ones; for such a system can also be a critical component of an effective management plan for school discipline. Unless they have such data, school personnel are not in a position to determine the effectiveness of existing control procedures.

As indicated earlier, the possibility of coordination problems involving technical support functions has grown correlatively with the number of functions. Individuals performing particular functions are uncertain of where their responsibility ends and others' begins. For instance, is the school attendance clerk who keeps records on truants also responsible for notifying the parents of these students? Or is the counselor supposed to double as an ombudsman or should he keep all problems strictly confidential? Indeed, little is currently known about the relative advantages of task specialization in school discipline.

Quasi-official Functions

The previous functions are all officially recognized, formal organizational control functions. However, in conducting our field studies we became aware that a variety of quasi-official functions are in some way related to school discipline. These do not involve specific job titles, reimbursement for services, or official review by superordinates. Nonetheless, school personnel typically agree on which individuals are responsible for these activities and on what impact they have on the school-control structure. Among the quasi-official functions that have been identified are student advocacy, teacher advocacy, conflict resolution, and defense of tradition.

Student advocacy involves speaking out for student rights and welfare when these issues are challenged by the school-control structure. Usually one or two individuals can be expected to protest any new rule, sanction, or other disciplinary policy that tends to ignore student rights or interests. In schools attended by large numbers of minority youth, student advocacy also may entail the defense of certain unconventional behaviors on the grounds that they are acceptable within the context of the minority culture.

Teachers, too, have their spokespersons. These individuals, who may or may not represent the local teachers' organization, complain whenever new developments threaten teacher rights or welfare. In the realm of school discipline, protests may be made when the administration increases the faculty's supervisory responsibilities or requires additional clerical work for making student referrals. Teachers are, in fact, generally wary of efforts to improve school discipline because such efforts often come at their expense.

Conflict resolution is a third quasi-official function. When disagreements arise between groups of students or between students and school personnel, there are often a few people who can be called on to intervene and bring the disputants into direct communication with each other. Sometimes these people are respected school employees, while other times they are trusted students or community members.

A final quasi-official function involves the *defense of school traditions*. Individuals who perform this function frequently point out that students are not behaving as well as they once did. When a new control procedure is considered, the defender of tradition usually observes that it has been tried before. This individual constantly reminds people that the current situation does not compare favorably with the past. Typically, the defender of tradition comes from the ranks of older school employees, and he or she most often enjoys a following among parents as well as teachers.

Need for Coordination

The proliferation of functions related in some way to school discipline has increased the likelihood of role conflict for educators. One dimension of such conflict pertains to what Zaleznik (1965) calls the failure to establish reciprocal role relationships. The relationships potentially affected by coordination problems include those between the following:

1. Administrators and teachers
2. Administrators and counselors
3. Teachers and counselors
4. Administrators and attendance clerks
5. Principals and deans of students
6. Teachers and paraprofessionals
7. Deans and security guards
8. Counselors and school psychologists
9. Administrators and probation officers
10. Administrators and child welfare workers

Failure on the part of these individuals to establish reciprocal role relationships can have obvious consequences for school discipline. For instance, teachers may cease referring students to "the office" if they feel that administrators have unilaterally decided to function more as student advocates than as rule enforcers.

If the quality and frequency of communication between role groups are increased, such coordination problems can be eased. However, simply scheduling a lot of meetings may not be sufficient for communication. To maximize the likelihood that school personnel will utilize their interactions to reduce misunderstanding and conflict, training is probably necessary. This can focus on how to work in groups, how to express problems in constructive ways, and how to make effective decisions (Duke 1977; Duke 1979b).

Role Ambiguity

Zaleznik (1965) differentiates between role conflicts and role ambiguities in the following manner:

> In contrast to a role conflict where quite clear prescriptions point toward seemingly contradictory behavior, an ambiguity exists where the role expectations have not crystallized or are otherwise vague. (p. 590)

The lack of clear-cut expectations elsewhere has been referred to as "anomie" (Turner 1978, p. 363).

One manifestation of role ambiguity in the school-control structure is tension between the expectation that teachers will function as professionals (particularism) and the expectation that they will function as civil servants (universalism). As professionals, teachers may be expected to treat each student as a unique individual—in other words, in a clinical fashion. As civil servants, teachers may be expected to treat all students in the same way—an impartial, legalistic orientation. Nowhere is the resulting confusion more apparent than in the area of school discipline.

On one hand, an argument can be made that each student behavior problem is unique and deserving of an "individualized" response (Fuller and Brown 1975). Teachers who share this perspective may regard many dysfunctional student behaviors as opportunities to learn more about what is bothering the youngsters rather than simply as problems to be eliminated as expeditiously as possible. As soon as teachers begin to deal differentially with students manifesting the same dysfunctional behavior, however, they become vulnerable to criticism for favoritism and inconsistency.

Despite considerable pressure from parents and administrators to apply rules and sanctions uniformly, many teachers continue to respond differently to different students. What is difficult to determine is whether or not this behavior by teachers is purposeful or carefully planned; inconsistency which is intentional must be distinguished from that which is arbitrary or capricious.

Role ambiguity can be reduced, if not altogether eliminated, by establishing clear expectations for teacher, as well as student, behavior and by communicating these expectations to all members of the school community. Expectations can be developed collaboratively, with input from school personnel, students, and parents. It may also be useful to discuss the "professional" and the "civil servant" models of teacher behavior in an open fashion.

Multiple Roles

A third problem undermining effective role performance is derived from the fact that at any given time individuals may be called on to play multiple roles (Zaleznik 1965). Teachers, for example, function not only as instructors, but also as curriculum developers, evaluators, clerks, allocators of resources, disciplinarians, and advisors, as well as in a host of nonschool roles. Talking with teachers reveals that they tend to perceive some of these roles as incompatible— for example, the role of instructor and the role of disciplinarian.

To be an effective disciplinarian, many teachers believe they must behave in ways that do not stimulate the student trust and personal rapport deemed so important for productive learning. Teachers who one moment must censure a student and the next moment must inspire him or her to master basic skills complain that they have difficulty convincing the student of their sincerity and caring. And students with low ability and students from cultural backgrounds unlike the teacher's are often affected the most by tensions that result from trying to perform these roles simultaneously. If a teacher enforces rules based on white, middle-class norms, minority students may see him or her as rejecting their cultures and, in effect, the students themselves. As a result, they may stop trying to learn. Moreover, low-ability students sometimes misbehave precisely because they are frustrated by their lack of scholastic success. When teachers are expected to be student advisors, as well as instructors and disciplinarians, the aforementioned problems may only be compounded.

Perhaps teacher frustration over the seeming incompatibility of their concurrent roles as instructors and disciplinarians has led, as much as any single factor, to the increase in task specialization and the number of school personnel concerned with student behavior problems. Ironically, these trends have not lessened the expectation that teachers will be "in control" in class (Duke 1979a). This finding supports Sarason's belief (1971) that the more things change in schools, the more they remain the same.

One possible way to relieve teachers of some of the pressure to be "in control" all the time is to devolve a portion of the responsibility for discipline onto students. In his account of the differences between Soviet and American education, Bronfenbrenner (1970) notes that discipline in Russian schools tends to be handled by a peer-review process, with students monitoring behavior problems, determining guilt or innocence, and meting out sanctions. Teachers only function occasionally to reduce the severity of a sanction. It is tempting to consider what the impact of such a redefinition of responsibilities would have on relationships between students and teachers in the United States.

Role Dissociation

Role dissociation refers to the unwillingness of individuals to identify with a particular role or to make a commitment to performing the role as effectively as possible. We did not originally intend to discuss role dissociation as a problem, but data from the field studies strongly indicated that almost everyone who is expected to perform discipline-related functions—particularly deans of students and vice principals—is disgruntled and dismayed. Administrators complain that they must spend an ever-increasing proportion of their time dealing with problem students; they resent being forced to curtail other, more enjoyable activities, such as supervising extracurricular activities. Thus, teachers, counselors, and administrators frequently seem to be engaged in a three-way game of "pass the buck," a game in which the objective is to redirect the resolution of student behavior problems to someone else.

Discipline-related responsibilities appear to take their toll psychologically. Many educators complain of bouts of depression, anxiety, and paranoia. Most would like to have someone with whom to discuss the problems, a fact evidenced by the willingness of school personnel to talk with field researchers. Those who describe themselves as survivors seem to have cultivated a cynical view of schooling and contemporary youth, a view which leads them to have no expectations of productive learning or obedient students.

In some instances role dissociation may be an outgrowth of the previously mentioned role-related problems. Hence, an individual may begin to perform a disciplinary function with the best of intentions, only to discover that the conflicts and ambiguities of the task are more than he or she originally anticipated. In other cases, though, there are indications that educators never intended to identify with their disciplinary roles. This latter group includes deans of students and vice principals who regard their positions as stepping stones to principalships. They endure their disciplinary functions for several years, but at no time do they ever consider their positions to be careers. Those who spend more than a few years as deans or vice principals frequently do so because they have been "passed over" for promotion. Having few alternatives, these individuals go through the motions of performing disciplinary functions, but without much commitment or vision of their work's importance.

It is not difficult to speculate on the reasons why the performance of disciplinary functions inspires so little dedication on the part of so many. As they are conceptualized, these functions tend to have a negative orientation. Behavior problems, as mentioned earlier, are rarely defined as opportunities—positive occurrences permitting educators to identify and assist troubled students. Few extrinsic benefits exist for those who effectively perform disciplinary functions, while the potential costs for ineffective performance are relatively great. Teachers, for example, may lose their jobs if they do not maintain classroom control; for parents and students are quick to criticize teachers whose classes are disorderly. And again, the increased tendency for the conduct of school personnel to be subjected to judicial review and litigation points up another potential cost. School personnel and the systems for which they work may be sued for malpractice when the absence of adequate supervision endangers the safety or welfare of students.

Turner (1978) talks about *role strain* or the seeming impossibility of meeting all the expectations encompassed by a particular role or set of roles. It appears that many persons who work in schools are feeling such strain. They sense that they cannot be teachers and police personnel, surrogate parents and civil servants, or open-minded, accepting advisors and models of moral conduct all at the same time. And these individuals also feel that schools have been forced to deal with all the problems which other sectors of society can no longer handle. They resent the public's reluctance to provide additional resources to assist them in their efforts.

Overcoming role dissociation and role strain obviously is a complex process, one deserving more attention than it is given here. Rewarding those who deal with student behavior problems with higher salaries or more free time may help, but probably not without some basic changes in definitions of disciplinary roles. Assuring those who currently spend most of their time on discipline— deans, vice principals, crisis teachers, some counselors, security guards—that they will have opportunities to rotate periodically into less taxing, more pleasant activities also may be useful. Building support networks and administrative teams in schools so that disciplinary personnel do not become isolated can be critical, given the need of most individuals to share their concerns and ideas. Finally, it may be necessary to remove from disciplinary roles certain individuals who do not seem to possess the patience, tolerance, interaction skills, or problem-solving capacities so vital to dealing with student behavior problems.

Conclusion

To help contemporary schools deal with the perceived increases in student behavior problems, the traditional role of disciplinarian has been supplemented by a variety of new roles. Division of labor and task specialization have consequently occurred. Schools today are generally characterized by more people performing a greater variety of disciplinary functions.

Ironically, however, the proliferation of new functions and the addition of new personnel have not reduced student behavior problems enough to satisfy educators or the general public. Year after year the Gallup Polls of the Public's Attitudes toward the Public Schools find people more concerned about school discipline than any other educational issue. Regrettably, the aforementioned dictum of Sarason—that the more things change in schools, the more they remain the same—seems to apply.

Among the aspects of school-control structure that have tended to "remain the same" despite a host of new functions and personnel are the following:

1. The roles of lawmaker, accuser, and judge still tend to be embodied in the same individual—usually the classroom teacher in elementary school and the dean or vice principal in secondary school.
2. Despite its perceived incompatibility with the role of instructor, the role of disciplinarian is still expected to be a primary responsibility of classroom teachers.

Findings such as these suggest that role-related problems should be a major focus for those concerned with improving school discipline. In this chapter we have tried to identify four types of role-related problems that seem to undermine the performance of many individuals associated with the school-control structure; these problems include role conflicts, role ambiguities, multiple roles, and role dissociation.

Role-related problems appear to exert an impact on school discipline in two primary ways. First, by contributing to inconsistent behavior on the part of school personnel, they discourage student respect for the school as a just and rule-governed organization. Second, they frustrate and demoralize school personnel.

While some role-related problems probably can never be totally eliminated, it seems that their negative impact on students and school personnel can be substantially reduced. Among the organizational changes that we have suggested are greater coordination of activities among individuals performing disciplinary functions; clearer behavioral expectations for teachers as well as students; shared responsibility for discipline (between teachers and students); and greater incentives for school personnel who deal with student behavior problems. Particular attention must be paid to improving the jobs of deans and vice principals—individuals who often spend most of each day reacting to student behavior problems.

In the final analysis, the school-control structure is no better than the people who are responsible for maintaining control. It is to the advantage of no one—student, school employee, or taxpayer—to make the performance of disciplinary functions so onerous and unrewarding that talented and sensitive educators avoid them whenever possible.

10 The Creation of Deviant Behavior in American High Schools

John C. Phillips

There is an old debate among sociologists who study what is called "the prison community." On one side are those who contend that the values and behavior of inmates are produced by conditions inherent in the prison setting itself. The other camp contends that much of what is termed the "inmate culture" is imported from outside the prison, that criminals learn how to behave in the prison setting before they ever physically set foot inside it. Both are probably partly true; some prison behavior is produced by the institutional setting, and some is due to the predispositions of the people who enter prisons. The same dispute will undoubtedly develop between investigators examining the phenomenon of school crime—and both sides will probably be partly right.

I wish to present a plausible "institutional product" theory of school crime, along with relevant evidence and a preliminary test of the theory. Let me emphasize at the outset that this theory seeks to explain some, perhaps the lesser part, of what is termed delinquent behavior.[1] Factors outside the school are probably responsible for most delinquent behavior in and out of the institutional setting; but that delinquency which is produced by school conditions may well be eliminated by school reforms. Such factors as the family, chronic economic problems, and racial discrimination are less amenable to change than is the organization of the school.

In 1955, Albert Cohen proposed one of the most influential theories of delinquent behavior to appear in recent decades: the "delinquent subculture" theory. This chapter will present a brief review of Cohen's thinking; a restatement of Cohen's theory in terms of "balance theory," a social psychological approach; hypotheses derived from the theory; and a synopsis of evidence related to the theory.

The School and Delinquency: Albert Cohen

Albert Cohen's general theory of subcultures (1955, ch. 3) begins with the premise that culture may be understood as a collective solution to problems faced by members of a social system. Given certain conditions, these individuals may develop a special cultural solution to their special problems. Since the new "solution" serves the special needs of a limited number of actors, it may be called a subculture.

Cohen was chiefly concerned with the solution to one kind of problem, the achievement of status. In effect, the values which provide the basis for according status constitute a cultural solution to certain problems faced by the collectivity. Cohen explains precisely how this "solution" may create problems for those who lack the attributes or abilities to achieve status in a given social system:

> Status problems are problems of achieving respect in the eyes of one's fellows. Our ability to achieve status depends upon the criteria of status applied by our fellows, that is, the standards or norms they go by in evaluating people. These criteria are an aspect of their cultural frames of reference. If we lack the characteristics or capacities which give status in terms of these criteria, we are beset by one of the most typical and yet distressing of human problems of adjustment. One solution is for individuals who share such problems to gravitate toward one another and jointly establish new norms, new criteria of status which define as meritorious the characteristics they *do* possess. . . . Such new status criteria would represent new subcultural values different from or even antithetical to those of the larger social system. [1955, pp. 65-66; emphasis in original]

Cohen emphasizes that certain conditions must obtain if a subculture is to develop. The "problem" must be shared by a number of individuals and these individuals must have the opportunity for sustained interaction. No single person can adopt his or her own criteria for status and reject those held by others. Even if several individuals experience similar problems, no shared solution can develop without interaction. Neither can a new cultural form be sustained in the absence of continuing social support.

As an oppositional subculture develops, those who share it may become increasingly alienated from conventional members of society. This is especially true with regard to people who reject conventional criteria for status and adopt alternate ones. The extreme case of such alienation occurs when the subculture accords status to individuals specifically because the activities in which they engage earn the disapproval of the larger system: "Certain kinds of conduct, that is, become reputable precisely because they are disreputable in the eyes of the 'out group' " (Cohen 1955, p. 68).

While Cohen's general theory of subcultures has many virtues, it lacks precision; and, of course, it does not directly address the subject of this chapter—failure in school. The following section will provide an interpretation of Cohen's theory in terms of balance theory, a social-psychological approach which is probably as unfamiliar to many criminologists as Cohen is familiar.

An Interpretation of Cohen: Balance Theory

Cohen's general theory can be restated in terms of a social-psychological approach called "cognitive balance theory." This posits that a person will tend not to harbor conflicting perceptions about two related objects. Rather, he will tend to view a given pair of related objects in the same terms—either favorably or unfavorably (Heider 1958; Newcomb 1953, 1961).

Suppose, for example, a person, P, likes another person, O (figure 10-1). Suppose also that P believes that O likes X (which may represent an idea, a way of behaving, or an individual). Balance theory would predict that P would tend to like X. Likewise, if P already likes X and believes that O also likes X, P will tend to like O. On the other hand, negative feelings toward O will tend to produce dislike for any X that P associates with O. Should P already like X and believe that O dislikes X, P will tend to adopt a dislike for O. What ought to happen, then, according to balance theory, is that P will tend to adopt consistent or congruent cognitions of O and X. If P loves O it is difficult for him not to love O's dog. If P hates dogs it will be difficult for him to love O, unless, perhaps, P can induce the dogcatcher to eliminate the dog. Should P dislike O and know that O likes fast cars, P should tend to dislike fast cars.

How does the balance theory apply to the boy who is failing in school? The boy (P) must either accept the school's negative evaluation of himself (X) or adopt a negative evaluation of the school (O) (figure 10-2). Most people want to think well of themselves and resist efforts by others to put them down. In order to resist the school's negative evaluation, a boy has only limited options. He may try to change the school's evaluation by working hard to improve his performance. He may escape the problem by withdrawing—leaving school. He may try to trivialize the situation, viewing the school's negative evaluation as unimportant. None of these options works very well. It is not easy to improve grades, and many will be unable to do so; track assignment may prescribe low grades (Schafer and Olexa 1971). Parents (and the law) may require attendance, and teachers and counselors will most likely emphasize the gravity of poor school work. There are no constraints, however, that prevent the student who is a school failure from adopting a dislike for the school (see Rhodes and Reiss 1969).

Once the student adopts a dislike for the school, he is ready to adopt

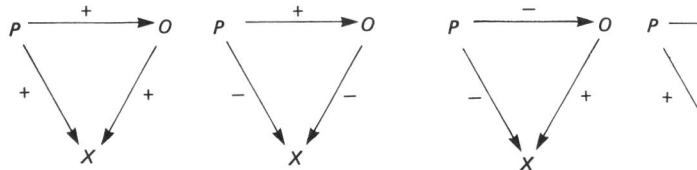

Where P likes O, P tends to adopt an attitude toward X consistent with the attitude of O.

Where P dislikes O, P tends to adopt attitudes toward X opposite the attitude of O.

Figure 10-1. Congruence of Attitudes toward Related Objects

Figure 10-2. Balance Theory and School Failure

attitudes consistent with this feeling toward objects, people, or ideas which he associates with the school; whatever he believes the school likes, he will tend to dislike, and whatever the school dislikes, the boy will tend to like (see figure 10-3).

The failure who has come to dislike the school may tend to be attracted to other failures; the school disapproves of failures, and the boy dislikes the school, so the boy should tend to like individuals who fail. Attracted to each other by their mutual antagonism toward school, such students are likely to come together and form a group; and tracking practices in schools facilitate this (Schafer and Olexa 1971; Hargreaves 1967). This new group, bound together by common antagonism, may now provide support for deviant behavior, much as the school provides support for conforming behavior[2] (figure 10-4).

Balance theory is a theory of cognition, not of behavior, so it is not strictly appropriate to move from readiness to approve antischool behavior to actual behavior. It is easy to imagine, however, a boy who has forsaken efforts to gain the approval of his teachers and has turned to antischool peers for the kind of respect and recognition we all seek. He would probably be ready to engage in behaviors that express a disdain for the school and what it stands for in order to gain the approval of his peers.

The scenario here is the same as that suggested by Cohen: Failure in school leads to dislike for school which leads to involvement with antischool peers and,

P tends to adopt certain orientations toward values, norms, individuals, or symbols (X), perceived by P as associated with the school (O). These orientations tend to be consistent with P's dislike for the school. That is, if P perceives X as approved or liked by O, P tends to adopt a negative orientation toward X. If P perceives X as disapproved or disliked by O, P tends to adopt a positive orientation toward X. Specifically, P tends to adopt a positive orientation (liking, approving) toward individuals and behaviors which, in P's perceptions, are disliked or disapproved by the school.

Figure 10-3. Attraction to Antischool Norms and Individuals

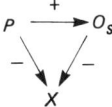

P is attracted to a subgroup, O_s, within the school. This subgroup shares with P a dislike for the school and what it stands for.

Figure 10-4. Formation of Deviant Subgroup

stretching balance theory a little, to antischool behavior. The balance theory argument has a virtue that Cohen's argument lacks—it is far more systematic. Given the assumptions inherent in balance theory and a few more about the nature of school failure and the limited options available to the person who fails, the process described above is logically necessary. Cohen, on the other hand, adopted an eclectic approach, a theory much less explicit about its assumptions and much less subject to criticism on purely logical grounds.[3]

Following the Causal Chain: Some Evidence

The next section will review evidence that connects the links of the causal chain.

From Low School Status to Dislike for School

Several authors have suggested that failure in school can be a painful experience (Hargreaves 1967; Kvaraceus 1945; Polk and Richmond 1972; Vinter and Sarri 1965; Ahlstrom and Havighurst 1971). Cohen (1955) recognized that in a competitive system such as the school, where (at least ideally) status is almost totally achieved rather than ascribed, success for some implies failure for others:[4]

> However sincerely one may desire to avoid invidious comparisons ... it is extremely difficult to reward, however subtly, successful conformity without at the same time, by implication, condemning and punishing the non-conformist. (1955, p. 113)

Vinter and Sarri (1965) suggest that the school behaves more actively when it deals with failures. They point out that although grades are used as rewards for acceptable conduct and/or achievement, grades are often used even more effectively and aggressively as the operating mechanisms for a variety of negative sanctions designed to curb student malperformance. They point out that students performing "below a certain standard received adverse grades and might (as a consequence of poor grades) be *denied* . . . a wide variety of privileges and opportunities within the school" (1965, p. 9). Pupils would then lose face among their peers when they were no longer selected for "minor but prestigeful classroom or school assignments (or) . . . excluded from participation in certain extra-curricular activities" (1965, p. 9).

Of course, failure in school would be no problem to boys who have no desire to succeed in the first place. That is, poor grades, seeing one's peers excel, and lack of opportunity to enjoy extracurricular activity could hardly bother a boy who, for whatever reason, does not care. The evidence indicates, however, that the vast majority of high-school boys do care about success in school. Vinter and Sarri (1965) found that almost all the students they studied were concerned with at least passing their courses. Turner found that all the boys he studied wanted to finish high school and that fully 85 percent desired at least some postsecondary education (1964, p. 43). In a study of a national sample of high-school boys, Bend (1968) discovered a pattern much the same as that found by Turner. There is evidence that high-school boys also seek to engage in prestigeful extracurricular activities in schools (Colemen 1961; Hauser 1965; Spady 1970).

The punishing experiences associated with low status constitute a problem, then, for low-status individuals. Indeed, Cohen is skeptical about whether many boys can tolerate the censure and disparagement that occurs at school:[5]

> The contempt or indifference of others, particularly of those like schoolmates and teachers with whom we are constrained to associate for long hours every day, is difficult, we suggest, to shrug off. It poses a problem with which one may conceivably attempt to cope in a variety of ways. One may make an active effort to change himself in conformity with the expectations of others; one may attempt to justify or explain his inferiority. . . . One may tell himself he really doesn't care what these people think; one may react with anger and aggression. But the least probable response is simple, uncomplicated, honest indifference. [1955, pp. 123-124]

We might add that teachers and school counselors often intensify the student's inability to remain indifferent toward his failure. The school's mission is to encourage behavior (getting good grades, extracurricular activity) at which the failure is doing poorly; so such personnel are likely to remind the failure of his substandard performance and to encourage him to "work harder." The negative sanctions associated with failure constitute a "problem of adjustment," a problem difficult to evade or ignore.

What reactions might result from the inability to "shrug off" repeated failure (or the punishment associated with it)? The term "status frustration" describes the supposed dissatisfaction arising from a desire for status coupled with a failure to achieve it. As Cohen suggests in the quotation above, we seek solutions to our problems; we do not tolerate the "feelings of tension, frustration, resentment, guilt, bitterness, anxiety or hopelessness" (1955, p. 53) that persist until the problems are solved. Undoubtedly, many boys who are failing react by striving to achieve better grades or more active participation in activities. But in a competitive system someone must "lose" if others are to "win." Many boys will never be able to earn the respect of others in the school.[6]

A very likely response to continued low status would be the adoption of a dislike for the bestower of that low status—that is, the school. In the above quotation Cohen's use of the words "resentment" and "bitterness" suggests such dislike. And a good deal of evidence supports this notion (Frease 1969; Gold 1963; Kelly and Pink 1973; Glueck and Glueck 1950; Kvaraceus 1945; Hargreaves 1967; Schafer and Polk 1967).

From Dislike for School to Antischool Friends

That people tend to be attracted to other people whom they perceive as having similar attitudes is well documented (Newcomb 1953, 1961; Byrne 1961, 1969; Clore and Byrne 1974; Aronson 1969). Thus, assuming "dislike for school" to be a salient attitude, we might expect boys who share it to be attracted to one another.

A recent experimental study using college students as subjects (Harvey and Kelley 1973) provides further reason to expect boys who dislike school to choose each other as friends. Subjects who had failed at an experimental task tended strongly to dislike others who had succeeded and to be attracted to others who also had failed. This study (albeit not conducted in the field nor with high-school students) provides a link between failure, adopting a dislike for successful peers, and being attracted to other failures. Hargreaves (1967) found a similar pattern in his study of English secondary-school boys. Boys who were doing poorly in school were attracted to similar boys and tended to dislike the more successful ones.

Schools may contribute to this tendency of boys who dislike school to associate with one another. Boys doing poorly in school (many of whom, we argue, will dislike school) are likely to be in the same classes; for students are very often assigned to classes according to achievement or perceived ability (Schafer and Polk 1967; Schafer and Olexa 1971; Rosenbaum 1975). Hargreaves (1967) found that boys in the lowest stream, who were by definition low in status, shared an antipathy toward the school. This antipathy became normative, in that boys of low status who attempted to do well academically received negative sanctions from their classmates.

The concept of *subculture* may also help explain the apparent mutual attraction of boys who dislike school. If more than one subculture exists, or if only one subculture exists alongside a dominant culture in a social system, each may "compete" for the allegiance of the actors in that system (Korbin 1951; Lerman 1968; Matza 1961; Sugarman 1967). Of course, subcultures do not really compete and individuals do not select subcultures; rather, one individual is attracted to others who say or do things that please him. Teachers and others who support the official school culture say and do things that punish failures in school. Supporters of an antischool subculture might manifest their antischool orientation in their dress, language, behavior, and verbal expressions of dislike for the school (see Lerman 1967; Riggle 1965; Stinchcombe 1964; and Veld Huisen 1972). That is, they say and do things which are pleasing to the boy who dislikes school. Thus, a boy who has been unable to gain the approval of his teachers and proschool classmates may be attracted to those individuals whose approval he can obtain.[7] This transfer of loyalties from one subculture to another or from the dominant culture to a subculture may be facilitated by the fact that many, if not most, boys experience an antischool orientation on occasion, even though the experience might only be vicarious (see Matza 1961, p. 105).

From Antischool Friends to Antischool Behavior

The most compelling reason to expect deviant behavior of boys who have antischool friends is that empirical evidence strongly supports the expectation. Empey and Lubeck (1968), Jensen (1972), Short (1957, 1958), Reiss and Rhodes (1964), Hirschi (1969, p. 99), Erickson and Empey (1965), Matthews (1968), Loft (1969), Hindelang (1970), Stanfield (1966), Stratton (1967), Gold (1970), and Voss (1964) all found a strong tendency among boys who had deviant friends to engage in delinquent behavior. ("Delinquency," as used here, included minor misconduct along with more serious offenses.)

The assertion that those involved in antischool groups will tend to engage in antischool behavior could stand on its own. But Cohen takes up the obvious question of why membership in a group should result in behavior consistent with the shared attitudes of group members. Recall that balance theory does not, strictly speaking, predict behavior, so we rely on Cohen alone for theoretical guidance on this issue.

According to Cohen, antischool groups, like all groups, accord status (respect and recognition) to individuals on the basis of group norms. Boys who are attracted to such groups usually have given up their efforts to achieve status according to school criteria, but they have not given up their quest for status. That we all seek status in one group or another is a basic assumption of Cohen's theory.

Failures, unable to succeed in the eye of the school, share a dislike for the school; Cohen suggests that they therefore tend to establish their own status criteria different from, and probably antithetical to, those of the school. That is, antischool groups tend to accord status on the basis of antischool behavior (1955, p. 65-66). If a boy hopes to gain status among his antischool peers, he must flout school norms—or at least give the impression of doing so.

Surprisingly little evidence connects group norms with individual behavior. Authors often simply infer the existence of group norms from the behavior of group members. The few studies that have attempted to explore the connection between norms and behavior conflict with one another. Matza found no relationship between various forms of adult criminal behavior and approval of such behavior (1964, p. 49). On the other hand, Hindelang (1970) and Hargreaves (1967) did find such a relationship regarding delinquent behavior. Buffalo and Rogers (1971) found that, while delinquents personally opposed delinquent behavior, they believed their peers approved of it. This indicates that group norms (as perceived by group members) may take precedence over the individual's notions of right and wrong and produce deviant behavior. A recent study of college students (Acock and DeFleur 1972) found that while neither the attitudes of the individual nor the perceived attitudes (norms) of one's peers predicted behavior very well, taken together, these factors sharply increased the accuracy with which behavior could be predicted. This indicates that group norms, combined with individual attitudes, are more likely to produce behavior than is either one alone. Thus, while the evidence is not final, the argument that boys will tend to misbehave to gain the approval of peers is very plausible.

The arguments above boil down to a simple chain of events. School status (success or failure) leads to affect toward school (liking or disliking), which leads to involvement in an antischool subgroup (or a lack of such involvement), which leads to behavior (deviant or conforming), as shown in figure 10-5. The final section of this chapter will describe hypotheses derived from this hypothetical chain (figure 10-5) and a synopsis of findings from a study conducted to test the hypotheses.

Hypotheses and Evidence

An examination of the causal chain in figure 10-5 suggests several relationships between its parts. If the chain is correct, the following hypotheses should be supported.

First, the parts in any causal chain should be related. Hence:

Hypothesis 1: School status should be (a) positively related to affect toward school, (b) negatively related to involvement in an antischool subgroup, and (c) negatively related to deviant behavior.

Figure 10-5. Theoretical Causal Chain

Hypothesis 2: Affect toward school should be (a) negatively related to involvement in an antischool subgroup and (b) negatively related to deviant behavior.

Hypothesis 3: Involvement in an antischool subgroup should be positively related to deviant behavior.

The next hypothesis is based on the idea that the relationship between the dependent variable (deviant behavior) and the other variables should be stronger for the variables which are closest to deviant behavior and weaker for those farthest removed. Hence:

Hypothesis 4: The relationship between involvement in an antischool subgroup and deviant behavior should be stronger than the relationship between affect toward school and deviant behavior which should be stronger than the relationship between school status and deviant behavior.

The next group of hypotheses is based on the expected effect on a relationship between two variables in the causal chain when an intervening variable (or variables) is controlled (see Rosenberg 1968, pp. 58-66).

Hypothesis 5: When affect toward school is held constant, the relationships between school status and involvement in an antischool subgroup, and between school status and deviant behavior, should disappear or be substantially reduced.

Hypothesis 6: When involvement in an antischool subgroup is held constant, the relationships between affect toward school and deviant behavior, and between school status and deviant behavior, should disappear or be substantially reduced.

Hypothesis 7: When affect toward school and involvement in an antischool subgroup are held constant, the relationship between school status and deviant behavior should disappear or be substantially reduced.

If variables which do not intervene between other variables in the causal chain are controlled, no change should appear in the original relationship between two variables. Two final hypotheses stem from this principle.

Hypothesis 8: The relationships between affect toward school and involvement in an antischool subgroup and affect toward school and deviant behavior should be unaffected when school status is held constant.

Hypothesis 8a: The relationship between involvement in an antischool subgroup and deviant behavior should be unaffected when school status, affect toward school, or both are held constant.

A study was conducted to test these hypotheses (Phillips 1974). Anonymous questionnaires were administered to 469 boys in two high schools in central New York State. The data generally supported the hypotheses with the exception of those related to the position of affect toward school in the causal chain; the data did not support the idea that affect toward school intervened between school status and the subsequent variables.

A reasonable explanation of this exception (more viable than the simple notion that the causal chain is wrong) involves the impact of tracking in the schools which were studied. It is possible that feelings about the school are irrelevant in a system which creates subgroups of failures (who tend to dislike school) by placing them together in "general" or "vocational" classes. In any event, involvement in an antischool subgroup was shown to intervene between school status and deviant behavior and between affect toward school and deviant behavior.

It is not the purpose of this chapter to suggest solutions to the problem of misconduct. However, if failure in school begins a process resulting in misconduct, it would appear that reducing failure (or, rather, increasing success) should result in less misconduct and more conforming behavior. There is some evidence that deviant behavior is reduced in schools where students feel wanted and able to do well in at least one school activity (Barker and Gump 1964; Wicker 1968; Schafer 1969). If this is correct, then presently feasible school reforms may eliminate at least part of the problem of school crime.

Notes

1. The term "delinquent behavior" should not be taken lightly. For some, "delinquency" means people who have a "delinquent character" or "antisocial attitudes." There is good reason to believe, however, that most delinquent *behavior*, especially minor offenses, is enacted by youths who are generally well behaved and who do not view themselves as delinquents (Gold 1970, ch. 1).

2. For a similar argument in the case of individuals who reject the "general culture" in a college setting, see Flacks (1963).

3. This is not to suggest that balance theory is ready to be elevated to the status of an axiomatic theory. But it is far closer to that ideal than is any eclectic approach such as Cohen's.

4. This suggests Thibaut and Kelly's (1959) discussion of *subjective status*. A person may evaluate the desirability of a relationship in terms of how his outcomes (rewards and costs) compare with those of others. If an individual believes that others like him are enjoying better outcomes, these better outcomes may constitute a "comparison level" or standard by which the individual perceives his own outcomes as failure.

5. While Cohen pays little attention to the psychological processes by which one might simply absorb or redefine the negative sanctions imposed by the school, those constitute an interesting issue, Stinchcombe (1964, pp. 124-128) suggests that girls might become committed to a future goal (marriage) for which school success or failure is irrelevant. School simply provides a period of waiting and dating prior to marriage. Some boys may have occupational goals (for instance, military, working for father) for which school is irrelevant or for which only minimal success (a diploma) is required. Some failures may be principally related to activities outside the school (religion, perhaps), so failure will have little real import. Some boys may consider themselves inferior and be happy to be barely passing. Some, of course, may not make an emotional response to the obvious low esteem in which the school holds them. We contend that such cases are unusual and that most boys find it difficult to accept their inferior status with equanimity.

6. Given a system such as the school where status is based primarily on achievement, there are at least three possible reasons that some people are almost sure to fail (be low in status). First, as Coleman (1961) points out, "status by its very definition is in scarce supply" (p. 143). This is especially true in an achievement-oriented system, since success and failure are determined by comparison to performance of others. Second, there is the matter of talent or aptitude. Some students lack the ability to do well in school, either in the classroom or in extracurricular activities. Third, there is considerable evidence that certain school practices and conditions produce failure in some potentially able students (Schafer and Polk 1967, pp. 234-246).

7. A number of authors (Stinchcombe 1964; Sugarman 1967; Veld Huisen 1972; Phillips and Schafer 1970; Riggle 1965; Polk and Halferty 1966; Polk and Pink 1971) have found evidence that different groups of students tend to have different kinds of interests and to be involved in different kinds of activities. One cluster of interests and activities centers on school achievement and activities, while another centers on nonschool activities such as drinking, smoking, and "making the teen scene."

The idea of competing subcultures is suggested by several authors.

Hargreaves (1967, ch. 8), Sugarman (1967, p. 162), and Stinchcombe (1964, ch. 5) all observe that students with nothing to gain from loyalty to the conventional school culture may shift their loyalty to a competing subculture that they find more rewarding. Lerman (1968) found that individuals were likely to perceive their friends as holding values similar to their own, suggesting that the "attractiveness of a subculture" is more correctly the attractiveness of certain peers.

11 School Crime and Conduct Disorder

Herbert C. Quay

While this volume focuses on crime occurring within the context of the school, it would be a serious error to consider this form of behavioral deviance as somehow independent of other forms of disturbed and disturbing behavior in children and adolescents. As we shall attempt to demonstrate, the almost limitless number of behavioral acts that are generally considered legally or socially deviant can be regarded as members of a very limited number of classes or subgroups of behaviors. It would be fruitless to seek causes or cures of crimes occurring in school believing that these represent isolated and discrete forms of deviant behavior or that individuals involved in them are all members of a behaviorally homogeneous subgroup. One may solve problems of cause, prevention, and remediation of school crime only by putting them into a broader framework which relates school crime to the major subcategories of behavioral deviance.

The Basic Constellations of Deviant Behavior

Since the pioneering efforts of Hewitt and Jenkins in 1946, there have been a host of studies which have demonstrated that the myriad specific forms of problem behavior exhibited by children and adolescents can be incorporated within one of four basic constellations. Utilizing modern multivariate statistical techniques to analyze data, most recent studies have followed Peterson's (1961) model study of the dimensions of behavior problems in normal elementary-school-age children. These studies have dealt with normal junior-high-school and high-school youth (Quay and Quay 1965; Peterson, Quay, and Tiffany 1961); children in special classes for the emotionally disturbed (Quay, Morse, and Cutler 1966); juvenile delinquents, ages twelve to seventeen, (Peterson, Quay, and Tiffany 1961; Quay 1964, 1966); and children under treatment in child guidance clinics (Patterson 1964; Miller 1967).

The majority of these studies have demonstrated with remarkable consistency that the relationships between most behavior problems can be reduced to four major clusters of interrelated characteristics. These clusters are perhaps most frequently referred to as conduct disorder, personality disorder, inadequacy-immaturity, and socialized delinquency.

Conduct disorder, somtimes called unsocialized-aggressive or unsocialized-psychopathic disorder, consists of behaviors which are almost always clearly at variance with societal expectations and are clearly aversive to both adults and other children. Characteristics consistently associated with conduct disorder are disobedience, disruptiveness, fighting, destructiveness, irresponsibility, impertinence, jealousy, profanity, attention-seeking, boisterousness, assaultiveness, defiance of authority, inadequacy, guilt feelings, irritability, quarrelsomeness, dislike of school, destructiveness of property, and negativism. A youngster consistently manifesting these will almost certainly be noticed by social institutions designed to control behavior: the home, the school, and the juvenile justice system.

Personality disorder is sometimes called anxious-withdrawn or neurotic disorder. Most of the characteristics of this pattern differ considerably from those in the first group. They contain strong elements of subjective distress, but the behavior generally has much less negative impact on the child's environment. Typical characteristics of personality disorder are social withdrawal, shyness, anxiety, crying, hypersensitivity, chronic sadness, seclusiveness, worrying, timidity, lack of self-confidence, and inability to have fun. Clearly, these behaviors represent more of a retreat from the social environment than an aggressive and hostile response to it. Still, children manifesting these characteristics appear in the courts; thus this pattern is obviously associated with delinquent activities, especially when it is coupled with impulsiveness stemming from high anxiety.

Typical characteristics of the *inadequacy-immaturity* syndrome are preoccupation, short attention span, clumsiness, passivity, daydreaming, sluggishness, drowsiness, excessive giggling, messiness, and being easily flustered and confused. Many of these characteristics seem to exist in almost all children at some stage in their development. However, when such behaviors appear in quantity in elementary-school-age or older children, they constitute problems, especially for the parent and classroom teacher. With regard to frankly delinquent behavior, children manifesting these characteristics are more often followers than either leaders or "lone wolf" delinquents.

The fourth pattern, *socialized*, or *subcultural, delinquency* represents behavior which is neither a source of personal distress nor maladaptive, considering the social conditions under which it appears to arise. Neither does it involve alienation from the peer group. Instead, the pattern encompasses behaviors that seem to be rational responses to environmental circumstances. Children manifesting these characteristics most often live in deteriorated urban areas. Typical characteristics are gang activities, cooperative stealing, habitual truancy, acceptance by and identification with a delinquent subgroup, and participation in the "street culture." Adolescents manifesting these characteristics cannot be regarded as psychologically disordered. Rather, they have adopted patterns of behavior which have been reinforced by their peers and by the delinquent or criminal subculture which provides their socialization experiences.

The appearance of these subgroups in all populations sampled by the above research suggests that they are ubiquitous. It is clear, then, that all our social institutions responsible for socializing or resocializing the young are dealing with the same basic subsets of problem behaviors.

While these four basic subgroups have been described by multivariate statistical techniques, experimental research still needs further to examine them in terms of additional psychological and educational variables relevant to both causes and cures.

Conduct Disorder

Because of the pervasive and serious social problems members present, this subgroup has been the subject of more research than has any other subgroup. Much school crime, particularly assault and property destruction, is probably attributable to members of this subgroup. We will, therefore, deal in some detail with studies of individuals with conduct disorder, looking first at works which provide additional information about the pattern's characteristics. (These also help validate the original formulation of the subgroup.)

Correlates of Conduct Disorder in Institution and Classroom

Among delinquent children, conduct-disorder pattern has been variously related to recidivism (Quay, Peterson, and Consalvi 1960; Mack 1969); to incarceration for a crime against a person; to problem behavior during institutionalization (including assaults on staff and other residents); to lengthy institutionalization (Quay et al. 1960; Quay and Levinson 1967); to failure to respond to a counseling-oriented institutional program (Quay and Levinson 1967); and to probation failure (Devies 1975).

Within the public-school context, the pattern has been related to hyperactivity (Victor, Halverson, Inoff, and Buczkowski 1973) and to frequency counts of specific deviant behavior (for instance, being out of one's seat, having physical contact with others, being noisy in the classroom) (Werry and Quay 1969). With regard to academic skills, Glavin and DeGirolamo (1970) found that conduct-disorder children were likely to make spelling errors because they refused to write or finish writing a word.

Cognitive and Perceptual Functioning

While members of this subgroup differ little, if at all, from those of the others with regard to measured intelligence (Quay et al. 1960; Quay and Levinson

1967; Prentice and Jurkovic 1976), several studies have discovered potentially useful information about perceptual and cognitive functioning within the conduct-disorder group.

A number of these studies have been motivated by the speculation that extreme conduct-disordered individuals are driven by an inordinate need for stimulation (Quay 1965, 1977), and will thus be intolerant of boredom and routine and inclined to behave so as to increase their level of arousal. Orris (1969) was the first to test this hypothesis. He demonstrated that conduct-disordered delinquents performed more poorly on a task requiring sustained attention than did either his personality-disordered or socialized-delinquent subjects.

In a complex experimental study, Skrzypek (1969) tested the hypothesis that conduct-disordered delinquents who were institutionalized preferred novel and complex stimuli to simple and conventional ones. In demonstrating this, he also found that even a brief period of isolation from sensory inputs increased these preferences. Working with much younger children in a residential setting for the emotionally disturbed, Whitehill, DeMyer-Gapin, and Scott (1976), and DeMyer-Gapin and Scott (1977), also demonstrated such heightened stimulation-seeking among conduct-disordered subjects.

In a sample of institutionalized young-adult offenders, Wheeler (1974) found that on tasks requiring cognitive restructuring, members of his conduct-disordered group performed much better than they did on problems necessitating only automatic mental responses. However, Prentice and Jurkovic (1976) found that the thought of conduct-disordered adolescent delinquents was highly concrete, and that these youths had less moral maturity and used more immature modes of moral reasoning than did members of other groups.

Taken together, all these studies suggest that the conduct-disordered individual is one who seeks more novelty and excitement and a higher level of sensory input than do other individuals.

Responsiveness to Social Cues and Rewards

In our society the behavior of most children and adolescents is usually controlled by such social cues and rewards as other people's facial expressions, gestures, and words. An individual not under the control of these social reinforcers will find it difficult to fit into most settings. A considerable amount of research has attempted to investigate the extent to which conduct-disordered children and adolescents are susceptible to social reinforcers. Most of these studies have involved a methodology employing verbal approval in efforts to increase subjects' performance on experimental tasks.

In an early study of elementary-school children who manifested the conduct-disorder pattern, Levin and Simmons (1962) found that verbal rewards actually decreased performance, rather than increasing it. While the literature on the responsiveness of adults with severe conduct disorders to social reinforcement has been equivocal (see Johns and Quay 1962; Bryan and Kapche 1967; Bernard and Eisenman 1967), a recent study by Stewart (1972) has suggested that Levin and Simmon's finding also applied to a group of institutionalized adolescent delinquents. Clearly, if the conduct-disordered youngster is to be brought into the social mainstream, he must become responsive to those social reinforcers which control our behavior in the home, school, and larger community.

Physiological Factors

The hypothesis that serious conduct-disorder might involve a physiological factor has also generated some research. Borkovec (1970) contrasted conduct-disordered, personality-disordered, and socialized delinquents on a measure of autonomic nervous system reactivity and found some evidence for underreaction in the conduct-disorder group. This finding accords with expectations based on the stimulation-seeking hypothesis discussed above; for chronic underreaction could lead to a less than optimal state of arousal, which in turn could be subjectively experienced as unpleasant, thus motivating stimulation-seeking behavior.

Along completely different lines, Webb and Oski (1974) contrasted iron-deficient-anemic black junior-high-school males with their hematologically normal peers and found that, according to their classroom teachers, the former manifested most characteristics of conduct disorder. The researchers suggested that the iron deficiency might cause heightened activation which manifested itself in restless, irritable, and disruptive behavior.

The Antecedents of Conduct Disorder

There has been an immense amount of inquiry, much of it unproductive, into the causes of abnormal behavior in children as it affects the family. But the relative amount of research on the possibility of differential antecedents for the four major patterns has been quite limited. However, some studies do permit the inference that, by and large, the conduct-disordered child suffers from a lack of adequate parenting and socializing experiences.

In their early research, Hewitt and Jenkins (1946) suggested that the conduct-disordered child came from a family situation marked by active parental rejection of the child. Hezel (1968) reported on conduct-disordered individuals' retrospective views of their parents; remembering their childhood experiences of the parents, these subjects felt hostility, rejection, and hostile detachment.

Megargee and Golden (1973) similarly noted that their sample expressed hostility toward earlier parental treatment. Observing conduct-disordered adolescents and their parents in actual social interaction, Hetherington, Stouwie, and Ridberg (1971) found that these adolescents participated minimally in family interaction and decision making. Recently, Murrell (1974) found that such children were more likely to be middle- or last-born children in somewhat larger than usual families.

Taken together, these studies at least suggest that the severely conduct-disordered child is reared in a situation unlikely to produce strong affectional bonds with parents (and thus with other adults) and unlikely to provide experiences needed for developing internal controls and responsiveness to usual social means of control.

However, before we uncritically indict parents who ostensibly reject their children, we must consider the role that the conduct-disordered child may have played in the family. We have suggested in detail elsewhere (Quay 1977) that an overactive, stimulation-seeking child may precipitate parental rejection, which may lead to a paucity of effective socializing experiences for precisely that child who most needs them.

Treatment of Conduct Disorder

To reduce school crime, researchers have suggested a host of measures which seem to involve almost everything but efforts to resocialize those who perpetrate the crimes (see Greenberg 1974). Almost certainly, however, little progress can occur until schools and communities adopt procedures for dealing with conduct-disordered youth. Fortunately, over the last fifteen years, there has accumulated an impressive body of knowledge indicating that the systematic use of behavior modification techniques can at the same time dramatically reduce deviant behavior and increase the acquisition of prosocial behavior and academic skills. These techniques, to be illustrated in greater detail in our later discussion of specific programs, principally involve precisely assessing the behavior to be changed; structuring the classroom or other setting to minimize deviance; and the contingent using of rewards by teachers, parents, and others. The method's effects also may be measured precisely on a continuous basis.

This line of research began by focusing on a single deviant child in the classroom (Zimmerman and Zimmerman 1962; Patterson, Jones, Whittier, and Wright 1965); was extended to small groups of deviant children (Quay, Sprague, Werry, and McQueen 1967; O'Leary, Becker, Evans, and Saudargas 1969); and then was used with entire classrooms of deviant children (Quay, Werry, McQueen, and Sprague 1966; Hewett, Taylor, and Artuso 1969). This research has also indicated that a variety of models of service delivery can be successful. Positive results have been reported for all-day special programs

(Hewett et al. 1969; O'Leary and Becker 1967; Heaton, Safer, Allen, Spinnato, and Prumo 1976); for resource rooms where children spent only a portion of the school day (Glavin, Quay, Annesley, and Werry 1971; Quay, Glavin, Annesley, and Werry 1972); for school-clinic cooperation in consulting regular classroom teachers (Kent and O'Leary 1976); and for programs in which outside agencies provide direct service to pupils (Stuart, Tripodi, Jayaratne, and Camburn 1976).

While much current research has focused on elementary-school children, several recent studies of children up to age sixteen are of particular interest to the student of school crime; for the conduct-disordered older child can present the most serious problem. Heaton et al. (1976) developed a motivational environment for behaviorally deviant junior-high-school students who had all had multiple suspensions from school and records of prolonged misconduct. They grouped these students into a single class and provided a special morning and afternoon program. Although the former involved traditional academic work, the pupils were given points for starting, maintaining, and completing assigned work as well as for appropriate social behaviors. Along with the points, teachers also gave these students such social reinforcers as smiles, gestures of approval, and verbal praise. Depending on their morning performances, in the afternoon students were allowed to choose what they would do; they could use points earned in the morning to "pay for" games, activities, soft drinks, candy, movie tickets, and bowling passes, and possibly even early dismissal. In three-fifths of the cases these investigators also succeeded in involving parents with their children's programs; they encouraged parents to establish at home such reinforcers as late privileges, TV privileges, and allowances contingent on school progress.

While ten out of thirty-two controls left school, only one out of fourteen of the experimental children did so. The latter also showed better attendance, fewer disciplinary problems, and some significant gains in academic achievement. Thus this program successfully served what was obviously a group of rather severely conduct-disordered junior-high-school students.

Stuart et al. (1976) took a somewhat different approach, although they were still operating within the framework of behavior modification. Based upon what they called "the operant interpersonal" approach, their strategy was aimed at helping develop negotiation skills necessary for successful social interchanges among adolescents, their parents, and their teachers. To create an environment in which each person was free to express his or her desires, a therapist was employed as a mediator. The therapist also offered rationales for changing behaviors on the part of all parties, so that each participant could make concessions without losing face. Moreover, this professional also provided a structure for carrying the negotiated changes into community life.

To implement their procedures, the investigators established a family and school consultation project which received referrals from principals and counselors. In the main, their clients were males, ages thirteen to sixteen, from lower socioeconomic status, one-parent homes. The schools were asked to assess client progress and needs and to reorganize such reinforcers as privileges and grades so that these would be contingent on the client's improvement, not on his class standing. For each boy, a formalized program was developed and agreed to by all parties.

Families received aid in developing contracts promoting specific behaviors in the school and home, and their responsibilities were pinpointed with regard to keeping appointments and fulfilling the children's contracts. The therapist was responsible for facilitating communication and cooperation between teachers and parents. Each therapist devoted a total of about twenty hours to the treatment of each case, over half of which was spent in person-to-person contact with families, with most of the remainder involving person-to-person contact with teachers.

Results indicated that the clients had improved behavior ratings from those who had referred them and from participating teachers, and improved parent-child interaction as reported by the parents. School grades also improved, but not to a statistically significant degree.

The Utilization of Less Restrictive Alternatives

According to current philosophy, all children who are handicapped in terms of school performance must be provided with an appropriate educational program in the least restrictive setting; they should participate in the regular school program to the greatest possible extent. Recent studies have indeed indicated that it is possible to modify both problem behavior and academic achievement without labeling a child as emotionally disturbed and without making him or her attend all-day self-contained classes.

The writer and his colleagues (Quay et al. 1972) utilized the resource room concept to deal with problems presented by conduct-disordered elementary-school children in the inner city. Children referred by their teachers attended such a room for one or two periods a day and received instruction in arithmetic, reading, or both. The classroom was structured so as to give pupils individual work areas and minimize mutual distraction and interference. Token reinforcers could later be traded for food, toys, games, or free-time activities. At the end of a sixteen-week period, social behavior and both reading and arithmetic had improved significantly; these academic improvements were in fact roughly double those of an untreated control group.

The resource room obviously involves considerably less financial expense than do all-day programs. We estimated, for instance, that a minimum of seven or eight self-contained classes would have been required to serve the sixty-nine children dealt with in our three resource rooms. Moreover, psychological and psychiatric examinations, costly in terms of both time and money, were not necessary prerequisites to participation in the resource room program. And attendance in the resource room did not seem as stigmatizing as attendance in an all-day program for "emotionally disturbed" children.

The results of these and many other studies clearly indicate that the conduct-disordered child and adolescent can become a functioning and productive member of the family, school, and community. All these efforts work at restructuring the social environment, not at changing some vague process occurring within the mind of the deviant child. Thus, prevention is probably achievable if, at an early point, the home and school are restructured so that they no longer facilitate the development of deviance. It is also apparent that while parental cooperation is helpful, the school can, by itself, do a great deal for the conduct-disordered child.

Outcomes

Most follow-up research on deviant populations has not utilized the fourfold classification discussed in this paper. However, it would appear, through inference, that conduct-disordered individuals have generally been found to have persisting problems.

In what is now regarded as a classic follow-up study, Robins (1966; see also Robins 1972) determined that antisocial children (and adults) had a higher frequency of psychiatric hospitalization and difficulty with the law, with their jobs, with their families, and with social relationships in general than did either neurotic or control children.

Two more recent studies, with follow-ups of much shorter duration, have also suggested that conduct disorder persists over time. Victor and Halverson (1976) have provided a two-year follow-up of a sample of ostensibly normal public-school children in terms of rated problem behavior. Correlations between teachers' ratings taken two years apart for the conduct-disorder cluster were 0.57 for boys and 0.74 for girls; and a smaller group of extreme cases showed similar persistence over a one-year span.

Gersten, Langner, Eisenberg, Simcha-Fagan, and McCarthy (1976) studied children in a sample of 732 families over a five-year period; they examined a number of dimensions of deviance, including delinquency and conflict with parents. Deviant behavior increased over time on these two dimensions just specified, and the authors concluded that "In general, then, the aggressive or Conduct Disorder types of behavioral disturbance continue over time at same or increased levels of expression" (p. 124). Upon breaking down the data according to the child's age at his or her first examination, the authors concluded that "antisocial behavior appears to become an established pattern of behavior only at or after 10 years of age and its power for predicting adult antisocial behavior should be maximal when assessed in middle adolescence" (p. 124). These follow-up studies clearly indicate that conduct disorder is not a self-limiting phenomenon. Thus, it becomes important to intervene successfully at least by the beginning of adolescence in order to avoid the social consequences of delinquency, later adult criminality, and other manifestations of social dysfunction.

Conclusion

The notion that school crime is primarily a manifestation of conduct disorder permits a better understanding of the phenomenon's nature, origin, and treatment. If the principles of behavior modification are used, successful treatment within the context of the school itself is obviously possible. On the other hand, failure to treat the problem will clearly have continuing untoward consequences for the children involved and for society as a whole.

12 Deviant Subcultures and the Schools

James William Coleman

The laws of physics state that for every action there is an opposite but equal reaction, and in many ways this is true of human society as well. No matter what the official objectives of a particular social institution or program, it inevitably produces a variety of unintended consequences. The remarkable advances in public sanitation and medical care have slashed the death rates, but they have also left many parts of the world facing staggering problems of overpopulation. Our prisons, which were intended to deter crime, have too often become its breeding grounds. This chapter examines some of the ways in which our educational system unintentionally encourages deviance among the young. More specifically, the focus will be on the school's role as a shelter and breeding ground for the deviant subcultures which promote juvenile crime.

The Nature of Juvenile Crime

In order to understand the school's role in juvenile crime, we must first formulate a clear picture of the nature of that behavior. Contrary to some popular stereotypes, juvenile criminals are not just younger versions of adult criminals. The crimes committed by youthful offenders have marked qualitative and quantitative differences from those committed by adults. In fact, somewhere between a quarter and a third of the juveniles in correctional facilities in the United States are status offenders and have been incarcerated for behavior that would not even be against the law for an adult (Sanders 1976, p. 65).

Data from several different sources clearly show that the patterns of offenses for juveniles differ from those for adults. The FBI data on the crimes reported to the police are of no value here because it is impossible to determine if the reported crimes were committed by juveniles or adults. *The Uniform Crime Reports* does, however, break down its arrest statistics by age. These statistics show that adults are more likely to be arrested on charges relating to the use of alcohol (drunkenness, driving under the influence, or disorderly conduct) than for any other reason. A distant second are the property crimes (burglary, larceny-theft, and fraud). Third are the violent crimes, particularly the various forms of assault. For offenders under eighteen, however, property crimes, particularly larceny-theft, head the list. Next are the status offenses (runaway and curfew are the only two status offenses listed in the FBI arrest statistics). The third most common reason for the arrest of a juvenile is violation of narcotics laws (*Uniform Crime Reports*, p. 190). So from these data it appears that violent and alcohol-related crimes are significantly less important among juveniles than adults, while drug-related offenses are more important. However, the use of arrest records as a measure of actual behavior is open to serious question. The number of persons arrested for various crimes reflects the enforcement priorities, procedures, and expectations of police agencies as much as the actual amount of crime.

Another important source of data on juvenile crime is self-reports—surveys which ask juveniles to report crimes they have committed. Obviously, the absolute reliability of such surveys is questionable; for some respondents undoubtedly try to conceal their criminal behavior. Nevertheless, these surveys do provide a valuable source of data which is entirely independent of the official criminal justice statistics. Moreover, surveys of self-reported crime among juveniles by Short and Nye (1958), Erickson (1971), and Gold and Reimer (1972), among others, generally agree on the relative frequency of the major types of juvenile crime. These surveys found drinking to be the most commonly reported deviant behavior among juveniles. Other frequently mentioned offenses included theft and various types of status offenses, particularly truancy. Fights between single individuals were also commonly reported, but gang fights were more rare. These surveys do not, however, agree about the extent of juvenile drug use. The earlier surveys show very little drug use, while the later surveys show a general increase, particularly in the use of marijuana. After surveying juveniles in 1967 and again in 1972, Gold and Reimer concluded that the use of marijuana and other illicit drugs had increased substantially, but other forms of delinquency had declined among boys and remained steady among girls.

One of the most significant conclusions which emerges from the study of juvenile crime is that it is not a solitary activity. The vast majority of juvenile offenses are committed in groups, not by single individuals. Major sources of data supporting this conclusion are the studies based upon official criminal statistics. Erickson (1971) analyzed eleven such studies conducted in the 1920s, '30s, and '40s, and found that 85 percent of the over 19,000 cases studied involved more than one offender (also see Clinard 1959). Of course, it is possible that juveniles are simply more likely to be caught when they commit crimes in a group. But self-report data also show a high percentage of "group crime." In Gold and Reimer's 1972 survey 92 percent of the boys and 97 percent of the girls who smoked marijuana reported that they did it in groups. Erickson's own survey found only one of the eighteen juvenile offenses he investigated to be more commonly committed by single individuals than groups. He found the rates of group participation to be between 70 percent and 80 percent for theft, drinking, and narcotics use, and only slightly lower for violent offenses such as armed robbery and fighting.

The Impact of Deviant Subcultures

A complete explanation of the causes of juvenile crime is beyond the scope of this chapter. However, in order to understand the role of the school in juvenile crime, it is necessary to investigate the role of one major criminogenic influence—the deviant subculture.

The Definition of a Deviant Subculture

First popularized by Milton Gordon (1947), the concept of the subculture has proven to be one of the most useful in all of social science. A subculture is essentially a "culture within a culture," that is, a segment of the main culture which has its own unique characteristics, yet still shares some of the characteristics of the main culture as well. Many sociologists define a subculture as a distinct set of norms and values shared by a specific group within a society. However, subcultures contain more than just norms and values. Each also contains its own construction of reality, which gives meaning and order to the lives of its members. Through this web of meanings, definitions, norms and values, a subculture encourages certain types of behavior and discourages others.

Although all subcultures are different in some way from the dominant culture, they are not necessarily deviant. A subculture is considered deviant only if it holds ideas and beliefs which the dominant culture condemns. So while the subculture of fundamentalist Christians may merely be different from the dominant culture, the subcultures of orgiastic Eastern cults are usually considered deviant.

Deviant Subcultures and Juvenile Crime

The fact that most juvenile offenses are committed in groups supports the contention that deviant subcultures are important in the etiology of juvenile crime; but in itself, this is hardly conclusive. Fortunately, there is a considerable amount of independent evidence on this point. A great deal of research has been devoted to the "drug culture," and there can be little doubt that the use of marijuana and other illicit drugs is clearly a subcultural phenomenon (see Coleman 1976; Goode 1972; Brecher 1972; Becker 1963). Indeed, it is doubtful that any substantial number of people would use marijuana or other illicit drugs were it not for the influence of the "drug culture."

A quick examination of one of the many descriptions of violent juvenile gangs shows that they too are part of a very distinct subculture (for example, Dawley 1973; Keiser 1969; Thomas 1967). The gangs have their own norms, values, and perspectives which are obviously conducive to criminal behavior. Even young people who are not actually members of a gang are likely to be influenced by gang culture if they live, work, or go to school in an area with a great deal of gang activity.

While it is generally recognized that drug users and the members of violent gangs are part of their own distinct subculture, that is not the case for young property offenders. Since most adults who commit property offenses are not part of a clearly definable subculture, young property offenders are often thought to be single individuals out for personal profit. Current research, however, shows that most young property offenders are part of what Irving Spergel (1964) calls a "theft subculture." As we have already pointed out, most juvenile property crimes are committed in groups. These groups tend to have a very specific set of attitudes and values which encourage or justify property crimes, while often rejecting other sorts of deviant behavior (Short 1968).

While the subcultures of juvenile drug users, gang members, and thieves are highly conducive to criminal activity, they tend to be narrow in scope and limited in membership. In contrast, the so-called "youth culture" influences a much larger number of young people but is less conducive to criminal activity. The central theme of the youth culture is the rejection of teenagers' subordination to adults. Thus, it often includes a rejection of parental standards and/or a rejection of the authority of the schools. The youth culture primarily manifests itself in relatively harmless expressions of individuality and separation from the adult world—a special style of dress, a unique set of slang expressions, preference for a particular style of music. However, because the youth culture weakens the effectiveness of parental controls and encourages youthful rebellion, it also promotes juvenile crime (see Wolfgang 1967; Polk and Pink 1971).

Of course, the theory of deviant subcultures does not completely explain juvenile crime. It cannot explain why some juveniles participate in a deviant subculture while others with similar opportunities do not, or why some juveniles commit crimes "on their own." Nevertheless, an understanding of the powerful influence deviant subcultures exert on many young people is critical to the understanding of juvenile crime and the role the schools play in its development.

Theories of Subcultural Formation

The origins of many subcultures can be understood better through a particularistic historical analysis than through more general theoretical formulations. For instance, the origins of the Irish or Italian subcultures in the United States are most easily explained by the historical circumstances surrounding the immigration of those groups and the reactions of the society into which the immigrants entered. Nevertheless, theory does help us to understand the reasons historical events unfolded as they did. And, more importantly, theory provides the grounds for predicting the future course of events and making concrete policy decisions which historical analysis alone can never provide.

Many social scientists have put forward hypotheses concerning the general causes of subcultural formation (Hollingshead 1939; Lewis 1961; Gans 1962; Shibutani 1955; Spergel 1966), but few have carefully investigated this issue. The first sustained attempt to develop a theory of subcultural formation was made by Albert Cohen (1955). Following the lead of many earlier writers, Cohen holds that subcultures are essentially a response to problems shared by a group of people. Indeed, Cohen believes that all human action is an ongoing series of efforts to solve problems. Since human problems are caused as much by the perspective of the actor as by the external situation, Cohen feels that effective solutions must entail some change in the actor's frame of reference. Subcultures, then, develop out of a group's effort at problem solving and the shifts in perspective that are required to help resolve those problems.

The principal alternative to Cohen's theory was set forth by David O. Arnold (1970). The focus of Arnold's theory of subcultural formation is differential interaction among groups of people rather than their common problems. More specifically, Arnold argues that two things are necessary for the development of a subculture among a group of people. First, members of the group must have the same structural position in the social system. Second, they must have more frequent interaction with each other than with people from other segments of society. Arnold feels that subcultures develop out of intensive interactions of people in the same structural position as they develop their own beliefs, norms, and values.

Although these two theories emphasize different aspects of the process of subcultural formation, they need not be considered contradictory. In fact, they complement each other quite well. The conditions specified by both Cohen and Arnold—common structural position, mutual problems, and differential interaction—all contribute to the likelihood of the development of a subculture.

While the works of Cohen and Arnold have helped to create a comprehensive theoretical framework for the explanation of subcultural formation, they tell us little about the forces which promote the development of deviant rather than nondeviant subcultures. In many cases it appears that the deviance actually precedes the subculture, which then develops in response to the problems the deviants share. For example, this kind of subcultural formation occurred among opiate users in the United States. Before the prohibition of opiates, most users were isolated individuals having little contact with each other. They often did not even consider themselves deviant. But the prohibition of opiates forced those who continued to use the drugs into closer and closer association in order to secure their supplies and protect themselves from society's hostility. As a result, a distinct subculture soon developed (Coleman 1976).

On the other hand, the development of a new subculture may be the stimulus for various sorts of deviant attitudes and behavior, rather than a reaction to it. The chances that a developing subculture will become deviant are influenced by many variables. The more deviants who are in the group in which a subculture is developing, the greater the likelihood that a subculture itself will be considered deviant. Structurally, there is a greater chance that a deviant subculture will develop among subordinate groups which are not politically, socially, or economically integrated into the dominant elites. The more status and rewards a group receives from the dominant culture, the less inclined its members will be to risk their favored position by challenging the dominant value system. On the other hand, the more powerful a group is, the less likely it is to be labeled as deviant (Becker 1963; Lofland 1969). For instance, it seems doubtful that marijuana would ever have been prohibited if it had originally been popularized by business executives or government officials, rather than by the poor and the minorities.

The School Environment

Albert Cohen's (1955) influential study of delinquent boys was one of the first comprehensive analyses of the role of the schools in the development of deviant subcultures. For Cohen, delinquent subcultures are a response to status deprivation among working-class boys, and he feels that the schools play a major role in creating and aggravating this problem. According to this theory, working-class boys feel status deprivation when they realize that they have less of those things valued by American culture than do middle-class boys. These things include material possessions and "status symbols," as well as social and academic skills. The working-class boys might solve this problem by simply avoiding contact with the middle class, but many cannot do so; for the schools they are forced to attend are middle-class institutions based upon middle-class values. So they reject middle-class values and attitudes and form delinquent subcultures—which give them status for the things they can do better than middle-class youths (that is, being tough and fighting).

As plausible as Cohen's theory sounds, it has several problems. For one thing, it is not clear that the rewards, such as high grades, that the schools give to middle-class students are really of such great importance to working-class students. More importantly, the theory fails to account for middle-class delinquency. Indeed, Cohen's basic assumption that working-class boys are more heavily involved in delinquency than middle-class boys has been challenged in many recent empirical studies (see Tittle, Villemez, and Smith 1978). If the contention of such researchers is proven correct, Cohen's line of argument collapses.

Cressey holds that academic failure promotes delinquency because it leads to a progressive "locking out" of failing students from the system for achieving legitimate success. As a result, these students become increasingly alienated from the school and "drift into association with delinquent subcultures" that are already present in the school environment (Sutherland and Cressey 1978, p. 249). Thus, in Cressey's view, delinquency is not a result of rebellion against an educational system that fails to reward lower-class students, but of association with the deviant subcultures students encounter in school.

Strong empirical support for the contention that the schools promote juvenile crime by fostering association with deviant subcultures comes from Elliott and Voss' (1974) longitudinal study of 2,617 junior- and senior-high-school students. After analyzing many variables, Elliott and Voss conclude that the schools are the most critical social milieu for the generation of delinquency. They find "association with delinquent classmates" and "commitment to peers" among the four best predictors of delinquency for both males and females. (The fact that commitment to peers is positively related to delinquency, even if those peers are not themselves delinquent, may reflect the influence of the youth subculture.) Elliott and Voss find that delinquents are more likely to drop out of school than nondelinquents. But contrary to the conventional wisdom, they find that delinquent students' rates of delinquency declined after they dropped out. Thus, separation from the school environment and its deviant subcultures decreases the incidence of youth crime.

Why do the schools harbor deviant subcultures despite the efforts they make to prevent delinquency? An examination of the school environment reveals the presence of all the conditions theory holds to be conducive to subcultural growth. By definition, students have a common structural position in the social system. They also share many of the same problems, some which are produced by the schools themselves—completing homework assignments, passing examinations, and dealing with the school bureaucracy. Other problems are common to all people of school age, for instance, the need to cope with parental authority or the ubiquitous problems of adolescence. Finally, students clearly engage in differential interaction for they have more contact with each other, both in and out of school, than with any other group of people.

Not only is the school environment conducive to subcultural development in general, but it also contains excellent conditions for the growth of deviant subcultures. By virtue of age alone, most students are cut off from the adult world of power and authority. And to aggravate the problem, the schools themselves are too often rigid authoritarian institutions run according to inflexible rules which impose harsh restrictions on the students merely for the sake of "maintaining authority." Feelings of frustration and alienation commonly result from this rigidity (see Kozol 1967; Silberman 1970). Yet most students can do virtually nothing to gain power over their own lives without violating the established standards for their behavior. It should, therefore, not be surprising that many students feel little allegiance to "the system." And at the same time, they have less to lose than most by challenging it. Few have families to support, good jobs, high status, or special social privileges. Punishments such as expulsion from school usually do not have immediate negative consequences and might even be welcomed by some. Even the criminal justice system gives special leniency to youthful offenders. In sum, the juvenile receives fewer positive rewards for going along with the dominant moral order, and less punishment for challenging it. Such conditions are obviously conducive to both individual and subcultural deviance.

Implications for School Policy

From a pragmatic point of view, the central question in the study of juvenile crime is obviously: "What can we do to prevent it?" Since it is extraordinarily difficult to change the family or neighborhood environment of potential delinquents, the schools often seem to be the ideal agency to handle crime prevention programs. However, there is only so much we can realistically expect of our school system. By the very nature of the institution, practically any school is likely to create conditions which foster the development of various subcultures. The key is to implement programs which discourage the formation and transmission of deviant subcultures.

Structural Change

One of the most appealing responses to the problem of juvenile crime would be to restructure the schools to eliminate the conditions which promote the development of deviant subcultures. Unfortunately, that is much easier said than done. Many of those conditions are not so much created by the schools themselves as by the position of young people in society as a whole. Nevertheless, some ameliorative programs are feasible.

One approach would be to improve lower-class students' academic performance in order to avoid the "locking out" process. In fact, several such programs have already been effected. The most well-known was the Head Start Program, which set up special preschools and compensatory education programs for disadvantaged children. Evaluation of this effort shows that the improvements its students made in the early years of school did not carry over into the higher grades. If compensatory education programs are to achieve any long-range improvements in academic performance among disadvantaged students, they will probably have to be continued right up through high school. And that, of course, means that the taxpayers would have to devote a great deal more money to education than they have so far shown themselves willing to do.

Another, less costly, approach would be to restructure the rules and regulations governing school behavior in order to reduce students' feelings of frustration and alienation. Many junior and senior high schools are guilty of petty authoritarianism which goes far beyond necessary discipline. What they, therefore, need to eliminate are rules and regulations which do not contribute to educational achievement. Dress codes, the prohibition of smoking, arbitrary restriction of the student's freedom of movement, and the prohibition of talking when it is not disruptive to the classroom are a few examples of unnecessary rules which can easily be changed. However, there is a limit to how far such reforms can go without jeopardizing the quality of education. A certain amount of discipline and control is required in any complex bureaucratic organization, and that is particularly true of the schools. The key is to make restrictions on behavior more reasonable so students can see that those restrictions are necessary for their education—not just arbitrary whims of the school administration.

Crime Prevention Programs

A number of schools have educational programs designed to prevent various sorts of juvenile crime. Drug education classes are probably the most common example. The basic idea behind such programs is to inform the students of the dangers of drug use and thereby discourage it. However, drug education programs often bring about the opposite result. Repeated discussions of drugs and their effects are just as likely to excite students' interest in drugs as they are to discourage it. When a drug subculture exists in the school (as it almost always does), its members are likely to challenge the conclusions of their instructors, and perhaps even launch their own campaign of proselytization. Other sorts of educational programs such as lectures by criminal justice officials or informal sessions where students meet local police officers are unlikely to produce such negative results. However, there is insufficient evidence to indicate whether or not such programs actually produce any positive results.

A different approach to the prevention of juvenile crime would be to encourage the students' participation in nondeviant subcultures. Hopefully, the students who are actively participating in such subcultures would have little time or interest left for deviant activities. Of course, many schools already have programs which encourage athletics, music, drama, art, and other extracurricular activities. But such programs might fruitfully be aimed more directly at those students who appear to be most likely to become involved in deviant activities.

Responding to Student Deviance: A Basic Dilemma

Subcultural theory points out a basic dilemma the schools must face when they attempt to deal with deviant students. If they allow the deviant student to remain in regular classes, they run the risk that he or she will help spread a deviant subculture to others. Thus the chances of spreading a deviant subculture are reduced by isolating deviant students in special classes or schools. But officially labeling these students as discipline problems, and putting them into special classes where they are forced to interact with each other, is likely to reinforce their deviant self-image and behavioral pattern. Special classes made up entirely of "discipline problems" provide an ideal environment for the solidification and reinforcement of whatever deviant subcultures may already exist among the students. So school officials are faced with a choice between two undesirable alternatives—one of which is likely to encourage the spread of deviant subcultures, and the other to encourage their solidification and development.

In making such a difficult choice, there is no substitute for sound judgment on an individual case-by-case basis. However, subcultural theory can provide some useful advice. From a theoretical perspective, the worst possible course of action is to separate deviant students into special classes in a school where there are also regular students. This not only encourages the development and intensification of deviant subcultures among the special students, but also puts them in close enough proximity to the rest of the student body to enable the subculture to spread.

In general, the best response to minor acts of deviance such as occasional drinking, marijuana smoking, or "normal" fights is simply to ignore them as much as possible, perhaps issuing minor reprimands. A more severe reaction risks stimulating the development of a deviant subculture, for it reinforces a deviant self-image in those students labeled as troublemakers and encourages differential interaction among them.

For more serious violations, the best response is probably to expel the students involved. Such action reinforces the unacceptability of their behavior, isolates them from contact with the deviant subcultures in the schools, and minimizes any negative influence they may have on other students. Arrangements should, of course, be made for their provisional readmission if they show a renewed willingness to conform to expected standards. However, it seems best to encourage these students to attend adult-education classes where their influence on other students and their exposure to juvenile subcultures is likely to be minimal. Indeed, Elliott and Voss' finding that former students' delinquency rates decline after they drop out of school indicates that we may be putting too much pressure on students to stay in school. Apparently, older students with behavioral problems and poor academic records ought to be encouraged to leave school and the adolescent roles that cause them problems. The weakness of this approach involves our economic system's failure to find them meaningful work or oftentimes any work at all. Our schools might take the money that would have been spent on the education of dropouts and finance job-placement programs. Such a "band-aid" approach could not, however, change the basic economic realities for most dropouts, especially for those from poor or minority backgrounds. Broadly based programs to attack underlying economic problems must first be implemented, before such efforts on the schools' part may be effective.

Conclusions

While it is clear that the insights gained from subcultural theory can help the schools deal with the difficult problem of juvenile crime, we must conclude with a cautionary note. Americans have an enormous, and in many ways excessive, faith in education. From poverty to racial discrimination, no matter what the social problem, we almost instinctively turn to our educational institutions for a solution. But the schools are only one piece in the intricate puzzle of juvenile crime. An effective solution to this vexing problem requires social changes which reach far beyond the schools into the basic fabric of our society. The schools are a logical place to begin addressing the problem of juvenile crime. However, if our efforts go no further, there is little hope for the significant long-term improvements that are possible through a more comprehensive attack on the problem.

13 The Social Patterning of Deviant Behaviors in School

Vincent Tinto

We can reasonably expect that in response to what is seen as the rising tide of criminal behavior in schools, there will be a flood of recommendations from various groups on what schools should do to stop such behavior. It is doubtful, however, whether these ideas will have much impact upon the overall rate of deviance among students. For while schools label and record behavior that is specifically *criminal*, this is only one of the more overt forms of *deviant* behavior. It is necessary, then, to make clear distinctions between those manifest behaviors thought of as criminal and less overt forms of behavior. Then it is necessary to pay serious attention to the latter forms. All criminal acts may be considered deviant, but many acts which are deviant, in the structural sense, may not be considered criminal. Similarly, there is not an equal likelihood that all persons who violate rules or norms will be thought of as criminal. Although those other behaviors and individuals are less noticeable than criminal ones, they are potentially just as destructive of the school's goals—and thus they are equally deserving of our concern.

Criminal behavior is the easiest type of abnormality to define; it violates the law. Homicide, rape, and burglary are obvious examples. As it is used colloquially, the word "deviance" applies to a more subtle kind of action that violates an accepted social norm or rule of group or society. The term "norm" is in turn a sociological one referring to all products of group interaction which regulate members' behavior in terms of expected or even ideal behavior. A norm tends to include not only expected behavior, but also a range of tolerable behaviors, the limits of which define deviant acts (Sherif 1954).

For an act to be labeled deviant, it must meet four conditions: (1) a norm or rule must exist; (2) an act that we have called rule-breaking (deviant in the structural sense) must occur; (3) that act must be interpreted as deviant (for instance, criminal); and (4) sanctions must be applied against the perpetrator. Thus, as Erickson (1966) points out, "Deviance is not something inherent in certain behavioral acts. It is a property conferred upon specific acts by the audiences (interpreters) which directly or indirectly witness them." The labeling of acts as deviant depends then both on the nature of the act and on the attributes and interests of the actors and audiences involved. For instance,

---

The author is particularly grateful for the assistance given by Elena Paolillo and Francis Cullen in the preparation of this chapter.

overt forms of deviance (such as rebellious behaviors) are more likely to be labeled as deviant than are covert or less overt forms (such as ritualism).

It is this less obvious type of deviance which the forthcoming recommendations to schools are likely to overlook. Those studies which fail to place such behaviors within the context of deviance run the risk not only of vastly underestimating the extent of deviant behavior in schools, but also—and more importantly—of seriously misinterpreting the roots of such behaviors.

This chapter attempts both to describe the range of deviant behaviors and the place of criminal behavior therein, and to explain the sources of their occurrence and social patterning among students. We will be asking two questions: (1) what gives rise to deviant behavior? and (2) what factors explain the types of deviant behavior that are adopted by differing types of students? In so doing, we will attempt to isolate those structural characteristics of schools which may contribute to the occurrence of deviant behavior. It is suggested that such deviant behaviors, criminal and noncriminal, reflect tensions which exist in schools (and in society generally), and which result from the goals espoused in schools and from their limited means of attainment.

In the following sections we will first delineate a theoretical model of deviant behavior in schools, drawing upon the work of Robert K. Merton (Merton 1938, 1959, 1964, 1968a, 1968b; see also Cole and Zuckerman 1968; Cole 1975).[1] Then, to specify the factors determining which types of deviant responses individuals make in school situations, we will synthesize existing research in the field. We will seek to extract from the literature some general propositions concerning the distribution of deviant role behaviors in school among different social groups, especially those defined by sex, race, and social class. Finally, we will offer some policy recommendations directed toward the reduction not only of criminal student behavior, but of other forms of deviant behavior as well.

Merton's Model of Deviance

Merton has argued that deviant behavior can be seen as an individual's response to the disjunction between valued goals and the legitimate means available to achieve them. Merton's basic premise is that when people are socialized toward a particular cultural goal but lack legitimate means to attain it, they will experience structurally induced pressure to engage in nonconforming behavior—that is, deviant behavior. Applying this scheme to American society, Merton contended that in a significant segment of the population widespread socialization to the goal of economic success combined with restricted economic opportunity produces pressures to deviate from accepted patterns of behavior.

He further suggested that because of a disjunction between a valued goal and the availability of legitimate means for attaining it, an individual would make one of five possible adaptations, four of which constitute deviant responses.[2] A significant majority of people would probably respond with conforming role behavior; that is, they would continue to ascribe to the valued goal and legitimate means despite the pressure to deviate. The four nonconformist responses for which others might opt are:

1. innovation—continuing to ascribe to the goal, rejecting legitimate means, and seeking out illegitimate means and/or creating new means which may become legitimate in the future;
2. ritualism—rejecting the goal while continuing to ascribe to the legitimate means to attain it (that is, going through the motions);
3. retreatism—rejecting both goals and means, which results in the individual's withdrawal; and
4. rebellion—rejecting both goals and legitimate means, which brings about the creation of opposing goals and means.[3]

We propose that similar conditions hold in schools. Specifically, we suggest that schooling in America is characterized by blocked goal attainment—by a disjunction between the goal of academic success and the legitimate means for attaining it. Moreover, we point out that existing data on deviant behavior in schools support our notion of parallels there to Merton's four categories of deviance.

Of course, we do not intend to deny that deviant behavior in schools may arise from sources other than means/goals disjunctions; for obviously, some rebellious behaviors (such as riots, vandalism, drug use) may have other primary causes. Clearly, schools contain numerous nonconforming student cultures as well as numerous psychologically unstable individuals. We are simply using Merton's model to suggest that much of the deviant behavior occurring in schools does result from blocked goal attainment.

Because Merton's model does not enable us to explain and predict which deviant role behaviors different individuals might adopt, we must develop variables specifying conditions and situations conducive to the assumption of each particular type. With regard to the school, we need to examine such factors as formal and informal social structures which influence the distribution of opportunities for academic success. We must also consider student/teacher and student/student relationships; for these affect the meanings that academic goals will have for the individual, as well as his perception of the opportunities available to him.

The situational nature of deviance is in fact crucial to the concept of deviant role behavior. For while staff and administration (representing the formal organization of the school) may regard a given student's behavior as deviant, his peers (representing the informal social system) may regard that same behavior as conformist. A student caught cheating, for instance, will have violated the school's expectations of normative behavior; but the youngster's peers may perceive the very same actions as appropriate to the student role as they define it, and so they will actually reinforce that behavior.

The notion of role adaptation also helps to clarify the situation and time-dependent character of deviant role behavior. In brief, the adoption of deviant roles may be seen as an individual's situational adaptation to specific means/goals disjunctions which occur at various times during the school year. Many students are probably deviant at some point in their school careers. Most return, however, to conformist behaviors once they achieve specific goals. Some do not.

We will attempt both to delineate the specific conditions which affect the social patterning of different deviant behaviors in schools, and to formulate a longitudinal quasi-path model of deviant careers which argues that deviant behaviors often occur sequentially; that is, it argues that when one deviant behavior fails to achieve a desired goal, the individual may go on to attempt other deviant responses. We hope that our efforts will highlight the situational, as well as the time-variant, character of student deviancy, and lead to the development of more effective policies for reducing or preventing it.

Sources of Deviancy in Schools

Before we can formulate a model of student deviancy, we must show that a significant proportion of students do want to attain academic success. We must also demonstrate that the differential distribution of legitimate means of attaining goals in schools gives rise to differentially distributed pressure to deviate from accepted patterns of academic behavior.

The Academic Success Goal, Legitimate Means, and Deviant Behavior

Many studies indicate that a great number of youngsters in school do indeed ascribe to the goal of academic success, Coleman's (1961) research notwithstanding. Studies by Hill (1951), Holloway and Berreman (1959), and Reiss and Rhodes (1959), and data drawn from Project SCOPE (Boocock 1972), reveal that from 66 percent to 79 percent of students surveyed believe that getting good grades is "very important" to future success. Moreover, a recent survey of studies of high-school students' plans indicates that over half of these students strongly desire to go to college;[4] getting good grades, therefore, has to be an important goal of a majority of high-school students.

Assuming for the moment that the goal of academic success is not only widespread among the student population but is also uniformly distributed among different types of students, the question remains: Are the legitimate means for the attainment of that goal uniformly available to all aspirants? The answer is clearly negative, if only because the very nature of school dictates that some people make it and others do not. As a number of commentators have noted, one of the primary functions of the school is that of separating the able from the unable (Havighurst and Neugarten 1967; Heyns 1974). Most persons believe that this screening is highly legitimate, and that it does not, in itself, call for deviant responses. Indeed, according to strictly meritocratic ideals, schools are supposedly programmed to deny academic success to that segment of the student body which does not have a high level of learning ability.

But we know that measured ability is not entirely objective, nor is it the only predictor of academic success. Both within and between schools, it is clear that such factors as social status origins, home environments, community characteristics, sex, and race are independent predictors of the potential success of persons of similarly tested abilities (Boocock 1972). Thus, although no exact figures are available, it seems reasonable to contend that the combination of meritocratic and ascriptive forces constrain a significant number of students from winning in the academic contest.

Given that a large proportion of students hold the goal of academic success and that a portion of these are blocked from achieving that goal, the logic of Merton's model leads us to suggest that the interaction of these two conditions—the "means/goal disjunction"—is a major source of deviancy in schools. Indeed, numerous researchers have documented the relation of academic failure to school deviance—so our notion seems to be well-supported (Feldhusen, Thurston, and Benning 1970, 1973; Hangstrom and Gardner 1968; Heath 1970; Jablonsky 1970; Thurston 1964; Watternberg 1967; Elder 1971; and Hill 1951).

The Distribution of Pressures and Deviant Behavior

The interaction between the goal's distribution among students and the distribution among them of legitimate means to achieve it yields pressures to deviate which are themselves distributed in specific ways. Presumably, those personal attributes associated with low likelihood of success in school and society would also correlate with the degree to which individuals in school experience pressures to deviate from accepted patterns of academic behavior.[5]

Limiting our focus to those attributes found to be most closely linked to success in school, namely social status, race, and sex, we find that they are indeed also associated with the distribution of pressures to deviate.[6] Regarding the general category, social status, the picture is not at first clear because status is positively related both to ascription to the goal of academic success and to access to legitimate opportunities for goal attainment[7] (Boocock 1972; Bowles 1972; Heyns 1974; Rist 1970).

We do not possess information on the exact numbers of pupils within each socioeconomic status (SES) group whose attainment of the success goal is blocked. However, we may roughly estimate by utilizing an indirect measure of means/goals disjunction employed by Spergel (1974), Short and Strodtbeck (1965), and Della Fave (1974). Della Fave found that the existence of a gap between aspirations and expectations was inversely related to SES among high-school students. Indeed, a reanalysis of his table (see Della Fave 1974, p. 160) revealed for each socioeconomic group the following percentage differences between those aspiring to four years or more of college and those unlikely to achieve that goal: 1 (highest SES) = 3.8 percent; 2 = 8.3 percent; 3 = 15.6 percent; 4 = 27.6 percent; 5 (lowest SES) = 26.6 percent. Because of these data, we submit that means/goal disjunctions and the pressure to deviate are more prevalent among students from lower social status backgrounds.

Regarding the status characteristic of sex, data from SCOPE reveal that the importance of earning "good grades" is similar for girls and boys (Boocock 1972); and other research indicates that even more boys than girls may be committed to this goal.[8] However, as an extensive review of the literature by Boocock (1972) suggests, in both elementary and high schools, boys fall far short of girls with respect to actually attaining academic success. This latter finding indicates that boys, perhaps due to such factors as maturational differences, sex-role expectations, and personality characteristics, do not have equal access to their goal. Following the logic of Merton's model, we thus propose that, as a result of similar commitment and differential opportunity, a greater proportion of boys than girls experience pressure to deviate.

Regarding race, the data consistently suggest that a greater proportion of blacks experience pressure to deviate in school than do whites (Elder 1970, 1971). Contrary to the general stereotype, more blacks ascribe to the goal of academic success than do whites (Boyd 1952; Brown 1965; Gist and Bennett 1963; Phillips 1972a, 1972b; Reiss and Rhodes 1959), while also experiencing a relative deprivation of opportunity to achieve that goal (Boocock 1972). But it is as yet unclear how race, sex, and social status interact in the specification of pressures to deviate. Since blacks tend to be overrepresented in the lower social ranks of society, and since low-status persons tend to experience greater pressures to deviate, it is unclear to what degree being black is independently related to means/goals disjunction.

Our survey of the literature on such topics as attendance, cheating, classroom behavior problems, dropping out, labeling, school-related alienation, and student rebellion has revealed that, with few exceptions, the occurrence of deviant behavior has in fact been found to be proportionately greater among blacks, among low-SES students, and among boys (Elder 1970, 1971; Heussenstamm and Hoepfner 1971; NEA, 1963; Ptaschnick 1973; Silverman and Blount 1970; Varner 1967; Worcester et al. 1972; Cloward and Jones 1962; Curley, Griffin, Sawyer, and Savitsky 1971; Dentler 1964; Glidewell 1961; Hill 1951;

Jablonsky 1970; Leveque and Walker 1970; Mullin 1955; Thurston 1964; Watternberg 1967; Balow 1966; Hangstrom and Gardner 1968; Rouman 1956; Schab 1969; Zeitlin 1957). It is noteworthy, in this respect, that a recent study of deviancy within schools (Backman, Green, and Wiranen 1971) reveals that overall rates of this phenomenon decline markedly after youngsters leave school (by graduating or for other reasons). This supports our contention that much of the observable deviancy among students is specific to the context of the school.

Innovative Behavior in School

Faced with a means/goal disjunction, most persons first attempt to adopt an innovative response; that is, they will first try to attain their desired goals through alternative, illegitimate means. Only after failing in this attempt (or finding that they have absolutely no oppportunity for innovation) will most people resort to other forms of deviance (Cloward 1959; Cloward and Ohlin 1960; Cohen 1966).[9] Cheating, purchasing term papers, "brown-nosing," as well as more creative responses to traditional problems, are some forms of behavior falling under the rubric of innovation. Such behaviors are deviant for two reasons: (1) they may challenge traditional practices in education, and (2) they undermine the moral force of the formal organization and the means to achievement it designates as legitimate.

But neither creativity nor the availability of illegitimate means are distributed at random in the school's social system. The distribution of illegitimate means appears to be very much controlled by the nature of the school's informal social systems; that is, access to such means depends both on the youngster's position within student subcultures and on his or her ability to develop effective relationships with representatives of the formal organization of the school, especially with the classroom teacher. As we know from past research, an individual's ability to effect these relationships is a function of such variables as sex, race, social status, physical attractiveness (especially for females) and behavioral styles (Rist 1970; Clifford and Walster 1973).

Given these findings, it is not surprising that we find that innovative deviant behavior is more likely to occur among whites than among blacks, among males than among females, and among students with higher social status backgrounds than among those with lower ones (Kingston and Gentry 1961; Hill 1951). Moreover, of the various forms of deviance which may occur in schools, only innovative responses have a significant likelihood of enabling the individual to achieve the valued goal.

Ritualism in School

To the outside observer, the least noticeable of the other forms of deviance would be ritualistic behavior–giving up the goal of academic success while publicly maintaining behaviors appropriate to that goal. This process is one of "going through the motions," and it is attractive as a mode of adaptation largely because its manifestations are primarily internal and, therefore, it does not elicit negative sanctions. The individual adopting this mode can always claim that he/she "tried."

Because of the internal nature of ritualistic responses, school authorities rarely consider them to be deviant. For these behaviors result in little, if any, overt conflict in the classroom or in any overt threat to the school's value structure. While ensuring the maintenance of attendance figures (and, therefore, funds from the state), ritualistic behaviors may also act to reduce the overall workload of teachers in classrooms. But though it is functional in this one sense, ritualistic behavior is dysfunctional for learning (Jackson 1968). Indeed, ritualistic behavior on the part of a significant number of persons in a classroom is hardly conducive to the learning of the whole class; in the long run such behaviors may result in the lowering of academic standards for all students.

Past socialization patterns and present norms of the school's informal social system are critical in determining patterns of deviant responses to disjunctive situations. Females appear much more likely to adopt ritualistic responses than males in similar situations, presumably because of the roles society expects the different sexes to play. Girls are encouraged to be comparatively docile and passive in the school, so that their deviate responses tend to be ritualistic rather than innovative or rebellious (Boocock 1972, pp. 94-95). Ritualism among females also appears to be a function of age and level of schooling. Boocock, for instance, cites evidence suggesting that ritualistic adaptations among females occur primarily in the later years of high school (1972, pp. 88-90). Specifically, a girl will find that though females generally outperform males in the earlier stages of schooling, in the last two years of high school—when performance is most relevant to college acceptance—the trend is reversed. This suggests that in education, underachievement, a possible reflection of ritualistic adaptations, may be a self-fulfilling prophecy.

The literature is unclear regarding social status and race. Because of differences between overall rates of deviancy among the various groups, it is difficult to pinpoint which of them, black or white, high or low status, is more likely to choose ritualism as a means of deviating. In those groups, responses appear to be highly dependent upon situations, varying according to school, peer-group, and family characteristics. Nevertheless, we do feel that persons of high or middle social status and white persons may be somewhat more likely to adopt ritualistic responses than are their opposite counterparts. Since ritualistic adaptations do not have much in the way of external manifestations which could disallow future conformist or innovative responses, individuals with a greater stake in the academic process may be more inclined to engage in them rather than in retreatist or rebellious responses. On the other hand, since the social structure of the school may affect the adaptation of deviant responses, blacks and/or lower status individuals may also have fewer opportunities for ritualism—so that they may be forced to be retreatist or rebellious, and thus to exclude themselves from future participation in the academic game.

Retreatism in School

Giving up of both goals and means very often leads to retreatist forms of deviant adaptations. Dropping out, truancy, and passivity are all examples of this type of response. In each of these, both the legitimate and illegitimate means are unavailable to the individual experiencing pressure to deviate. In response, the person gives up pursuit of the goal and withdraws from the situation. Unlike ritualistic behavior, retreatism is external in character and thus more likely to be noted by school officials, recorded in school records, and studied by social scientists and psychologists interested in student behavior in general and dropout behavior in particular.

The noticeability of retreatist behavior exposes the individual to possible recrimination and stigmatization at school and in the family. But since the retreatist individual takes the blame for failure, such behavior is frequently viewed as part of the normal attrition process. Therefore, it is likely that retreatism will be adopted when (1) there is little potential for recrimination by significant others (that is, little family or peer pressure for attainment); (2) the individual has alternative values which tend toward this behavioral mode (that is, the counterculture's attitude of "turning on" and "dropping out"); and (3) there are significant alternative peer pressures to take on this form of deviance (that is, deviant subcultures). Ritualism and retreatism are similar insofar as they both involve relatively submissive behaviors rather than aggressive ones. Thus, retreatism will probably follow ritualism in the student's deviant role adaptations.

The social system of the school would also seem to be related to the patterning of retreatist behaviors among students. The formal and informal social systems of the school may keep some youngsters from adopting alternative responses; such youths may be induced—or forced—to withdraw from school situations. This may be as much of a cause as is support from alternative subcultures. Indeed, teachers may even encourage students to withdraw from large classrooms when such actions do not threaten the teachers' position—that is, when they might not affect attendance-based funding or teacher evaluations.

Regarding which students will tend to adopt retreatist behavior, the evidence suggests that males may be somewhat more likely than females to have such responses. The latter apparently feel significant social and normative constraints against retreatism; there is, for instance, the prevalent notion that it is simply not "proper" for girls overtly to retreat. Moreover, there are not many alternative support mechanisms for females (peer groups in particular) which would offset the social consequences of dropping out.

Although the literature reveals no simple relationship between retreatism and social class, we believe that this type of behavior may be somewhat more likely among lower social status groups of certain racial and ethnic characteristics than among many higher status groups. Not only are higher status persons less likely to participate in deviant subcultures, they are also more likely to encounter stiff parental resistance to any activity that would jeopardize their future chances for acceptable employment in the conventional order.

With respect to race, it would seem that blacks of lower status are more apt than whites of similar class origins to withdraw from disjunctive situations (Heussenstamm and Hoepfner 1971; Phillips 1972a, 1972b; Ptaschnick 1973; Silverman and Blount 1970). Apparently, this is due largely to the groups' slightly different value orientations and to the former's experiencing less peer-group and family pressure for academic success. Taking our cue from Turner (1960), we suggest that unless they have particular values predisposing them to rebellion, blacks are most likely to retreat from disjunctive situations. Elder (1971), for instance, gives evidence that blacks categorized as integrationists were prone to retreat in the face of disjunctive situations, whereas, in similar positions, blacks categorized as black nationalists tended toward more aggressive, even rebellious, responses.

A factor which may help explain the prevalence of retreatism among blacks is that the school affects the type of adaptation an individual will choose. School staff may consciously and unconsciously encourage blacks to adopt retreatist modes of behavior, if only because such ultimately dysfunctional responses do not disrupt the classroom as do rebellious responses. Indeed, one might argue that overburdened teachers in crowded ghetto schools may actively encourage such behaviors (both ritualistic and retreatist) as a means of reducing their workloads to manageable levels (Rist 1970).

Rebellion in School

Of all forms of deviant behavior, rebellion is the most obvious, and is therefore much more likely to be noted in school records than other forms of student deviancy. Involving as it does the rejection of established goals and means and frequently the attempted substitution of new goals and means, rebellious behavior also poses the most direct threat to the established order of the school. Vandalism, interpersonal violence such as assault, school-directed violent demonstrations and riots, student strikes, and classroom outbursts against other students and/or teachers all, in varying ways and degrees, directly threaten the established order of the school, its value system, and its distribution of rewards. They are direct threats to the school because they immediately challenge the prevailing structure of authority. Rebellious behaviors also indirectly threaten the school insofar as they demoralize both faculty and students. The rebellion of a few students may lead others toward deviance—as, for instance, in the case of the "snowball effect" of student demonstrations.

Studies show that, next to academic problems, inability to adjust to the school's behavioral expectations results in the referral of more students for psychological evaluation—and in their subsequently being labeled deviant—than does anything else (Parmer 1960; White 1966). However, while not all of these students are, in fact, rulebreakers, not all rulebreakers are so labeled in official records; for again, the application of this label is highly situational and contingent upon such attributes as sex, race, and social status. Studies of student deviancy which utilize school records alone are therefore likely to substantially underestimate the total amount of deviant behavior and inaccurately emphasize rebellious responses over other types of deviant adaptations. Such studies will tend, therefore, to indicate that only certain members of the student body are prone toward deviant behaviors.

Because of their potentially disruptive consequences, rebellious acts of deviancy tend to evoke direct and immediate school responses aimed at reestablishing social control. Such punitive measures as immediate or threatened ejection from the classroom and/or school, forced isolation from the larger student body, and the utilization of security forces are not uncommon, especially if rebellion among a large proportion of students seems likely (for instance, in inner-city schools with large minority student populations).

For the immediate participants, especially students, rebellion offers little in the way of positive returns. Since it is so overt, rebellion immediately exposes the individual to direct response by the institution, which could involve punishment and/or banishment from the classroom and the school. Faced with the removal of academic credentials such students then face an uncertain future with regard to employment. At the very least, the rebellious individual may be haunted by school records which label him as a "troublemaker."

As with other forms of student deviancy, rebellious behaviors appear to be patterned in the social system of the school and to occur more frequently among certain groups and in particular school contexts. Several mediating factors seem to influence who takes on rebellious responses to disjunctive situations, among them (1) the sequence of deviant behaviors; (2) the perceived legitimacy of the existing distribution of means and goals; (3) peer-group orientations; and (4) past history of goal attainment. It is likely that, for a large majority of students, rebellion is the last resort, the last phase in their histories of deviance (Cloward and Ohlin 1960). Having failed at all else and being unwilling or unable to take on retreatist responses, youngsters may move toward rebellion as the only remaining mode of expression other than final conformity. For most students, rebellion against school officials and/or expectations entails the rejection of a wider set of values regarding proper behavior in society; therefore, they engage in it only after all other forms of adaptation fail. Of course, for a number of students, rebellion may be the first and most immediate response to means/goal disjunctions; in their cases, personality attributes, peer-group pressures, and past failures at conforming adaptations appear to be critical determinants.

Not surprisingly, we find that blacks are more prone to rebellious responses to disjunctive situations than are whites (Phillips 1972a, 1972b; Ptaschnick 1973; Elder 1971). Except for a small, though increasing, number of students, whites are more likely than blacks to see themselves as having equal opportunity and less likely to be strongly attracted to such powerful counterideologies as "Black Power." And, as evidence demonstrates, more whites than blacks believe that conforming, nonrebellious responses will lead to rewards after graduation.

Many of the preceding comments also apply to differences between male and female rates of rebellion. Simply put, females are considerably less likely than males to engage in rebellious role behaviors. Because of the different ways in which the two sexes have been socialized, girls are expected not to exhibit aggressive reactions to disjunctive situations.

Among students of differing social class backgrounds, differences in rates of rebellious responses are not as clear. One might anticipate that lower status persons, especially minorities, would be more likely than higher status persons to take on rebellious adaptations. But members of the former group, especially white ones, are less likely to be exposed to radical ideologies that tend to promote rebellion. It is still difficult, however, to determine the precise relation between social class and rebellion, since there are conflicting data (Stinchcombe, 1964) and since lower status persons tend to have higher rates of nonconformity for all adaptations.

Concluding Comments

Our discussion was not intended to explain all deviant behaviors in school. Undoubtedly, for many people deviancy is rooted in norms and personal attributes developed prior to schooling, so that their behaviors are relatively unaffected by the social structure of the school. Nevertheless, we argue that to develop a more thorough understanding of deviant behavior among students, it is necessary to scrutinize those structural aspects of schooling which influence the attainment of the goal of academic success. In our view, the disjunction between the valued goal of academic success and the availability of legitimate means to attain that goal is a primary cause of student deviancy. But again, even these disjunctive pressures do not by themselves sufficiently explain either the taking on of nonconformist behaviors or the types of deviant reponses. For that, a number of mediating variables are needed, variables which include school, teacher, and individual characteristics. We argue, then, that knowledge of the pressures to deviate and of the structure and process of the

Social Patterning of Deviant Behaviors   163

school's social system can provide significant insight into the patterning of responses taken on by different types of students.

It has also been suggested that there may be distinct longitudinal sequencing of deviant behaviors; that is, that deviant behaviors occur in time-dependent patterns, with individuals moving from one mode of adapation to another according to their measures of success at each point in the sequence. Figure 13-1 presents what we consider to be the most common sequence of deviant role adaptations.[10]

Most importantly the diagram indicates that most persons socialized into the goals of society would first be inclined to adopt innovative responses to disjunctive situations and only to adopt other, more "defeating" responses when innovation fails or is not possible. This suggests that the majority of youths in the United States hold so strongly to the goal of academic success and to its sequential counterpart, occupational success, that they continue trying to attain these before experiencing any diminution of the goals' importance.[11] Still, the model recognizes that for some persons, especially those not having a strong commitment to the goal of academic success or those ascribing to alternative ideologies, rebellion and/or retreatism may follow immediately upon means/goals disjunctions.[12]

Regarding questions of policy, it should be evident from the preceding analysis that we would argue that the overall rate of deviancy in schools will not be significantly reduced through attempts to deal with particular isolated forms of student deviancy and from their root causes. Current attempts to restrict rebellious behavior among students, through the use, for instance, of police in schools, are particularly suspect. Undoubtedly, such actions will

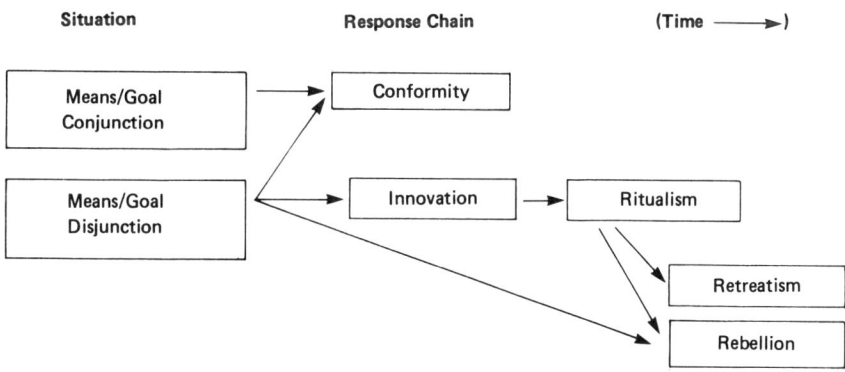

Note: Only paths of greatest likelihood are shown.

Figure 13-1. Suggested Sequential Chain Model of Deviant Role Adaptations

discourage some students from participating in more overt forms of rebellion and will induce some others to leave school entirely (that is, to become more extremely retreatist). But many openly or potentially rebellious students are just as likely to adopt less overt deviant behaviors. While these alternative modes of deviant behaviors may be less noticeable than those they replace, in the long run their consequences for effective schooling may be as severe, if not more so; for one of the root causes of deviance—one which is amenable to social action—will not have been dealt with. Moreover, the use of such restrictive disciplinary measures as police patrols may actually increase deviancy among students. While police may help insure the safety of teachers, administrators, and students, their presence may lead the great majority of students who would not otherwise become deviant to question the very authority of the school. In turn, this will increase the likelihood that more students will adopt deviant behaviors in the future.

Anyone who has ever visited a school patrolled by policemen must have been struck by its stifling atmosphere. Such a school is reminiscent of other, more obviously custodial institutions—asylums, prisons, and concentration camps. Most obviously similar are the locked doors, the sense of entrapment, the air of despair and betrayal, and the almost "Big Brother" mentality. Is it surprising that students exposed to such environments frequently take on the behavioral characteristics appropriate to those environments? Are we not, in fact, advocating deviant behavior when we treat all students as if they were deviant? Perhaps it would be best for criminal behavior to be treated in the criminal system outside the school.

We believe that the root cause for much of students' criminal behavior lies in the very structure of the American school. Our schools intentionally seek to limit to a chosen number the fruits of academic success. Whether viewed as a meritocracy or as a stratified system of privilege, the school is designed to screen out those who, for whatever reason, are not deemed suited for higher levels of attainment. Insofar as that attainment is or is perceived to be functionally related to attainment in the broader society, the school pressures individuals to deviate from accepted patterns of behavior. And to the degree that such judgments of acceptability and/or merit are affected by considerations other than merit, the school creates pressures to deviate which are not distributed uniformly among members of the student body. Whether this is intentional or not is beside the point; that it is inherent in the structure of the school which thus creates its own deviants is to the point.

What can be done to remedy this situation is, however, no simple matter. The school serves a number of functions—socialization, screening, selection and differentiation, and training. Attempts to alter one function, in this case screening, will affect the manner in which the school carries out its other functions; for example, reducing screening in order to limit deviancy would result in a reduction of differentiation. Whether such changes in balance are acceptable is very much a question of personal judgment. And, though some commentators have spoken of disestablishing the school system, they have rarely suggested alternative structures for carrying out that system's other functions which are clearly necessary in our highly differentiated, complex society.

Our position is that screening's dysfunctional consequences upon student behavior are not entirely the result of this process, per se. Rather, they are in part the result of screening which recognizes only a very limited number and types of achievement. Should schools come to give equal rewards for a greater variety of skills and attainments (skills which cut across both personality and social-class distinctions), they will have done a great deal to reduce the frequency of student deviancy in schools. A better school will emerge. At present, however, our schools are in the unhappy position of attempting to control deviant behaviors which they themselves produce and which may be heightened by the very tools used for their control. The Queen of Hearts in *Alice in Wonderland* would have felt very much at home in the United States school system.

Notes

1. It must be emphasized here that Merton's model is only one of several competing approaches in the field of deviance, and that it has been the source of much debate. Our efforts do not rest on the claim that Merton's model is completely adequate or that it is the only framework capable of providing insights into the causes of deviance. Rather, we are attempting to assess the relevance that one prominent theoretical scheme, Merton's model, can have in the explanation of the phenomenon of school deviance at the elementary and especially the secondary level.

2. It should be underscored that for Merton these five adaptations "refer to role behavior in specific types of situations, not to personality. They are types of more or less enduring response, not types of personality organization" (1968a, p. 194).

Additionally, as Merton views it and as it is used in this chapter, deviance is any departure from institutionalized expectations, or norms, of a given social system or setting.

3. As we shall note in greater detail as a later point, one weakness in Merton's discussion of types of adaptation is that he failed systematically to explore the conditions under which any one adaptation will transpire. This we will attempt to do. Several theorists have argued that Merton's typology of adaptations can fruitfully be expanded (Dubin 1966; Harary 1966; Parsons 1951, pp. 256-276). We have decided not to utilize these typological extensions because we did not believe, in light of the limited scope of the current undertaking, that the complexity they introduce outweighed the debatable theoretical advantage they offer.

4. The list of relevant works is too long to note here. For a complete listing see Cullen and Tinto (1975) from which the current work is partially drawn.

5. Failure to achieve academic success has been posited as a source of deviance outside school as well as within it. See Cloward and Ohlin 1960; Cohen 1955; Palmore and Hammond 1964; Silberberg and Silberberg 1971.

6. We have chosen to employ status characteristics as the central variables of our analysis for two reasons. First, they have traditionally been the dimensions along which work in the field of deviance, particularly that utilizing Merton's model, has proceeded; second, our endeavor is one of social structural investigation, and status position is the basic unit of analysis for this mode of sociological theorizing. Also, due to the lack of data, our study has been limited almost totally to the effects of one status at a time. That is, the consequences of possessing a particular combination of statuses (or "status set") have not been examined.

7. Again, the list of relevant works is too long to note here. For a complete listing of those items see Cullen and Tinto (1975).

8. Again, for a complete listing of all the relevant works see Cullen and Tinto (1975).

9. We would like to thank Richard A. Cloward for personally impressing the importance of this point upon one of the authors.

10. The paths, though suggestive, are not to be taken as representing the outcome of longitudinal path analysis, even though such analysis seems to offer some hope of tracing out such deviant response chains. And the arrows (unattached) to ritualism, retreatism, and rebellion are meant to suggest that some of these behaviors arise from causes other than means/goal disjunction.

11. For some, even failure at innovation may not lead to continued deviancy; instead the strength of other normative orientations may lead them to reconforming behaviors. Such persons may perceive the costs of other forms of deviancy to be too high or in conflict with other important values.

12. The need for more detailed research in this field is apparent. The very limited research that does exist often focuses only on one form of deviancy (most frequently cheating and rebellion) and for data usually relies on self-reports and/or school records. But, as we have pointed out, such school records are less than reliable indicators of the actual rates and distribution of deviant behaviors in school.

14
Perspectives on Absenteeism in High Schools: Multiple Explanations for an Epidemic

Beatrice F. Birman and
Gary Natriello

Rates of absenteeism are reaching epidemic proportions in many high schools across the nation (*Newsweek* 1979). School administrators see this as their major discipline problem (Wright 1978; Duke 1978a; Meyer, Chase-Dunn, and Inverarity 1971). Even in suburban high schools, absence from school is a cause of great concern (*Time* 1977).

Because of what many see as high schools' frequent failure to provide students with even the most rudimentary skills they need for facing the responsibilities of adulthood, public attention has recently been focused on problems of absenteeism in high schools. High rates of absenteeism have been cited as one cause of the persistent decline in SAT scores (Wirtz 1977). Absenteeism has also been linked to school violence and vandalism; students who are involved in delinquent behavior are likely to have the greatest number of absences from school (Rubel 1977). Still, little attention has been devoted to analyzing the complexities of this phenomenon.

While the fact of a high-absenteeism rate may pose a single and discrete problem for the school administrator, absenteeism is really composed of many problems. As a consequence of the multiplicity of problems involved in the phenomenon called "a high-absenteeism rate," diverse solutions have been proposed; these range from interventions targeted at individual students to far-reaching changes in the structure of secondary education and society at large. Likewise, students, schools, and society all have different perspectives on absenteeism, leading to a variety of explanations of the phenomenon. And analyses by social scientists develop according to the theoretical perspectives and disciplinary paradigms adopted in their training and shared by their professional colleagues.

The purpose of this chapter is to bring some order to the diverse phenomena

---

An earlier version of this chapter appeared under the title "Perspectives on Absenteeism in High Schools," *Journal of Research and Development in Education* (Summer 1978). Reprinted with permission. The authors would like to thank Dr. Amnon Igra of the California State Department of Health for his most helpful comments on this earlier version.

embedded in the problems of high-school absenteeism and to the multiple ways in which the problem might be explained; we wish to clarify the reasoning which leads educators to adopt specific interventions for minimizing high rates of school absence. We will explore the variety of causal theories for high-school absenteeism which social scientists might offer. We will also describe some educators' approaches to the problem. Here we assume that the actions taken by educators to combat high absenteeism reflect their definitions of the problem, and that the success of their interventions will depend, in part, upon the soundness of these underlying definitions.

We will also document a shift in social scientists' and educators' thinking about high-school absenteeism, discussing both the nature of this shift and its implications for proposed intervention strategies. In the most general terms, we are concerned with the fact that today's policymakers and researchers discuss absenteeism, like other educational problems, in broader social terms than did their predecessors.

This chapter is divided into four parts. In the first, we will outline the dimensions of high-school absenteeism and how it has grown in recent years. Second, we will discuss the individual, school, and societal levels from which absence can be viewed as a problem. Third, we will describe some explanations which have been proposed at each level of analysis. Finally, the intervention strategies which have grown out of the proposed explanations will be presented. This analysis is not to assess the probable success or failure of proposed interventions, but to place them, along with the discussion of the problem of high-school absenteeism, within a broader, more analytical and theoretical context.

High-School Absence: The Incidence

Accurate statistics on the dimensions of high-school absenteeism are difficult to find, for school attendance records are frequently misleading. According to Meyer et al. (1971) such records are inflated for at least two reasons. First, teachers and students themselves tend to protect students from the negative consequences of being listed as absent. Students might attend their homeroom classes in order to be marked present even if they do not attend any other classes; and teachers may not follow up on students who cut a few classes but are present for part of the day. Second, school records may systematically exaggerate attendance in order to protect the school's resources, which are based on measures of average daily attendance. As a result of these two factors, "Many students who make only an occasional or brief entry into the school may be continuously listed as present . . ." (Meyer et al. 1971, p. 131).

In spite of these probable overestimates of school attendance figures, it is clear that rates of absenteeism are on the rise. For example, in comprehensive high schools in San Francisco, absenteeism almost doubled between 1966 and

1968; in 1966, mean unexcused absences ranged from 5.5 to 18.4 per student, while in 1968, the range was from 10.6 to 36.5 per student (Meyer et al. 1971). More recent figures indicate that the high rate of absenteeism in these same San Francisco schools has continued; a 1974 study found that 22 percent of all high-school students there had accumulated ten or more unexcused absences in a single year (Dornbusch 1974). Other cities also report high rates of absenteeism. For instance, recent figures indicate that of the sixty-seven comprehensive high schools in New York City, none reports average daily attendance (ADA) rates of more than 84 percent (Garner 1978; Brodow, in progress)—and close to half of them report ADAs between 50 percent and 70 percent. In Boston high schools the rate of absenteeism has doubled since 1974 to 25 percent, while it runs about 15 percent in St. Louis and Philadelphia (*Newsweek* 1979).

The increase in absenteeism is not limited to a few urban areas; it is a nationwide phenomenon. In 1965, 12 percent of the 517 high-school principals in the Equality of Education Opportunity Survey reported average attendance figures of 90 percent or less, while in a similar survey in 1970, 36 percent of the principals reported average attendance figures of 89 percent or below (cited in Meyer et al. 1971). Across the country, at least 2 million students regularly cut school without an excuse (*Newsweek* 1979).

In certain areas, school administrators are responding to the increasing severity of this problem with unusual and, for some, offensive solutions. For example, a recent report on a national TV news program portrayed the attempts of administrators of one school in Dade County, Florida, to encourage school attendance by giving rewards to students merely for attending school. However, the trend of rising absenteeism shows no signs of being reversed.

High-School Absenteeism: Many Problems

The problem of high-school absenteeism is only as old as compulsory-attendance laws. For it is only when school attendance becomes universal that nonattendance is viewed as deviant (Everhart 1977; Tyack 1976), and only when attendance is mandated does truancy become a crime. In fact, there is some historical evidence that compulsory-attendance laws were passed only after high-school attendance became essentially normative. Because of the increasing American emphasis on education that began in the late 1950s and 1960, it may be easy to forget that absence from school is not a new phenomenon—that only in the past twenty-five years have high schools been attended by more than 50 percent of adolescents (Martin 1974). But the negative impact of absenteeism on students, school, and society as a whole is perhaps greater now than it used to be.

From the perspective of the individual student, absenteeism can lead to deficiencies in knowledge and those credentials necessary for future success in life. Although researchers are still trying to determine precisely which types of school experiences have positive effects on learning (Karweit 1976), time spent on learning does seem to be one clear factor (Begle 1971; Wiley 1973; Wiley and Harnischfeger 1974; David 1974; Pelavin and David 1977); absence from school certainly limits the time a student may devote to learning. Further, employers often require those they hire to have a high-school diploma, even though that may not guarantee its bearer possession of the skills and knowledge necessary for satisfactory job performance (Berg 1971). Indeed, a recent study of San Francisco high schools has discovered that school attendance alone may ensure that a student passes his or her coursework, perhaps regardless of what is actually learned in school. The study found that no student who regularly attended class failed a subject (Dornbusch 1974).

From the perspective of the school, absenteeism may be both a problem and a solution to potential problems. On the one hand, high-absenteeism rates threaten the school's legitimacy as an institution which is legally required to educate all young people. Some school administrators may also be concerned about the implications of high absenteeism in a somewhat more self-serving way; the problem may jeopardize funding, since the size of a school's budget is often based on calculations of average daily attendance. We do, in fact, believe that most school administrators are genuinely distressed with skyrocketing absenteeism rates and are concerned about meeting their responsibilities to the young people in their communities. However, absenteeism can still be seen as a solution to some problems for some educators. High-absenteeism rates obviously ease overcrowding in high schools, while they also cut down on behavior problems; for many of the students who do not attend school are likely to be those who would cause trouble were they there. Indeed, this notion that absenteeism serves to mitigate such situations is reinforced by the fact that high-school administrators often impose absence, in the form of suspensions and expulsions, on students who cause trouble in the school (Children's Defense Fund 1974). It is ironic that suspensions and expulsions are frequently used as a disciplinary measure for truancy.

From the societal perspective, high-school absenteeism presents both short-term and long-term problems. The former center on the delinquency and crime which occur when large numbers of adolescents out of school and unemployed are left with nothing constructive to occupy their time. Long-term difficulties involve the failure of these same students to acquire the credentials or basic competencies necessary for successful adult functioning both in and out of the work environment.

High-School Absenteeism: Many Explanations

The complex array of problems caused by absenteeism is paralleled by the range of explanations which might be proposed to account for the phenomenon.

Social scientists of differing persuasions view absenteeism as a manifestation of differing phenomena, and educators have proposed both explanations and solutions for the recent rise in rates of school absence. The next three sections of this chapter present an overview of the explanations offered by these groups.

Student-Level Explanations of Absenteeism

Perhaps most common among psychologists and educators are explanations which focus on the individual student. These professionals are primarily concerned with the question of why certain youth are chronically absent from school, tending to address it through one of two psychological paradigms—the psychodynamic and the behavioral. Explanations of absenteeism on this level also emphasize the family's impact on the behavior of the individual.

Psychodynamic approaches generally view school absence as one small part of a syndrome of such nonconformist behaviors and attitudes as rebellion against authority figures and poor superego controls. From this point of view, the roots of absenteeism might be seen as inadequate socialization in childhood— because of a broken home, for example. Popular portrayals of juvenile delinquency in the 1950s used this explanatory paradigm (Cohen 1955; Glueck and Glueck 1950).

Unlike the psychodynamic theorist, the behavioral psychologist is interested in the particular behaviors which a student exhibits and the factors in the student's immediate environment which might reward these behaviors. That is, those causes which may be traced back to early childhood are less important than reinforcement contingencies which lead to continued absence from school. From this perspective, students fail to go to school because attendance is not rewarding or because other activities are more rewarding (Morgan 1975). A behavioral psychologist might also emphasize the contributory nature of school characteristics which are aversive to students, or determine that chronic absence is a form of "school phobia" (Patterson 1965; Wheeler and Wheeler 1974).

In analyzing absenteeism, other social scientists focus on current conditions in the student's family. Research on the relationship between social class and parental values indicates that students from different family backgrounds will experience different patterns of interaction with their parents (Kohn 1963, 1974). That parental interest in schooling affects children is clearly indicated both by the historical literature on the educational experiences of immigrants (Tyack 1974), and in the contemporary portraits of the educational experiences of minority youngsters (Madsen 1973) and youngsters from lower class families in rural communities (Hicks 1976; Dillman 1979). This recognition of the family as an influence on student attendance, in fact, underlies a number of intervention programs designed to reduce absenteeism (Kimmel 1977); again, such programs concentrate on the situations of individual students.

Student-level explanations of high-school absenteeism have been popular among educators since high-school attendance became widespread. However, the methods of reducing absenteeism used by early truant officers differ significantly from those used by more contemporary school counselors and psychologists. The efforts of the former were largely directed at getting the children of immigrants to school so that they might be socialized into the American way of life (Everhart 1977; Tyack and Berkowitz 1977). Moreover, to achieve their goal of apprehending "lawbreakers" who did not attend school, truant officers generally employed coercion—never a particularly effective measure. This approach has been replaced by the more ameliorative one of school counselors and psychologists. But the orientations of the truant officer and of contemporary school psychological personnel do share one important similarity; both regard absenteeism as a disciplinary problem regarding which each student must be dealt with separately.

School-Level Explanations of Absenteeism

While educators have continued to rely on individualistic approaches to absenteeism in high school, they along with social scientists have come to give serious attention to school-based origins of absenteeism. Over the years, these school-based explanations have shifted from emphasizing the influence of peer groups to emphasizing school governance and curriculum change.

Many social scientists have proposed explanations of absenteeism which focus on the school. These researchers tend to ask why certain schools show higher rates of absenteeism than other schools. One body of social-science literature emphasizes the power of peer groups and student subcultures (Gordon 1957; Coleman 1961; Cusick 1973). If the student body in a school does not value school attendance, then rates of absence are likely to be higher than they will be in schools where attendance is valued. This argument also accounts for variability in rates of absenteeism within a single school for, according to it, students belonging to cliques whose members do not value school attendance will have higher rates of absence than those belonging to cliques whose members do value it.

Involvement in peer groups may as well be the key factor separating students who go to school but do not attend classes from those who do not attend school at all. For the former, the high school would seem attractive as a place to meet friends outside the home and off the street corner, a place where groups of adolescents are not immediately viewed with suspicion. In other words, schools can serve as such meeting places regardless of whatever activities might be going on in classrooms.

The discussions of peer groups have been supplemented with a growing body of literature on the effect of the school context on students (Davis 1966;

Werts and Watley 1969; St. John 1971). This literature proposes that a school-related phenomenon such as average achievement affects the performance of a given student independent of his or her individual characteristics (Meyer et al. 1971). For instance, given two students with identical social class or achievement, the one attending a school with a high average-achievement level will achieve at a higher level than will the one attending a school with a low average-achievement level. However, students in schools with high average-achievement levels will have more negative self-concepts than will students achieving equally in schools with lower average levels of achievement. In applying such reasoning to the prediction of high-school absence, one could argue that were two students to have identical individual characteristics, the one going to a school with a high rate of absenteeism would be more likely to be absent, but would also be less likely to perceive him or herself as having a high-absenteeism rate.

Going beyond the types of arguments just described, other social scientists look to structural arrangements within the school to explain high rates of absenteeism. In the wake of the high-school upheavals of the late 1960s, some social scientists have begun to explain high rates of absenteeism through the concept of alienation (Stinchcombe 1964; Bronfenbrenner 1973; Coleman et al. 1974). They claim that students' disaffection with school has stemmed from their lack of participation in school governance; that is, students, like workers in factories, became alienated from their work because they had no say in determining what that work would be. An indicator of students' lack of input into school affairs was, according to this group of theorists, the outdated or "irrelevant" curriculum. Along similar lines, such other structural characteristics as school size are seen as possibly affecting attendance; for instance, it might be argued that student alienation—and therefore absenteeism—would be greater in direct proportion to school size (Barker and Gump 1964). Thus it may be possible to decrease absenteeism by reducing student alienation. This might be accomplished by increasing student involvement in school governance, by creating smaller high schools or minischools, or by becoming more responsive to student behavior; school personnel might profitably reward students' improvements and place costs on their misbehavior (McPartland and McDill 1977).

There is now evidence that yet another aspect of the school's climate affects absenteeism: student fear and apprehension caused by violence in school. Four percent (or about 800,000) of the students surveyed in the NIE *Safe School Study* (National Institute of Education 1978) reported that they had stayed home in the previous month because they were afraid to go to school. While absenteeism may be linked to school violence and vandalism insofar as these are all manifestations of student discontent with school, absenteeism may also be seen as a reaction to the level of violence and vandalism in a given school.

During the late 1960s and early 1970s many educators replaced their individual-level explanations of problems in high schools with school-level ones, sometimes asking themselves what structural elements made schools inhospitable for adolescents and so discouraged attendance. Consequently, a significant number of educators began to call for the reorganization of schools as institutions, and many became active in the alternative schools movement (Deal and Nolan 1978).

Perhaps this interest arose in response to changes in the political environment; for the late 1960s and early 1970s were years of rapidly shifting social values during which social institutions, rather than individuals, were increasingly held accountable for social problems. It is also possible that educators' increased interest in school-level explanations of absenteeism was at least partly due to the growing dimensions of the problem. When chronic absentees constitute a very small proportion of the school population, it makes sense to believe that absence is a student's problem. When the number of absentees increases, the schools must acknowledge at least partial responsibility.

Societal-Level Explanations for School Absence

Although societal-level explanations for school absenteeism might seem obvious to many social scientists, they are relatively new to most educators. This type of analysis addresses the question of why high rates of absenteeism are more common in some societies and historical periods than in others. On the societal level there are at least three prominent explanations for the problems of school absence: the correspondence argument, the citizenship argument, and the articulation argument.

The correspondence argument proposes that, despite the expressions of distress on the part of school administrators, the problem of absenteeism is beyond their control; differential rates of absenteeism and high-school completion reflect inequalities in the social order (Carnoy and Levin 1976). According to this argument, schools are structured to discourage attendance by certain groups of students as a way of preparing them for their later social status. High-absenteeism and dropout rates rationalize future high rates of unemployment among disadvantaged groups in a society which is not committed to full employment policies; that is, these problems in high school legitimize the existing social order, especially the low levels of social mobility experienced by some groups.

The citizenship argument, on the other hand, is derived from the notion that perceptions of the student role are changing in accordance with changing social values. Because this perspective is based on a new notion that adolescents are really adults and citizens who have legitimate needs and interests capable of fulfillment outside the educational system (Meyer et al. 1971), absentees are not necessarily seen as truants or rulebreakers; instead they are viewed as citizens attending to legitimate outside interests. The citizenship argument, therefore, attributes high-absenteeism rates to the schools' failure to recognize students' social status and to provide them with activities suited to their role as citizens.

The articulation argument views high absenteeism as a reflection of the increasingly loose linkages among institutions. In other societies and in earlier periods of history, educational institutions have been closely connected with other institutions; high-school diplomas were entrées to the labor force, and the skills taught in high school were seen as useful for future employment. Since school no longer appears to guarantee future employment, students do not always perceive it as useful for meeting their future needs. They are thus likely to put little effort into schoolwork. In this view, regular attendance is a minimal indicator of effort in school (Dornbusch 1974); low attendance is an indicator of low articulation between school and the work place.

Societal perspectives on the problems of school in general and absenteeism in particular are reflected in the reports of recent commissions studying high-school reform. Between 1973 and 1975, at least four national commissions reported on adolescents and the institutions responsible for their education (Coleman et al. 1974; Martin 1974; Brown 1973; Porter 1974), while a number of states also turned their attention to educational reforms at the secondary level (North Carolina, 1974; California, 1975; New Jersey, 1977). As summarized by a RAND study (Timpane et al. 1976), these reports attributed the crisis in the high schools to three pervasive factors affecting individual students: the increase in age segregation in our society; the increasingly early biological and psychological development of youth (including the development of a youth subculture); and the lengthening delay between the time when the young are ready to assume adult roles and the time when they are allowed to do so. These explanations do not see high-absenteeism rates as being caused entirely by the psychological makeup of individual students. Nor do societal perspectives indicate that characteristics of the school are fundamental causes of absenteeism—though these notions clearly do have implications for school structure and operations.

Societal-level explanations of educational phenomena have long been common among some social scientists, Marxists in particular. But as is the case with school-level explanations, only rather recently have educators begun to accept this type of theory—perhaps because the problems they face have come to be so widespread and of such magnitude that student- and school-level explanations no longer seem adequate. While school-level explanations result in school-level solutions, societal-level explanations tend to place responsibility for student problems and for the solutions to them outside the school and on the larger society.

Interventions to Promote Attendance in High Schools

We have just reviewed a wide range of possible explanations for high-school absenteeism proposed by social scientists and educators. These explanations exist on three different levels: those of the individual student, the school, and the society. Each level of analysis suggests different modes of intervention to promote attendance, some of which we will briefly describe in this section.

Student-level explanations support interventions focusing on the individual student; such methods can take the form of punishment, rehabilitation, or facilitation. Absence is a disciplinary problem when students are considered nonconformist and rebellious because they break school-attendance rules. For many administrators with this orientation, effective solutions appear to be enforcing roles and meting out such punishments as detention or suspension. In the rehabilitation mode, counseling, either in individual or group settings, might be used to help students change their attitudes and behavior patterns. When the problem is perceived as related to the student's family situation, schools attempt to facilitate attendance by increasing communication with parents with regard to student absenteeism; these efforts could include assisting parents who have difficulty ensuring that their children get to school as well as parent-education programs designed to convey the serious consequences of continued absence (Kimmel 1977).

Interventions suggested by school-level arguments take one of two forms. If these are directed at the peer group, they might seek to encourage peer attitudes which increase school spirit and attendance by strongly emphasizing attractive extracurricular activities or competitive athletics. On the other hand, these interventions might simply focus on fostering a warm, friendly atmosphere in the school and so improving its social climate. However, attempts to encourage positive peer attitudes by fostering a relaxed school climate can backfire, for students already attend some schools primarily to socialize with their friends, not to attend classes (Meyer et al. 1971).

School-level interventions based on alienation arguments might take the form of increasing student participation in school governance or increasing student input into the curriculum. While the former would presumably heighten students' commitment to school, the latter could make coursework more "relevant," thereby increasing the likelihood of attendance. Whereas recommendations for such intervention were popular during the late 1960s (Deal and Nolan 1978), the idea of student input into the curriculum recently has been criticized as a cause of the decline in high-school academic standards (Wirtz 1977).

Some societal-level arguments do not lend themselves to workable interventions aimed at promoting school attendance. For instance, the correspondence argument is not compatible with interventions short of complete societal restructuring. The citizenship and articulation arguments, on the other hand, support the three major reforms of secondary education proposed in the reports of the national commissions; dispersion of the education of youth to institutions other than the school (that is, to the workplace and the community); increased individualization and flexibility in the arrangement of the high school as an institution; and modernization of curriculum (Timpane et al. 1976).

These interventions which the commissions have proposed seem to suggest that the future high school might become an institution with flexible hours and schedules. Instead of being characterized by a structured, departmentalized curriculum, it would emphasize learning opportunities in which skills are more important than course content.

Moreover, many of these reforms intend to encourage out-of-school activities which help students become oriented to the world of work. Although legitimate outside work commitments on the part of students, of course, are not new, the notion of restructuring schools to facilitate them is; it is based on the new conception of students as "citizens."

The societal-level arguments espoused by some commission reports go beyond restructuring the high school. Some have even challenged the very concept of compulsory schooling, suggesting, for example, that the age for leaving school be lowered, or that the number of hours for compulsory school attendance be reduced. This theme has been most recently repeated in a report by the Carnegie Council (1979).

Some recent interventions, notably the introduction of competency-based graduation requirements, will also alter the traditional meaning of compulsory school attendance. More than ever before, students will be graduating from high schools without having completed four years of regular course work. Likewise, such other policy changes as the recent decriminalization of truancy in the state of Washington (Washington State Department of Social and Health Services 1977) can be seen as both responses to and redefinitions of the problem of absenteeism. Such interventions appear to be aimed at minimizing a variety of school problems such as student unrest, vandalism, and violence, as well as absenteeism.

Thus the commission reports represent a major shift in the approach of educators seeking solutions to these student problems; for they look for causes and cures in the school's structure—and, more importantly, in its links to the larger community. Previous discussions of the high school have tended to regard its structure as fixed, and they have viewed deviant student behaviors as problems to be corrected. Even discussions of school-level reforms during the late 1960s did not consider a large-scale restructuring of all high schools to be feasible, their reforms being aimed at small numbers of disaffected students.

Final Comment

We began this chapter by describing the magnitude of the problem of high-school absenteeism and analyzing the problems which absenteeism presents for the student, the school, and the society. We went on to review an array of explanations proposed by social scientists and to argue that the views of educators are shifting from explanations based on the characteristics of individual students to ones based on societal problems. Likewise, we indicated that proposed strategies for solving many problems in high schools have shifted accordingly. While it may be possible to deal effectively with the problem of absenteeism in high schools on either an individual or a school level, its current magnitude suggests that societal interventions increasingly are likely to be proposed. Recent legislative initiatives to address the problems of youth and high schools have indeed recognized the need for broad-based interventions (White House 1980).

It is beyond the scope of this chapter to provide a detailed evaluation of the various attempts to reduce high-absenteeism rates. Besides, such global approaches to student problems as changes in compulsory-attendance laws and the creation of legitimate substitutes for high-school attendance require long-term evaluation efforts. Data on the success or failure of such attempts are not yet available.

In the wake of attempts to reform high schools through basic changes such as the redefinition of attendance patterns, educators must be careful not to define away the problem of high absenteeism without addressing its negative individual and social consequences. For high-absenteeism rates continue to deprive students of the skills and credentials needed for later occupational attainment; and if they are not rigorous, or if they are viewed as providing a "second-class" diploma, minimal competency exams will not mitigate these effects. Nor will lowering the age for finishing school negate the ill effects of high-absenteeism rates on society if such a change leaves large numbers of students unoccupied and lacking the skills or credentials to obtain future employment.

Finally, both educators and social scientists should continue to monitor trends in absenteeism rates, being careful not to assume that these will necessarily keep rising. Even from the brief perspective of the past four years, some would argue that the high-school upheavals and widespread student disaffection of the late 1960s and early 1970s were caused by a unique set of historical circumstances sparked by the Vietnam war and political unrest related to it. Attitudes of the nation's high-school students have clearly tended to follow the lead of the nation's college students and, since the end of the Vietnam war, college campuses have experienced a shift to a more calm, business-as-usual atmosphere. As college students have become more career-oriented, they have come to seem less politically alienated and perhaps more observant of academic responsibilities. Similar attitudes may filter down to the high schools. The result might be a shift to greater attendance rates in high school, regardless of which intervention strategies are employed.

**Part IV
Vandalism:
A Special Case**

15 Intrinsic Rewards in School Crime

Mihaly Csikszentmihalyi and *Reed Larson*

Enjoyment and the Survival of School Systems

On the most abstract level, the problem of school crime can be conceptualized as a systemic one. Each school is a social system which exists insofar as it can place appropriate constraints on the behavior of persons who are part of the system; to the extent it is unable to constrain the relevant behavior of students, its existence as a functioning system is in jeopardy.

Like any other social system, schools can survive only as long as people are motivated to act according to patterns of constraints which characterize the behavior complex we call the school. Unless the community is motivated to pay taxes, the teacher to teach, the janitors to keep the plant in order, and the students to abide by the rules of behavior required to make learning possible, institutions of learning will cease to exist.

In this context we are interested primarily in the students' lack of motivation to accept the constraints of school systems. In practice, this lack translates into the phenomenon of school crime, as manifested in acts of vandalism, burglary, larceny, assault on other students and on teachers, and so on (U.S. Senate Subcommittee on the Judiciary 1975). The question with which we must deal is, then, why increasing numbers of students act to subvert the systemic constraints which allow the existence of schools (Marvin et al. 1976). We shall approach this issue from the viewpoint of motivation theory.

People accept the constraints of a social system for one of three possible reasons, or for a combination of these. First, a system may compel constraint through a combination of extrinsic rewards and deterrents—the "stick-and-carrot" mechanism of social control. This serves to convince persons that their survival or comfort is best served by accepting the system's constraints. Schools rely on grades for rewards, and on various disciplinary measures for deterrents to obtain compliance; these are supported by the more informal social controls of public opinion and parental attitudes.

A second set of reasons for students' acceptance of the school's constraints concerns the perceived means-end relationship between their present place in the system and their future goals. As long as youngsters believe that by being good students they get closer to valued statuses—of affluence, power, self-esteem—they will be motivated to comply with the constraints of school. Extrinsic and means-end reasons are presumably orthogonal; at least theoretically they are independent of each other.

The third and final group of reasons that may motivate a person to belong to a system, and so to accept its constraints, comes under the rubric of "intrinsic motivation." When people enjoy the activity which a system makes possible, they spontaneously abide by its constraints. For instance, basketball as an action system requires development of certain skills and observation of specific rules. Young people usually accept these constraints even in the absence of extrinsic rewards or deterrents, and even though playing basketball will not help them to reach a desirable future goal. The activity is an end in itself because its immediate experience is intrinsically rewarding.

The increase in school crime could be attributed to failures in any and all of these three motivating systems. It could be argued that the extrinsic reward-punishment mechanisms which used to keep students more or less in line are becoming less effective. Or it could be argued that for an increasing number of students the means-end relationship between education and desirable future goals is becoming less believable. Both these arguments are probably sound. But here we shall focus on the third possibility, which is usually ignored; that schools are less fun; that intrinsic motivation for becoming educated is decreasing; that "criminal" activities provide students with more enjoyment than do schools.

Scholars studying delinquency tend unwisely to dismiss the need for enjoying what one does by giving it the derogatory label of *short-run hedonism* (Strodtbeck and Short 1964; Cohen 1970). It might be better to recognize that in the absence of clear extrinsic or means-end-motivational supports, an individual's most functional response is to do what is most enjoyable. Thus if we wish them to accept the rules on which schools are based, we need to understand what students enjoy; then, schools may provide intrinsically motivating experiences so that youngsters will not have to seek those in contexts disruptive to the school system. This approach is certainly not new. Almost twenty-four centuries ago, Plato recognized that the main goal of a sound education is to train people to find "pleasure and pain in the right objects" (*Laws*, II; see also Aristotle, *Ethics*, II, 3). Considering this historical basis, it is indeed surprising that we have done so little to achieve this goal.

Crime and Enjoyment

School crime occurs when a person acts according to constraints of an antisocial system rather than those of the school system. Through his actions, the individual is then in effect identifying himself with a criminal system; he ceases to belong to the school system. The recent literature usually explains the decision for this action in terms of delinquent subculture pressures placed on the person (Sutherland and Cressey 1974; Cohen 1955); that is, a student resorts to criminal action in order to gain or keep his status in a peer group.

There is no question that socialization into a deviant subgroup is an important reason for rejecting the school's rules. However, it is insufficient. To understand a person's decision to identify with a deviant system, we must also understand the motivation for delinquent action. We believe that part of this motivation is intrinsic; in other words, many adolescents find criminal acts to be more enjoyable than behaviors available in socially sanctioned settings. Unless we understand why this is so, we will be unable to build intrinsic motivation into school activities; and we will lose the most efficient deterrent to antisocial behavior that a social system can have.

Many observers have noted that delinquency, at least in its early stages, is an enjoyable activity. Thrasher (1936) thought that stealing was the result of a "sport motive" rather than of desire for a material gain; McKay (1949) and Tappan (1949) both saw delinquency as form of play; and more recently, Cohen (1970) reached the same conclusion. In affluent suburban school crime, intrinsic motivation presumably plays an even larger role. Tobias (1970), for example, found that middle- and upper-middle-class offenders mentioned boredom as a major reason for engaging in delinquent acts, while they usually discounted the need for money as a contributing factor.

The connection between enjoyment and delinquency has not been thoroughly investigated, even though many researchers have recognized it. This is at least in part due to the lack of a viable theory of enjoyment, and to the widely shared assumption that only youths with peculiar personality traits enjoy crime. The purposes of this chapter are to present a general theory of enjoyment, and to argue that criminal acts are perfectly suited to providing enjoyment to normal individuals who lack access to alternatives.

A Theory of Enjoyment

In the past decade, there has been a resurgence of interest in the topic of intrinsic motivation. Two partially converging theoretical approaches have been most influential in explaining the sources of the enjoyment people derive from certain activities. The first approach, based on the neuropsychological models of Berlyne (1960), Hebb (1965), and Hunt (1965), assumes that there is an optimal arousal level which the organism seeks to maintain. When stimulation is too monotonous, a person will be motivated to vary environmental input; when stimulation is excessively varied, the motivation is to reduce input variability. For a person in the optimal arousal range, the given experience will be intrinsically rewarding (Ellis 1973; Hutt 1970).

A second approach with wide currency has grown out of the work of White (1959) and de Charms (1968, 1976). The emphasis here is on the concept of competence, control, and personal causation. If a person perceives his or her acts as voluntary, he will experience them as qualitatively different from acts which he or she perceives to be controlled by an outside agency. When action is attributed to extrinsic causes, then, extrinsic contingencies are necessary to sustain it. Recent works by Kruglanski (1975), Lepper and Greene (1975), and others have shown the power of intrinsic motivation in experimental settings, at the same time demonstrating how fragile such motivation is—just a few cues suggesting outside control can transform an enjoyable activity into a chore.

The personal causation approach attacks the issue of enjoyment at a different level, that of a person attributing causality to his or her actions. This is not necessarily in conflict with the arousal theory, since the approaches focus on phenomena having different levels of complexity. While the first is relatively more molecular, the second is more molar. Both theories have numerous implications for making the school environment intrinsically motivating, thereby reducing behavior which conflicts with the institution's systemic requirements.

A third model of enjoyment, which is in some respects a synthesis of the two mentioned above, has been developed by this author (Csikszentmihalyi 1975a, 1975b, 1976a, 1978). It will be summarized here, and its relevance to the problem of school crime will be examined in detail.

In a series of studies begun four years ago, we interviewed several groups of people who devote much time and energy to activities that have few extrinsic rewards and lead to no future goal: chess masters, rock climbers, dancers, athletes, and so forth (Csikszentmihalyi 1975b). Their explanations of feelings involved in engaging in these activities converged on a few central points, leading us to a theoretical explanation of the experience of enjoyment and its preconditions.

Briefly, an activity seems to be enjoyable when a person perceives that his or her capacity to act (or skills) match the opportunities for action perceived in the environment (or challenges). People find that in this balanced state of interaction, which appears to be the subjective counterpart of the optimal arousal state, they have a peculiar dynamic experience which we have called the *flow state.*

Flow is a state in which one concentrates on the task at hand to the exclusion of other internal or external stimuli. Action and awareness merge, so that one simply does what is to be done without a critical dualistic perspective on one's actions. Goals tend to be clear, means are coordinated with the goals, and feedback on one's performance is immediate and unambiguous. In such a situation, a person has a strong feeling of control—or personal causation—yet, paradoxically, ego-involvement is low or nonexistent, so that one experiences a sense of transcendence of self, sometimes a feeling of union with the environment. The passage of time appears to be distorted; while some events seem to take a disproportionately long time, hours generally seem to pass by in minutes. It is because of the flow experience that games, creative activities, and moments of religious ecstasy are so enjoyable as to be intrinsically rewarding.

The main contribution of our research, however, has been the suggestion that all kinds of serious, work-related activities can also produce flow, and, therefore, be intrinsically rewarding. Physicians claim that performing surgery is addictive for essentially the same reasons that rock climbers find climbing or gamblers find poker addictive (Csikszentmihalyi 1975b). Mathematicians describing the intrinsic satisfaction of working with numbers indicate similar experiences (Halprin, in progress), as do high-school students discussing their favorite courses (Mayers 1977).

In the absence of the properties which produce the experience of flow, activities become boring, frustrating, or anxiety-provoking. Workers who get no feedback on the quality of their efforts quickly become uninterested. If a situation provides no challenges, boredom is virtually inevitable.

Flow and its lack are characteristics not of the physical environment, but of the person's interaction with it. While the objective environment makes it easier or harder to achieve systemic interaction, the balance of skills and challenges necessary for flow ultimately depends on the person's perception of what the skills and challenges are. For example, loud noise hinders the concentration needed for maintaining flow, but it does not make flow impossible for those who can disregard it. Currently we are studying large numbers of workers in industrial and clerical settings. Many of them find their jobs boring and unchallenging. But others, who are in every other respect similar to members of the first group, look on the same jobs as stimulating and enjoyable. The two groups appear to differ only in that persons in the latter group have an ability to restructure their tasks and create personal challenges which make their work intrinsically rewarding. The environment's contribution to creating flow should not be disregarded, however. It is certainly easier, for instance, for people to experience flow in a game than in a dentist's waiting room, and most people would perceive fishing as more enjoyable than working on an assembly line.

It is important to realize that while it is personally rewarding, the flow experience is socially neutral. Like physical energy, it can be used for productive or destructive ends. Battle veterans, for example, often nostalgically say that during front-line war experiences they felt more intensely alive than at any other point in their lives. Warfare is in fact an excellent flow activity because it provides clear goals, unambiguous feedback, total involvement, and potentially matched challenges and skills. Despite the fear and misery it also generates, war simplifies the life of many men to such an extent that it overcomes its own drawbacks and becomes intrinsically rewarding.

In general, competing physically seems to be the most obvious ingredient of flow-producing activities, both for participants and for spectators. From the Balinese cockfight (Geertz 1973) and the Spanish bullfight to football, hockey, roller derby, and boxing, violent confrontations provide the most easily understood match between challenges and skills, the clearest goals, the most immediate feedback. It takes no special skill to see the challenge of a confrontation and to act in a setting that requires violence.

It is for this reason, presumably, that so many of young children's flow experiences involve violent or destructive acts. Fighting with peers (or with parents) is one of the most available flow activities for children. Challenges and skills are at hand; goals and feedback are clear. Thus, children who learn no other skills or see no other opportunities for action find in violence and destruction a ready source of enjoyment. By the same token, one would expect that grown-ups who are frustrated in their efforts to find flow in more complex forms will regress to simpler forms.

The main goal of a truly civilized education is in fact to teach children to experience flow in settings that are not harmful to self and others. Again, this is the goal Plato established for his own educational system: to train youths in how to find pleasure in action which strengthens the bonds of human solidarity instead of weakening them. Most subjects taught in schools are synergistic (Maslow and Honigmann 1970), in that they are symbolic skills which serve to unite people rather than set them against each other. But, unfortunately, school activities often fail to provide flow experiences, so students do not become intrinsically motivated to take part in them. And, all too often, the only source of flow that students do find is the negative opportunity to hurt or destroy. It is the mechanism of this negative process that we now need to examine in more detail.

Flow and School Crime

From the point of view of intrinsic motivation, schools are engineered all wrong. To paraphrase a point made by Shore (1971), the wonder is not why some students commit crime, but rather why so many do not. The manifest function of schools is to teach youth a set of abstract skills which supposedly are useful in the performance of adult roles in society. To students, the school's goals should appear to be challenges. And the learning of math, biology, and so forth constitute the challenge that schools ostensibly present to their students; quite often, the challenges are not matched to the students' skills. According to a recent pilot study (Mayers 1977), for example, high-school students felt that 34 percent of their classes presented them with more challenges than they could handle, while 26 percent of them presented challenges lower than their skills. Only 40 percent of all classes were rated near the optimum level of balance between skills and challenges. On the other hand, the youngsters rated their favorite activities (which ranged from drama to basketball), at the optimum balance a much higher proportion of the time. In another study (Csikszentmihalyi, Larson, and Prescott 1977), teenage students consistently rated themselves as more bored in school than in any other setting. Unpublished data from this research showed that students indicated that during classes they thought about school-related activities less than half (45 percent) of the time. Instead, their minds were on such unrelated topics as "my boyfriend," "how much I hate Mrs. Green," and "how soon the bell would ring and release me from this boredom." When these students did think about things that were related to the classroom situation, their topics included "how hard this is" and "what word I could make to give me points."

Occasionally, some intrinsically motivated learning occurs under these conditions. In some cases the skills of the teacher and the skills of some students mesh, creating a situation in which these individuals provide an optimal challenge to each other. But the knowledge level of teachers (their skills in an activity) is typically so far above that of the students that balanced systems of reciprocal challenges are rare. Most learning in schools is motivated by the economy of extrinsic sanctions and rewards.

Unfortunately, these extrinsic sanctions and rewards, upon which the school is based, are destructive to any intrinsic motivation students still have. Research shows that persons who initially do things because they find them satisfying lose this intrinsic motivation when extrinsic motivators are introduced because the feeling of personal causality is subverted (Deci 1975; Lepper and Greene 1978; Kruglanski 1975). Thus, schools tend to destroy any enjoyment of learning which youngsters may bring to the classroom.

The inability of schools to provide engaging action systems helps to create bored, frustrated, dissatisfied people. Lacking opportunities for enjoyable involvement through school, such youths seek alternate structures of challenges to obtain flow experiences. Our research in progress suggests that the frequency of delinquent acts reported by secondary-school students is inversely correlated with the level of challenges they perceive in school ($r = -.43, p < .05$), while there is no relationship to the level of challenges perceived out of school. Delinquency appears to be one system of opportunities for action that is an alternative to the action system of the school.

These feelings suggest not only that challenges and skills are often mismatched in school, which is almost unavoidable in a mass-educational system, but also that some students do not perceive what the school has to offer as challenging at all. There is an obvious paradox here; the abstract, symbolic tasks provided in academic settings can be seen as challenges only by persons who have enough abstract, symbolic skills to act within that system of action. In other words, to those who develop the curriculum, math problems and history quizzes are real, but to most students they are not. Students see those as challenging only insofar as they are artificial obstacles to be circumvented. This is true even of highly intelligent, motivated students. When we asked an outstanding fourth-grader about the most special event in his school year, for instance, he spoke with obvious animation of the time his teacher sent him to take the pupils' milk money to the principal's office. This stood out as the most exciting thing he did in school all year precisely because it was the only one involving concrete responsibility in a real situation. This example is quite typical

(Goodman 1964; Holt 1969). Children and adolescents rarely become completely involved in academic subjects; instead, their heightened experiences come from concrete activities in which they can recognize the challenge and match it with their skills. These tend to be interpersonal encounters, mostly involving peers, or school subjects such as gymnastics, music, or art.

Adult ambivalence concerning the usefulness of specific academic areas does not make it any easier for a student to recognize these subjects as meaningful challenges. As Jules Henry (1963) pointed out, our culture tends to convey conflicting messages about the validity of scholarly pursuits. Perhaps the only subjects which most communities endorse wholeheartedly are athletics for boys and the glamour-consumer role taught in home-economics classes for girls. Not surprisingly, these challenges will seem real to a majority of adolescents, and, as a result, many of them will experience flow only in settings that involve glamour or competitive athletics.

Yet, most of the time in school is in fact spent in activities that students cannot structure as flow experiences. Therefore, the characteristic states of many students are boredom and worry, rather than total involvement and peak performance. "As a result," writes Bronfenbrenner (1973, p. xxv), "the schools have become one of the most potent breeding grounds of alienation in American society."

Antisocial Action Systems

In the prototypical crime movie, high suspense is created as the protagonists execute an elaborate plan for committing the crime. The elements of the situation with which they are dealing (the bank, the watchman, the timetable) are never entirely predictable, and the viewer thus feels a sense of excitement and vicarious challenge. But the plan and the crime are only possible by virtue of the predictability of the system that is about to be subverted.

In a similar fashion, a school provides a predictable structure of actions and possible reactions. Indeed, more and more high schools are becoming mechanical systems ruled by constraints on timing, location, and behavior; the similarity between schools and jails is becoming ever more pronounced. In such a system, many students are capable only of experiencing the self-determining state necessary for enjoyment by disrupting the system's rules. Again, it is only through the existence of order that the opportunity for disruptive behavior can come into being. A student can subvert the order in a class session, the physical order of the building, the general control of the teachers, and the authority of the principals; the possibility for each of these provides a challenge to someone who is unable to find enjoyment within the constraints of the system.

At the simplest level, interrupting a teacher's lecture with wisecracks is a diverse and stimulating challenge. The immediate goal is to draw laughter without behaving so inappropriately as to be thrown out of the classroom. If a student is skillful at such endeavors, he can build an alliance with other members of the class and succeed in perpetrating progressively more disruptive acts. The teacher's authority is gradually weakened until he or she loses control of the class. But this destroys the action system, because there is no more order to disrupt. As with other parasitic interactions, the intruder must learn to moderate his disruptive effect lest it destroy its host system.

This classroom drama may also be played out through a different dimension of skills. The less verbally clever student may seek to achieve control of a situation through emotional combat; his challenges may involve exceeding the teacher in stubbornness, generating fear, being attuned to moments of vulnerability, and overcoming the class order by force of will. This is a dangerous game of emotional control, for it is capable of turning into physical violence. Moreover, similar escalating emotional duels may be played out with other students or with principals.

These opportunities for antisystem enjoyment involve competitive interactions, the skills of the teacher being challenges to the student and vice versa. If the teacher is skilled, he or she can maintain control and experience satisfaction produced by teaching. But if the student is more skilled than the teacher or if several students join together, they may gain the upper hand and thus the satisfaction of control. The antisystem students have an advantage in that they can choose from any number of disruptive strategies. But, with experience, a teacher develops a repertoire of counterstrategies ranging from exploiting his own alliance with other class members to dismissing students at the first hint of disruptive behavior.

The frequent school crimes of theft, vandalism, and arson represent other levels of challenge for antisystem students. To say that vandalism results from negative attitudes toward the school (Goldman 1961) does not explain why the actual event took place. For instance, anyone who has ever looked at a bathroom wall recognizes that graffiti writers are interested in more than simple destruction. Similarly, those windows which students break are not always the easiest ones to hit. Thus, we need to recognize that it is all the obstacles to be overcome in order to steal or to start a fire that make these acts great adventures—adventures of the sort Tom Sawyer and his gang cherished.

We have presented only a suggestive overview of possible challenges for antisystem behavior that exist in schools. We do not mean to suggest that antisocial action systems can keep a student in a continuous state of enjoyment, nor that everyone will find this type of action to be intrinsically motivating. But when few other options are available, these are viable alternatives. A beginner in such systems needs few skills, and he can find gradual challenges which provide new opportunities as his skills develop.

Implications for the Reduction of School Crime

There are several strategies society can adopt in an effort to reduce school crime. One solution is to strengthen the set of contingencies which affect the extrinsic motivation of students; this can be accomplished by increasing security measures, enforcing behavior penalties, and providing stronger inducements for prosocial behavior. While such an approach will almost surely work, it does have some drawbacks. In terms of cost-benefit accounting, it is rather expensive. On the one hand, it requires cumbersome machinery of deterrence and prosecution; and on the other, it involves the expense of bribing young people to do what they ought to be eager to do naturally. In terms of long-range effects, a more serious consideration would be the destruction of intrinsic motivation caused by this increased reliance on extrinsic contingencies; for the more schools rely on coercion and inducements to make students accept their constraints, the more students will see schools as systems in which voluntary participation and, hence, intrinsically motivated behavior are impossible. When schools attempt to ensure predictability through extrinsic contingencies, they leave only one option for enjoyment: to disrupt the system's constraints. The ultimate consequences of socializing each generation into a pattern of extrinsic motivation (and the deviance which accompanies it) are at present incalculable, but they will inevitably be severe.

A second solution is to strengthen the means-end connection between adherence to school constraints and achievement of desired future goals. If all students could be certain that their futures depend on school performance, at least the extreme forms of disruption would be minimized. At the present time, however, such assurance is unrealistic. High schools perform a sorting function for a minority of students interested in future academic or professional careers. For the rest, there simply is no clear connection between performance in school and future success. Moreover, a substantial proportion of youths must feel realistically that their chances of success in school are limited. Since they are competing academically with better prepared middle-class students, ghetto teenagers suspect that participating in the school system will not add appreciably to their chances of achieving desirable life goals. Hence, adherence to the school's constraints becomes futile for them, at least in terms of means-end motivation. To change this state of affairs, a closer correspondence between school performance and future rewards must be created; this will be difficult, but not impossible. However, this solution has the same drawback as the previous one: the emphasis on external contingencies—in this case future rewards—trains youth to be extrinsically motivated, disregarding the need for enjoyable involvement in the present.

A third solution keeps in mind that intrinsic motivation is necessary for spontaneous involvement in a system, and starts transforming schools accordingly. Of course, such a task is at least as difficult and demanding of monies and energy as are the previous ones. However, this solution has the clear advantage of lacking the side effects of the other two; in fact, in addition to reducing school crime, it promises to socialize youth into a pattern of action that has long-term societal benefits. If youngsters learn to find enjoyment in work, as adults their dependence on extrinsic sources of reward will probably decrease; thus there should be a reduction in the burden of material bribes we now use to keep ourselves alive and more or less awake. If schools made their main goal teaching youth how to enjoy life, they would help accomplish the ultimate task of human liberation: to free people from the addiction to extrinsic rewards. It is this positive goal that should direct the action of educators, not the negative goal of reducing school crime. That problem will in fact be solved along the way, naturally.

At this point, the reader will surely expect some detailed suggestions as to how to reach the proposed goal. But were we to pretend to have solutions ready for application, we would be dishonest. Our purpose has been to diagnose what we see as the roots of a problem and to indicate the general shape of what might be its solution. Even to begin translating these abstract concepts into practical actions, the combined efforts of communities, teachers, administrators, and researchers are necessary.

But in order to avoid possible misunderstandings, it might be useful to clarify what our research suggests about that which is needed to teach making life enjoyable. In the first place, our theory most definitely does not imply that schools ought to amuse, entertain, coddle, or give pleasure. Although such experiences can be enjoyable, their positive effect is usually weak and transient, so that their motivational power is unreliable. A recent study found, for instance, that during an average week, high-school students reported watching television as their least positive experience, although this was a voluntary and frequent activity (Csikszentmihalyi, Larson, and Prescott 1977).

On the contrary, enjoyable experiences providing sustained intrinsic motivation are characterized by challenges that require the utmost extension of a person's skills and, in so doing, provide a feeling of mastery and growth. Theoretically, any activity could serve to produce flow experiences; nothing in the present curriculum of schools is inherently inimical to flow. It is crucial, however, that emphasis not be placed on mastery of the subject matter, but on the process of mastery itself. That is, what matters is not that students learn trigonometry, but that they learn to enjoy the act of learning. The more different symbolic media students learn to use in an intrinsically motivated way, the more able they will be to restructure everyday life so that it provides flow, and the less dependent they will be on extrinsic motivation to give meaning and purpose to life. So the key for making schools enjoyable is to change the goals of instruction.

While curriculum is not inherently an obstacle to flow, the organizational constraints of school systems are almost ideally suited to depriving students of any opportunity to experience enjoyment. As education becomes increasingly rationalized and centralized, students' chances to structure their activity, to feel free and in control, decrease in proportion. It seems inevitable that the trend toward making the school experience more predictable must be reversed if we are to develop intrinsically motivated students. If strict schedules, unbending rules, and impersonal teaching situations continue to prevail, for their survival schools will have to rely even more heavily on extrinsic contingencies; and in the process, they will breed new generations of bored, alienated adults for whom violence is a logical way to assert existence.

Within these fairly general parameters, the flow model suggests a theoretical starting point from which concrete policies can be derived. The work of systematically generating and implementing such policies will be difficult and frustrating. Yet it seems to be the only viable alternative.

16
Aesthetic Theory, Perceived Control, and Social Identity: Toward an Understanding of Vandalism

Vernon L. Allen and
David B. Greenberger

The term vandalism is used to encompass a vast array of destructive acts, the diversity of which seems limited only by the complexity of the environment and the imagination of young people. If vandalism has remained a stubborn problem for society to solve, it has been no less resistant to a satisfactory theoretical interpretation by social scientists. Over the years, a number of attempts have been made to explain vandalism, but most have been little more than descriptive accounts or typologies that reduce the wide diversity of acts into a few homogeneous categories (Cohen 1973; Madison 1970; Martin 1961). Other approaches have explained vandalism in terms of problems of personality dynamics and social maladjustment (Feldman 1969; Reiss 1952). Still other theories emphasize situational factors such as symbolic aggression or conformity to peer-group norms (Cohen 1973; Wade 1973). However, while most of the extant theories are indeed useful for explaining some instances of vandalism, most of them are very restricted in scope.

We shall attempt to develop a theory that takes as its conceptual point of departure a set of assumptions far different in three important ways from those underlying the approaches mentioned above. First, we assume that there is no discontinuity between vandalism and socially acceptable behavior with regard to basic psychological processes. Second, we assume that factors inherent in the distal stimulus are at least equally as important as traits of the individual; they may, in fact, be even more significant. And third, our approach assumes that destruction produces important positive cognitive and social consequences for the individual.

The theory we propose consists of three main components—affective, cognitive, and social. The first portion of this chapter discusses aesthetic theory, which can be used to specify the type of dynamic stimulus configurations in the physical environment that produce varying degrees of positive affective experience in the individual. Relevant studies designed to test this portion of the theory are presented. The second portion discusses the consequences of

---

This chapter was written while the senior author was a Fellow at the Netherlands Institute for Advanced Study in the Humanities and Social Sciences.

destruction for an individual's perception of personal control and efficacy. Pertinent experiments designed to test this aspect of the theory also are included. The third section introduces the concept of social identity which is necessary for providing theoretical unification of aesthetic factors and perceived control. In addition, this concept supplies a link between the psychological processes that we discuss and such other conceptual units in the social environment as role, group, and social structure. Finally, the fourth section describes a few of the practical implications of our theory.

Aesthetic Factors

Anecdotal evidence suggests that one factor important in vandalism is the sheer pleasure and enjoyment an individual experiences as a consequence of committing destructive acts. This reaction is pervasive among both adults and children; for instance, youngsters often say that destruction is simply "fun." Piaget (1952) noted that destruction is one of the types of play activities of children. In our own research we have been struck by the relish with which people related their experiences of breaking objects. Previous attempts to explain vandalism have not paid sufficient attention to the enjoyment produced by destruction.

We hypothesize that destruction is pleasurable because it has the characteristics of an aesthetic experience. That is, the variables that account for the pleasure of socially acceptable aesthetic experiences in art, music, and literature are also responsible for the enjoyment associated with acts of destruction; and the degree of enjoyment in any act of destruction depends upon the presence and strength of the variables that determine any aesthetic response. Indeed, artists as well as psychologists have noted the close affinity between art and destruction and between creative and destructive acts. This apparent paradox is explicable in terms of our theory, for the transformation of material into a new structure activates the same basic set of psychological variables in both creative and destructive acts (Allen and Greenberger 1978).

Recent psychological research in aesthetics and related areas has identified several variables that determine the level of positive affect. According to Berlyne (1971), under certain conditions both arousal and dearousal relative to adaptation level will produce positive affect. Until the individual reaches a point of very high arousal, he experiences pleasure from a moderate increase in arousal. He will perceive as unpleasant any further increment in arousal beyond this high-arousal point, and only a decrease in arousal will be pleasant.

Research has shown that the most important stimulus factors which increase level of arousal—and thereby contribute to a positive hedonic experience—are complexity, expectation, and novelty. In addition, organization or symmetry and psychophysical characteristics are significant. Applying aesthetic theory to destruction, we can predict that an individual will perceive that breaking one object will be more pleasurable than breaking another object as long as one of the destructive acts is more complex, novel, and unexpected than the other. On the basis of past experience, people learn to anticipate that objects will break in a characteristic way along the dimensions specified by aesthetic theory. Therefore, the theory further predicts that the object selected for destruction will be the one which maximizes involvement of the aesthetic variables underlying positive affect or enjoyment. Several studies provide empirical support for these hypotheses concerning the role of aesthetic variables in destruction.

Before, during, and after are three phases of destruction in which aesthetic variables are involved. Before the destructive act, objects may vary in their appearance on the basis of structural variables (such as complexity, novelty, and expectedness), psychophysical properties (size or intensity), and organization (pattern or symmetry) of stimulus elements. When an individual expects that changing the appearance of an object will make it more interesting or pleasing, he may try to effect such change, even if to do so he must use socially disapproved methods such as vandalism. During the process of destruction, enjoyment derives primarily from the visual, auditory, and tactual-kinesthetic cues that occur as an object is rapidly and radically transformed. Hence, the level of enjoyment an individual derives from breaking an object should vary positively according to the degree of complexity, unexpectedness, and novelty involved in the destructive process. After a destructive act, the appearance of the stimulus object can differ according to the variables specified in aesthetic theory. At this stage, the pattern and organization of the object's parts are important determinants of its appearance; for example, breaking a particular pane of glass in a large window might create an interesting pattern.

To test the role of aesthetic variables in destruction, a series of studies was undertaken using laboratory experiments and personal interviews. Studies were conducted to examine: (1) the relation between complexity before, during, and after destruction and a person's inclination to destroy an object; (2) the effect of unexpectedness on the enjoyment of destruction; (3) organizational factors involved in selecting a target for destruction; and (4) the influence of psychophysical factors and type of material on the enjoyment of destruction. Finally, personal interviews were employed to obtain information concerning the reactions of persons who have participated in destructive acts.

In one experiment, it was hypothesized that desire to break an object will be related to the complexity manifested in its destruction. A silent color film was constructed showing twenty-six panes of glass being broken in a standardized way, and judges were used to select the five of these which involved the greatest range of subjective complexity. When subjects observed the final film, they indicated how much they would like to break each piece of glass. A significant relation between the observers' commitment to break a pane of glass and its subjective complexity was found. The hypothesis was strongly supported: subjects preferred to shatter the objects that broke in a more complex way. Data from a related study revealed that both pleasingness and interestingness increased directly with greater stimulus complexity; this suggests that in the first experiment the pleasingness and interestingness connected with the destructive act may have accounted for the findings concerning desire to break.

A third experiment investigated the effect of expectation or uncertainty on the enjoyment of destruction. According to aesthetic theory, destruction should be most enjoyable when it does not confirm an expectation. To test this prediction, an experimental situation was established in which pieces of glass broke in a way that the subject expected on the basis of previous trials— with one exception. Two films presented four segments of glass breaking. In the fourth segment of one version, the glass shattered when it was initially struck, just as it had in the first three trials shown in the same film. But in the other version, the glass in the fourth segment did not break until the third time it was hit which disconfirmed the subject's expectation. The results indicated that subjects found the experience to be more enjoyable when it did not confirm their expectations.

A fourth experiment examined the role of initial complexity in selecting targets to be destroyed (Allen and Spencer 1977). Using wooden blocks, we constructed three pairs of buildings with initial complexity operationally defined in three ways: (1) tall versus short buildings (holding constant the size of blocks and shape of buildings); (2) small versus large blocks used in construction (holding constant the height and shape of the buildings); (3) irregular versus regular design (holding constant the size of blocks and shape of buildings). We assumed that subjects would expect the process of destruction to be more complex for one of each pair than the other. It was predicted that subjects would prefer to destroy the building of each pair having the more complex initial structure. Results showed that, indeed, subjects did consistently choose to destroy the more complex structure (82 percent overall).

A fifth study hypothesized that an individual will decide to destroy those elements of an object which when broken will result in the most pleasing pattern. First it was necessary to assess the aesthetic value of a large number of patterns consisting of nine adjacent white and black squares, in order to predict the "pleasingness" of various patterns that would result from breaking a specific portion. Then, a window was constructed with the same pattern as the abstract designs used in scaling. According to scaling data, three black squares across the diagonal creates a highly pleasing pattern; therefore, two panes were removed at the end of the diagonal, and subjects were allowed to select any one of the seven unbroken panes of glass for destruction. The frequency of choosing the middle pane was greater than expected by chance. After the first response, subjects were again asked which of the remaining six panes they would most like to break. As predicted, they chose the one that produced the most pleasing pattern possible with the existing configuration.

The psychophysical variable of size of stimulus was investigated in a sixth study (Allen and Sobel 1978). Since the destruction of large objects provides greater emotional arousal and probably a more interesting and pleasing type of breaking, it was predicted that subjects would prefer to break the largest windows available. Upon being shown a series of seven square panes of glass (ranging in size from 6x6 to 30x30 inches), subjects were asked to decide which one they would like to break. Results revealed a clear preference for breaking the larger windows. Data were also obtained concerning the subjects' expectations about the way the windows would break as a function of size. It was predicted that expectations about breaking the different-sized windows would be congruent with the preference data; that is, subjects would expect the larger windows to break in a more interesting and aesthetically pleasing manner than the smaller ones. According to the results, subjects did believe that larger windows would break in a way that would be significantly more complex, interesting, pleasing, novel, beautiful, exciting, and loud. Thus, a person's anticipation about the nature of aesthetic variables in destruction can help account for his choice among targets of varied sizes.

In a seventh study we explored the possibility that aesthetic variables can account for differences in enjoying the destruction of many common building materials (Chao and Allen 1978). Subjects rated how much they enjoyed each of twenty filmed segments portraying the breaking of different types of material (with or without accompanying sound). Interestingly, the level of enjoyment was highest when both visual and auditory information were available, with the visual-only condition being next, and with auditory information alone being rated as least enjoyable. Factors such as the complexity and unexpectedness involved in breaking were correlated with differential amounts of enjoyment of destruction across the twenty different types of building material. Categorizing the material into five different groups yielded the following ratings of enjoyment (from most to least): glass, tile, wood, metal. The importance of the aesthetics of destruction is emphasized by the strong correlation between enjoyment and desire to break a particular type of material.

Although we have discussed separately several aesthetic variables, in everyday life many of them are, of course, actively involved in any specific instance of destruction or vandalism. For illustrative purposes we shall describe a study conducted with a sample of young males to test aesthetic theory with data obtained from relatively unstructured interviews about destructive incidents. Respondents recalled all incidents in which they had engaged in destructiveness during the past five years; then, detailed questions were asked about the three most serious incidents.

Respondents were able to describe their acts of destruction in amazing detail, and there were indications that the object of destruction was a very salient and critical aspect of the act. Indeed, the subjects could explain why they had chosen one object instead of another nearby one; many said they had selected a particular object because of the way they expected it to break. For example, one person broke a certain light because the glass was very thick, indicating to him that it would break in an interesting manner. Some respondents, however, suggested other motives behind destructive acts; one felt that he had "accomplished something by the breaking"—a factor we shall discuss in the next section.

After completing the open-ended questions about a given incident of destruction, the respondents assessed it on a number of bipolar scales. The most important results concern the enjoyment scale, which we conceptualize as the dependent variable. Significant positive correlations were found between degree of enjoyment experienced during destruction and the complexity, interestingness, and unexpectedness of the destruction; this relation was consistent with our predictions and with previous experimental results. In addition, the interestingness of the destructive act was correlated with the level of excitement reported by respondents.

In summary, the aesthetic theory of destruction suggests that the psychological factors accounting for the pleasurable experience associated with such socially approved stimuli as art, music, and literature will also help explain the varying degree of enjoyment or fun experienced during acts of destruction. For purposes of simplicity, we have discussed the theory primarily in terms of information emanating from a single sensory modality—vision. Moreover, the empirical studies have dealt primarily with the visual sense. But other types of sensory cues can also be easily incorporated into aesthetic theory and subjected to empirical testing. In some cases of vandalism, it is indeed likely that cues from the auditory and tactual-kinesthetic senses will be very important. The nature of the relationship between cues from different sense modalities introduces further complications to the study of vandalism. Thus, there is a need for additional research in aesthetic theory not only regarding the role of information from each separate sense modality during destruction, but also regarding the relative contribution of visual, auditory, and tactual-kinesthetic cues to enjoyment across different types of vandalism.

Perceived Control

Our emphasis on the role of stimulus factors in vandalism suggests another important set of psychological variables that may be related to destruction. Destruction is a very simple and direct way for a person to exert successfully an impact on the external physical world; therefore, one of the consequences of destruction or vandalism may be that the individual develops a perception of increased personal control. Perceived control has proved to be a very important motivational construct in many areas of psychology. Although several terms have been employed in discussions of this psychological concept, the same basic idea underlies all of them, including: competence (White 1959); self-efficacy (Bandura 1977); origin-pawn (de Charms 1968); power (Seeman 1959); and internal-external control (Rotter 1966). All these concepts assume that people are motivated to believe they are capable of producing some effect upon the external world. Many researchers have been very successful in using this notion to explain a wide range of types of behavior.

We have proposed that under certain conditions the act of destroying an object in the physical environment will be an effective technique for enhancing an individual's sense of personal control (Allen and Greenberger 1980). Persons who have experienced a detectable decrease in their perceived level of control are likely to make a strong effort at restoring the previous level; they can accomplish this by behaving in a way which promotes feelings of effectiveness and success. While a variety of objective and subjective events can produce a decrease in the individual's sense of control, attempts to change directly the social and physical environment are an efficient way of enhancing the sense of control. When efforts directed toward the social environment have failed, an individual may resort to such simple and dramatic—though socially unacceptable—methods as vandalism.

An act of destruction can effectively increase perceived control, even if it bears no direct instrumental relation to the original cause of the decrease in control; that is, the destruction itself need not eradicate the source of the lowered control in order to be an effective ameliorative technique. All the specific instances of success (for instance, of vandalism) will be integrated into a more general feeling of control.

We conceptualize general control as being based both on a person's overt actions and on his beliefs about how malleable the environment might be. Therefore, this view of control is a highly dynamic one which depends upon the characteristics of a given individual, and also upon the particular physical and social environment in which he must participate.

A person's sense of control is affected when he produces a modification in the physical environment: this is so because the implications of that modification (especially when the modification is destructive) affect the probability of success and/or the individual's perception of the locus of the success. One of the special characteristics of destructive behavior is that the individual knows he has a high probability of success in it; most objects can be destroyed quite easily. When a person contemplates engaging in a destructive act, he believes that such behavior will require a relatively small expenditure of energy since the environment contains many objects that can be broken successfully. Moreover, the lack of difficulty and the high probability of success associated with destroying objects in the physical environment stand in marked contrast to the greater difficulty and lower probability of success involved in attempts to make constructive modifications in the environment. The possibility of a successful outcome is even more remote when an individual attempts to change the social environment.

As noted above, the connection between control and destruction also involves the nature of attributions made by individuals concerning success or failure in modifying the environment. Research has found that people tend to believe that their personal abilities are responsible for their succeeding in a given endeavor (Weiner et al. 1968). An individual will, therefore, attribute the successful execution of a destructive act to his own abilities; consequently, he will perceive an increase in his level of general control.

Another possible explanation for the effect of destruction on control concerns the relation between emotional arousal and cognitions about personal control. In his past experience, an individual may well have felt a clear connection between high emotional arousal in general—and strong positive affective responses in particular—and high perceived control. When one engages in behavior that produces strong positive affect (such as destruction), his perceived control is likely to increase as well.

We designed several studies to test hypotheses concerning the relationship between destruction and perceived control; all used undergraduate students as subjects. In these studies, perceived control was lowered experimentally; subsequently, the subjects engaged in destruction in a controlled laboratory setting. We expected that under such conditions a minor act of destruction would be sufficient to increase a person's level of perceived control. Specifically, in these experiments, the destruction entailed breaking a tower constructed of small wooden blocks (72 cm high). Each subject broke the tower by releasing a volleyball at the end of an inclined ramp in such a way that it would roll down and strike the tower's base. This ensured that the tower always broke in a standard way and that the subjects all expended the same (minimal) amount of effort.

Two experiments were conducted to examine the interaction of aesthetic variables (along with the moods associated with them) and perceived control. It was predicted that a direct relation exists between affect and control, and further than the aesthetics of the destruction which occurred would have an effect on perceived control.

In the first experiment, a positive or a negative mood was created through the technique developed by Velton (1968). Results showed first that, even before subjects broke the tower, their score regarding success or failure differed significantly according to which of the two moods they were experiencing. That is, subjects in the positive-mood condition reported perceiving themselves as more successful than did those in the depressed- or negative-mood condition. Second, scores on perceived success supported the initial hypothesis; for subjects who had been made to feel depressed, the simple act of breaking an object would increase feelings of success. Moreover, depressed subjects who did not engage in destruction did not reveal any change in perceived success. Likewise, results supported the hypothesis that being in a positive or negative mood would influence a person's sense of control over the outcome of destruction, which in reality always occurred in a standard way. That is, subjects in the positive mood believed they had exerted significantly more control over the destruction's outcome than did subjects in the negative mood. In sum, then, the results of the experiments supported our predictions; apparently, the existence of positive and negative affect is sufficient by itself to influence a person's feelings of perceived success and control.

A second experiment examined the effect of the complexity of a destructive act on the enjoyment and perceived success produced by that act. This study tested the hypothesis that subjects will experience a greater sense of success when an object breaks in a complex rather than a simple manner. Complexity was experimentally varied by using blocks of different sizes to construct two towers identical in height and shape. While one structure used twenty-four large blocks (8×9×10 cm) and broke in a simple manner, the other used ninety-six small blocks (4×5×4.5 cm) and broke in a more complex way. The subject's degree of objective control over the destruction was varied. In one condition, the experimenter performed the act of breaking (low control); in a second condition, the subject produced the breaking (high control); and in a third, the subject both assembled the structure and was responsible for breaking it (highest control).

Replicating findings reported earlier, results showed that subjects experienced significantly greater enjoyment in destroying the complex structure (of small blocks) than the simple one (of large blocks). More importantly, the complexity of the destruction influenced perceived success in the predicted way; breaking the complex (small-block) structure resulted in greater perceived success than did breaking the simple (large-block) one. As for the effect of objective control, subjects reported significantly greater feelings of success when they actively produced the breaking themselves than they did under the condition of low control. In the high-control condition, participants also reported somewhat more enjoyment of destruction, but this was not statistically significant. Thus, data from this experiment indicate that there is a direct relation between an aesthetic variable (complexity) and perceived success: the more complex the process of destruction, the higher the perceived level of success.

In a third experiment, the initial level of subjects' perceived control was varied by means of feedback concerning success or failure on a task. Subjects were told that they had either succeeded or failed in performing an important task; thus their degree of capability in controlling an outcome was made salient. Results indicated that, as a consequence of later breaking the block structure, subjects who allegedly had failed on the task exhibited a dramatic increase in scores on sense of control. In contrast, subjects who were successful on the task showed little change in perceived control after breaking the structure. These findings indicate that, after experiencing a decrement in perceived control as a result of failure, persons can increase their level of felt control by destroying an object. The experiment also compared direct destruction by the subject as opposed to observation of the same destruction caused by the experimenter. Results showed that, when the subject simply watched while the experimenter broke the structure, their perceived control was affected only slightly, in marked contrast to what happened when they performed the breaking. This suggests that personal responsibility for a destructive act is a critical variable in restoring perceived control by modifying the physical environment.

We suggested earlier that two components comprise one's perception of general control: belief in the strength of one's own personal ability to produce changes in the physical environment, and beliefs about the degree to which the environment itself is malleable and, therefore, amenable to change by anyone. These beliefs are usually, but not always, highly interrelated. A successful act of destruction has implications for both of these beliefs. While destruction is a complex process, its central characteristic is that it results in changing the physical environment. Therefore, it is possible that any type of action—destructive or constructive—that produces a change in the environment will enhance an individual's perception of his general control.

An experiment was designed to compare the relative impact on perceived control of different kinds of environmental modifications—destructive and constructive. Because of the dynamic nature of destruction—a rapid and complete transformation of a structure—this form of modification is expected to have a greater impact on perceived control than other methods of changing the environment. In the experiment, subjects were initially placed in a situation of low control: after the possibility of free choice was made very salient, the subjects were deprived of their freedom of choice. Then, subjects either rested for a period of time or engaged in an act that caused a change in the physical environment in one of three ways: (1) destruction (as described in preceding experiments); (2) modification (taking blocks from the floor and stacking them in a box); (3) construction (building a structure of one's choice from the blocks). The same number of blocks was used in all three conditions. Dependent measures were obtained separately for the subjects' feelings about sense of personal control and about the malleability of the environment.

Results for personal control showed a difference among the three experimental conditions, with scores being highest for destruction, next for construction, and lowest for modification. Still, all three ways of altering the environment resulted in significant increases in levels of personal control over those that existed in a condition in which no environmental change occurred. Results were not so clear, though, regarding perceived malleability of the environment; the difference between the control and the three experimental conditions reached only marginal statistical significance.

These data make it obvious that construction and modification, as well as destruction, can exert some influence on perceived personal control. Furthermore, the results indicate that our findings for perceived control in this series of studies cannot be explained by a simple frustration-aggression hypothesis—that is, that inducing a state of low control in individuals will produce frustration capable of being relieved by breaking an object. Were this explanation valid, this experiment would not have shown an increase in perceived personal control through the two other ways of altering the environment. It should be remembered, however, that the change in perceived personal control produced by destruction was greater than that brought about by either of the other two modes of altering the environment.

Before closing this section, it should be stated that the procedures used in these experiments represent very conservative tests of the hypotheses. Subjects in all the experiments were required to engage in the destructive acts, and in their postexperimental interviews some indicated that they had been somewhat reluctant to participate in the breaking. Because in these experiments we hypothesized that destruction leads to an increase in perceived control, the fact that the subjects were placed in a low-control situation (that is, they did not have freedom of choice in the experiment) should have operated against obtaining positive results for perceived control. The destruction in these experiments was approved by the experimenter; so the level of emotional arousal is much lower than it would be in instances of such socially unacceptable behavior as vandalism. Obtaining significant results in the predicted direction for personal control—in spite of low perceived choice and minimal emotional arousal—strongly attests to the phenomenon's robustness. Moreover, the nature of the destruction that occurred was quite insignificant; had it been more serious and extensive, the impact on perceived success and control would no doubt have been much stronger.

Social Identity

We have proposed that there are two sets of important and closely related variables which seem to be implicated in vandalism; they have been discussed separately for ease of presentation. It is not only the case that a close and direct relationship exists between the affect produced by aesthetic variables (or other means) and perceived control; both these factors can also be viewed as components of a broader theoretical construct called social identity. Before discussing affect and control with reference to this more general construct, we should comment briefly on the relation between affective responses and perceived control in destruction and vandalism.

Our own results, as well as previous research findings, have revealed that there is a direct relation between affect and control; while a change in affect can influence a person's perception of control, a change in perceived control likewise alters one's affective experience. To explain this relationship, we assume the existence of a general class of affective states which can be characterized by a strong common affective component, but which has differentiated cognitive components. A change in magnitude or direction (positive-negative) of one affective state will influence certain other ones. Thus, if a person's positive affective state increases, his perception of control increases concomitantly; similarly, an increase in control should produce an experience of stronger positive affect.

The origin of the close association between positive affective states and perceived control must derive from a person's past history, in which many events have occurred that tend to elicit these affective states simultaneously or in close temporal contiguity. Therefore, during the process of destruction the activation of aesthetic variables evokes a positive affective response which also enhances a person's feeling of control. It is not really possible to ascertain the relative contribution of the affective response alone to perceived control, for this cannot simply be isolated from the contribution of the other factors mentioned earlier—probability of success and attribution of ability—that are also intimately involved in destruction.

We should now discuss the important concept of social identity (Ziller 1973), which is closely related to perceived control. *Social identity* is defined as the sum total of the social referents of the self-concept, and it consists of all the cognitive residues of past behavior as well as the inferences made by the individual and others about one's behavior (Sarbin and Allen 1968). It would be a great oversimplification of reality, of course, to think of a specific belief, such as sense of control, as being isolated and without extensive connections to other components of the individual's cognitive-social system. A specific act acquires its meaning and significance only in relation to the concept of social identity held by the individual and by other people who constitute the important links in the structure of his social relationships; without such a global concept, it would be difficult to understand fully a great deal of social behavior.

One of the functions of the social identity system is to control and modulate the impact of affective and cognitive factors presented earlier. For instance, for individuals possessing a positively evaluated, complex, and highly differentiated social identity system, the experience of destruction would be insufficient to produce a strong positive aesthetic response. Similarly, a social identity system that contains stable elements of competence in at least some social or cognitive areas will exert an influence on perception and behavior. In such cases, transient negative experiences are less likely to cause a diminution in perceived control, and accepted techniques that were successful in the past will be used in attempts to restore control.

It is clear, then, that the construct of social identity plays an important role for the individual by helping to unify many specific and apparently unrelated responses into a more general schema; and also by establishing standards or guidelines which the individual can use to evaluate his own behavior. Since perceived control of the social and physical environment is one of the central dimensions comprising the concept of social identity, any change in perceived control will produce corresponding reverberations more broadly across other psychological dimensions. Space does not permit a detailed discussion of the concept of social identity; suffice it to say here that this seems to play an important role in most acts of destruction.

The concept of social identity reminds us that in order to provide a satisfactory general theory of vandalism, we must try to integrate social variables with the major affective-cognitive factors presented earlier. Many instances of destructive behavior do not take place in isolation from other people. Vandalism often occurs in the context of a group and, therefore, should in such cases be viewed as a social act. According to our theory of destruction, what is the connection between the social group and a person's behavior or perception with regard to vandalism?

Social comparison theory is relevant to this question. Festinger (1954) posited that a person evaluates the correctness of his own attitudes and abilities by comparing relevant dimensions of self with other people. This theory hypothesizes further that an individual will choose to compare self with those of others who are similar—not dissimilar—in the relevant dimensions. Since perceived control is an important behavioral dimension, individuals are likely to engage in social comparison on this dimension. When perceived control is particularly salient (for instance, after a lowering of control), social comparison is especially likely to occur.

Support for our application of social comparison is provided by recent theoretical extensions of Festinger's theory. Jellison and Arkin (1977) have argued, for example, that ability or general competence is the basic dimension by which people make social comparisons; the authors assert that "any characteristic over which the individual is assumed to have some control can be treated by others as reflecting the individual's general competence" (p. 247). They further propose that people attempt to demonstrate competence to others by presenting themselves as being basically similar—but somewhat different—from the comparison group in a way that is socially approved by the group. Interestingly, such differentiation from the norm not only provides information about level of control, but also has implications for the person's social status in the group.

One way in which an individual can try to differentiate himself from the group is by engaging in risk-taking activity, since this form of behavior is associated with attributions of high ability. The attribution of ability or competence made by one's self (and others) will be related to the difficulty and the risk of the task (Weiner et al. 1968). Two principal types of risk are connected with destruction—lack of success and injury to the person. As indicated, there is a certain probability that most objects will break successfully on the first attempt. When an individual succeeds in destroying an object expected to be difficult to break, greater competence will be attributed to him and his social status in the group will rise.

Both the risk of physical danger (from flying glass, for example) and the possibility of being apprehended are present in acts of destruction. The seriousness of the risks will influence the strength of the attributions which are made about ability and control; that is, as the risk to the individual increases, there will be stronger attributions of personal control if the act is successful. It is important to note that risk-taking is also accompanied by high emotional arousal, and research had indicated that the cause of emotional arousal is often misattributed (Nisbett and Valins 1971). In other words, a person may misattribute the cause of high emotional arousal, believing that this state is brought about by the process of destruction itself rather than by the more general risk-taking situation; as a consequence, the individual would find an act of destruction to be more enjoyable than he would if his level of emotional arousal were low.

Implications

The theory of destruction or vandalism that we have presented is an attempt to provide a better understanding of the role of environmental or stimulus characteristics in destruction. The variables identified by our theory may play a very important role in vandalism in two ways. The crux of our theory is that certain factors intrinsic to the destruction of objects in the physical environment tend to elicit positive affective responses and positive cognitions about the self. Regarding psychological effects, then, we can say that people engage in destructive acts for both "fun" and "profit"; that is, destruction is pleasurable because of the aesthetic variables involved in it, and it is useful in that it enhances the individual's perception of himself with respect to control and competence. In turn, both these psychological consequences of destruction have implications for a person's social identity—for his self-concept and for evaluative responses from other people.

Our theory can be stated in either strong or weak form with regard to its practical implications for vandalism. The strong version of the theory would state that the appearance of certain objects in the environment, the anticipation of affective experience during and after destruction, and the expectation of increased sense of control will all serve as eliciting cues—cues that evoke or stimulate acts of vandalism. In its weaker form, the theory would state that the aesthetic variables associated with an object and the perception of enhanced control produced by destruction will serve as discriminative cues—cues that determine selection among potential targets when destruction is inevitable for other reasons. Furthermore, even in cases of vandalism that are produced by motives extraneous to the domain of our theory (by revenge or accident, for instance) the positive affective (enjoyment) and cognitive (control) consequences intrinsic to the destructive act itself will reinforce destruction and thereby increase the likelihood that vandalism will occur again in the future. Moreover, from past experience people will learn to select carefully the objects they will destroy, so as to maximize both their control and their enjoyment; that is, people will learn to choose targets according to their anticipation about the nature of the destructive process. In other words, the extent to which the experience of destruction is pleasurable and increases perception of control will be related to the characteristics of the object itself, as well as to the way in which the process of destruction occurs.

One of the straightforward implications of our theory is that school vandalism could be greatly reduced if destruction were simply made less enjoyable and beneficial for participants. According to the aesthetic component of our theory, the appearance of an object before and after destruction is important in vandalism. If an object looks as though it will break in an interesting and pleasurable way, it is more likely to be destroyed. Similarly, any object is a candidate for vandalism if it seems capable of being made more aesthetically pleasing by destruction.

Aspects of the physical environment or characteristics of the individual can be modified so as to make destruction a less positive cognitive and aesthetic experience. Vandalism would be less likely if architectural designs and type of materials were used that minimized processes that contribute to enjoyment and perceived control (for example, destruction that is complex, unexpected, novel, or intense in terms of visual, auditory, and tactual-kinesthetic information). From our point of view, then, it is less important to concentrate on a material's durability and resistance to destruction than on ensuring that a minimum degree of enjoyment and enhancement of control is associated with the destruction.

Acknowledging the important role played by aesthetics and perceived control in vandalism should also help suggest preventive programs directed toward the individual. It certainly should be possible to discover substitute activities—activities that are socially approved, but which still provide the same type of satisfying outcomes associated with destruction. A first step in this direction would be to make people more clearly aware of the psychological benefits they derive from the affective and cognitive processes which are intrinsic to the experience of destruction.

17 Preventable Property Damage: Vandalism and Beyond

Richard F. Thaw II

While vandalism in schools has increased enormously in recent years, so have efforts to stop it. But the proliferation of security devices, mechanical and human, has not been shown to combat effectively the increase in destruction. Neither alarms, trailers, polycarbonates, nor dogs have signaled the end of destruction. Moreover, the most effective short-range deterrents have in the long run, generally, become inviting challenges to would-be vandals. Newspaper accounts now indicate that a few districts are discouraging vandalism by turning out the schools' lights at night; ironically, these very lights were probably installed just to prevent property destruction. Police in the halls, supervisors for bathroom patrol, dollar rewards given to students for not committing destructive acts, and increases in parent-liability laws have not, over time, stopped the spread of vandalism. Nearly all such traditional measures presume an effectiveness upon acts of willful misconduct made against property.

The literature, however, points to the ineffectiveness of traditional measures used to prevent destruction, and indicates that recognition and reporting of destructive acts taken against property are arbitrary and incomplete.

We must, then, investigate the shortcomings of the traditional approach to the problem. First, it is evident from the unknown nature of losses that the problem is inconsistently perceived. Second, this inconsistency is caused by an adherence to well-known definitions that do not apply to the actual ways most destructive acts are committed. Third, the first two difficulties lead, in turn, to a remedial approach that attempts to treat only a part of the problem after the fact. Fourth, the search for causes of the growth of vandalism has been unproductive. Although that search has produced a list of causative social ills that helps explain the phenomenon of property destruction, it has not provided a way to come to grips with it. Fifth, the emotional connotations of the word "vandalism" make the problem a "third person" one. When perpetrators of acts against property are labeled "vandals," it is difficult for the speaker to feel any personal responsibility for the related issues.

Perception of the Problem

It is generally acknowledged that the reporting of vandalism is inconsistent. A given destructive act may or may not be reported as vandalism, depending upon the persons judging and reporting the incident. For example, were an administrator to report repairable or ignorable damage as vandalism, he would quite possibly be accused by his superiors of overreacting; his judgmental ability might be questioned. Likewise, other individuals might not report minor vandalism and graffiti because they believe those to be tolerable escape-valves for internal turmoil. The net result of such subjective reporting is an incomplete description of the facts.

According to the traditional approach, classifying an act as vandalism requires a qualitative assumption of intent or maliciousness. This attention to motivation prior to reporting results in the failure to report much preventable property loss.

As minor destructive acts are repeated without consequence, they begin to lose the quality of deviance from the norm and cease to be "abnormal." Furthermore, the traditional definition of vandalism fails to include routine minor acts against property, due to their high frequency and individually minor impact. If destruction is committed frequently, it ceases to be deviant behavior; and if each act has a minor impact, it becomes difficult to recognize the collective implications of property destruction until such destruction approaches crisis proportions.

Defining the Problem

Considering that current estimates indicate that only about 20 percent of actual property losses are reported by schools as acts of vandalism, it becomes obvious that preventable losses include much more than is encompassed by the common use of that term. The point is that once a problem is defined by an action's preventability, rather than by its motivation or intent, it then becomes possible to categorize it according to some schema.

Further, once a problem of destruction has been reclassified as being preventable damage, it is then possible to recognize various forms and patterns of that destruction. It is a specific advantage of this approach that it avoids treating vandalism as a symptom of a larger problem. The approach based on analyzing preventable property damage depends upon a recognition of what damage is committed and how it is being accomplished. This recognition exposes the destruction that has remained hidden under conventional reporting systems.

In review, vandalism is damage caused by willful misconduct or malicious mischief. If a prosecutor is to win a case, our judicial system requires the establishment of such intent. Thus a perpetrator who successfully pleads lack of intent can define the situation as something other than vandalism and somewhat diminish the consequences of the act. The shortcoming has been to define recognition of the problem upon willful misconduct or malicious mischief, rather than upon recognition of damage, regardless of why it occurred. A more practical approach would therefore be to recognize all preventable property damage.

Working Toward Preventability

Most traditional measures have been taken after some destruction has already occurred. Alarms are installed in schools where there have been break-ins; police appear in the halls following the development of a full-fledged problem; money goes into lighting once buildings and grounds have been damaged; and trailer-watches exist only where there has been a previous vandalism problem. Although some strategies do include school- and community-relations programs, they are not sufficient. More must be done to anticipate problems; the key to preventability is knowing first what is being done to property and then how it is being done.

Searching for Causes

The tradition of attempting to explain vandalism as a symptom of societal problems has yielded insights into violence on TV, family relationships, discrimination, gangs, drugs, territoriality, community, failure of the courts, frustration, alternative education, relevance of curriculum, and many other areas. But this approach has not provided a way of dealing directly with destructive acts. Instead, it has supported the contention that property destruction is a tolerable form of self-expression. It is clear, then, that treating property destruction as a symptom of a larger problem leads to interesting conclusions, but unmanageable solutions.

Emotional Implications

When an act against property is labeled as vandalism, those connected with the act are labeled as malicious, mischievous, destructive, and deviant. But, as has already been noted, persons who destroy property usually later attempt to redefine the act as something other than vandalism. Also previously noted, when vandalism is discussed as a current problem, listeners are unlikely to identify themselves as contributors to the problem: the vandalism problem, it will be felt, is one that is caused by a "third person." As a result of these points, recognition of a given act as vandalism usually requires that someone else perform it.

The establishment and acceptance of responsibility for vandalism has been a shortcoming of the traditional approach. This problem results from viewing acts against property as misbehavior on the part of an individual, isolated from the context of the larger group. It does not consider that the individual may be acting within the definitions held by the larger group. Regarded as such, the bulk of preventable property damage is seen as a low priority when pitted against the larger purposes of administering, supervising, and educating children.

Requirements

An effective approach would use a uniform measure to recognize all acts against property. This instrument should detect developing patterns of destruction and should anticipate future patterns. The overall approach should resist explanations of property destruction which neither bring one closer to a solution nor facilitate personal ownership of the problem on the part of the overall school community. Broad-based participation from the entire school community in the reduction of any property damage is also a requirement.

Such an approach will enable prevention campaigns to be carried out with participation from those that have contributed to the problem. Campaigns searching for "vandals" treat only part of the problem, and keep us from seeing our individual contributions to the problem.

Toward a New Approach

The first step toward a new approach is to determine where dollars are being needlessly lost in acts against property. It is only after this step that appropriate measures may be selected for saving as many of those dollars as possible. Traditionally, educators have treated a good deal of nonaccidental damage to school property as an expression of vandalistic intent and behavior. The shortcoming has been that many of those acts are not the expression of vandalism as the word is traditionally defined, but result from carelessness and thoughtlessness.

Heavy littering of paper towels in a restroom suggests carelessness and not necessarily an intent to waste supplies. The sight of bicycle or foot paths worn through on a landscaped slope suggests thoughtlessness. These typically unreported acts certainly, through repetition, cost money in labor and material. Most often, such acts do not declare an intent of maliciousness. They are preventable, but there is no accounting and little awareness of them.

There is evidence that the greatest dollar losses in preventable property damage in the schools are represented by acts which are excluded from conventional reporting systems. Carelessness and thoughtlessness have been the real source of $5 out of every $6 lost. The findings of a recent study show that, in one particular district, preventable property damage has cost six times more than the amount estimated and reported by the school district personnel. The three-year vandalism estimate of $748,000 does not include some $3.5 million in preventable property damage (Thaw 1976).

Beyond Vandalism

Nearly every school has areas where greenery has required constant maintenance against damage. This type of difficulty often develops through faulty landscape design—one that does not recognize the human tendency to take the shortest route between two points. Groundcover and bushes, for instance, are sometimes planted between a classroom door and a cafeteria door. Frequently, the terrain of the schoolyard provides sloping areas where bikes may career through the shrubbery. In cases where students have damaged property for sport or convenience, it may be obvious that there must have been an awareness of the damage they were committing. Although it is going too far to assume that the acts were hostile, one can say that there was an awareness of destruction: the action was directed by a priority for play or expediency.

Most of these individually minor and frequent acts are not reported: they are simply absorbed in the routine functioning of the school. To warrant inclusion in a conventional report of property destruction, acts must be sizable, uncommon, and clearly hostile. In addition, if damaged property requires replacement, rather than repair, the odds are better the act will be reported.

As long as there is little awareness of these minor acts and absence of consequences for these acts, deterrence to successive acts is lacking. Without consequences to actors for their misbehaviors, there is no way to alter the balance in their judgments about the opportunities and risks involved in the performance of an act against property.

Crisis Management

The organization of the school district reflects the inconsistency inherent in the traditional approach. District action is a forced reaction to events. Damage occurs prior to district decision making. Preventable property damage is hidden in the expenditures of such departments as audiovisual, maintenance, and grounds. There are few organized attempts for providing deterrence before acts grow sizable and out of the routine, and consequently recognized. Recognized acts are those which may attract public attention and cause public concern.

When acts included in a report imply student intent and anger, administrators are likely to feel they should record only the most obvious cases. A desire to protect the district's insurance rating also encourages the ignoring of routine, small acts against property. This partially explains why a district often does not include man-hours or repairable damage in a property damage report. The problem might seem to diminish if some incidents are not counted; there is little immediate reward (and some risk) in the truth.

Ignoring minor acts, except to distribute the resultant maintenance and repair among district employees, puts the district in a position of having to wait for acts to become large enough and singularly serious before they can be recognized. This late attention often requires outside assistance, and the final dollar-loss is frequently much greater than it would have been had early intervention taken place.

The "Acts Against Property" Approach

Acts taken against property are generally joint or collective—actions based upon meanings arising through human interactions. The meaning of an action grows out of the behavior of others toward the individual proposing it. Consequences alter this meaning. An effective strategy allows the development of consequences applicable to the ways the property damage is committed. Discovering the ways in which property is damaged requires a model that shows the generic dimensions of the damage and shows possible interrelationships. Such an approach provides both an understanding of patterned action and a capacity to predict future actions. This model will treat three kinds of behavior as generic dimensions of preventable property damage: hostility-directed acts, acts of carelessness, and acts of thoughtlessness.

Hostility-Directed Acts

These acts are expressions of hostility showing an intent to seek revenge, change, or gain. For example, if a student writes profanities on a classroom door after a reprimand from the teacher, he is committing a hostility-directed act. This is the traditional intent-laden vandalism act. It is against this type of act that traditional security measures are appropriate. The bulk of money allocated for prevention is directed toward this type of act. However, damage caused by hostility-directed acts represents only a minor portion of dollars unnecessarily lost.

Acts of Thoughtlessness

Acts of thoughtlessness are those characterized by an intent to play. Awareness of the consequent destruction of property fails to override the desire to proceed with play. For instance, several boys who were playing dodgeball against a school wall, using handfuls of mud as the ball, were certainly aware that the mud was sticking to the wall; but the enjoyment of the game overrode any awareness of probable destruction of property. A variation is when two boys, racing with a 16mm film projector on a cart, toppled the cart and smashed the projector. When confronted, the boys stated, "We didn't mean to do it!" They were attempting to have the act defined as not malicious in an attempt to be let partly off the hook. This act was expensive and preventable. It will probably not be reported as a preventable loss. Another typical response—"But, they were doing it too!"—can also result in such absolution of blame; because when an act becomes frequent or widespread, it loses the quality of deviance and thus cannot qualify as vandalism. The weakness of the traditional approach to defining vandalism is evident in the excuses often given for having destroyed property.

Acts of Carelessness

Acts of carelessness are closely related to littering. They are not necessarily characterized by any intent, and there may or may not be a degree of awareness in their performance. Students throwing soaked balls of paper towels onto a bathroom ceiling are, for instance, participating in an act of carelessness. A nonschool example would be that of a person having just loaded grocery bags into a car from a cart and failing to put the empty cart back in the stall a few feet away. Personal awareness of the careless action may, or may not, be present.

The Model

The Venn diagram (figure 17-1) presents the acts against property focus. Each circle represents one of the three groups of acts just described. Circle A stands for hostility-directed acts, B for acts of carelessness, and C for acts of thoughtlessness. All acts against property involve one, or a combination, of these three elements. Where the circles overlap, the areas of intersection represent acts that demonstrate a combination of characteristics. When all three elements contribute to an act, that could be plotted in the area shared by all three circles.

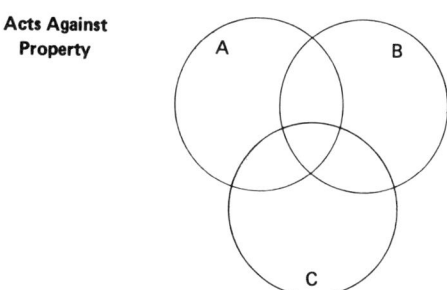

Figure 17-1. The Venn Diagram

The model considers all acts against property to be vandalism and beyond. The model is designed to escape the traditional trap of reporting the clearly shown hostility-directed act (unshared A) and ignoring the acts falling outside this area. The shared portions of the hostility-directed act (shared A) represent those acts that may or may not be reported under a traditional reporting procedure.

To illustrate, a window was broken near the playing field of a school. The perpetrators were a group of students who had a reputation for destructiveness and who had chosen to throw baseballs against the wall containing that window. Even if the youths' intent was unclear, use of this model would have caused their act to be reported: it would properly be placed in the intersection of circles A and C. The act was preventable and the loss is, therefore, recognized and reported as preventable.

Consider the present model in relation to the weaknesses characteristic of the traditional approach. In defining the problem, the model reflects all damage and destruction whether intentional, willful, malicious, careless, or thoughtless. The behavioral genotypes of the act are secondary to reporting any damage in excess of deterioration from normal use; questions about abnormality and deviance follow the basic recognition and reporting of damage. The model is based upon the assumption that acts against property occur in different ways. A focus on preventable damage does not initially assume abnormality in an act; it enables responsibility for, and ownership of, the problem to be assigned to "normal" people. This distribution of ownership also has implications for curriculum development in the area of shared responsibility. Additionally, the model permits an administrator to attend to the problem better; for his report will not necessarily convey information about angry students. The model requires only a determination of preventability, not an assessment of intent. It treats acts against property as a collective problem, not as one solved by focusing upon individuals. Damage is seen as resulting from the behaviors of persons who interact, and whose joint actions have their own collective meanings. Such persons decide whether to commit an act according to their past experiences with the balance between opportunity and risk. If one knows what is happening to property, one can reduce opportunity, raise risk, reduce accessibility, and predict the inspiration to commit destructive acts. Remediation of the problem should occur through the sharing of responsibility and through the appropriate selection of consequences for particular acts. Those consequences must be fit properly to the specific types of acts which prompt them; for example, installing an alarm system would not help save money that is being lost due to littering.

How the Model Is Used

The model is most important insofar as it provides a means to see all preventable destruction and to develop uniform definitions. The Venn diagram offers an economical way of tallying the pattern of events.

The model shows patterns of elements contributing to preventable property damage and allows a selection of consequences appropriate to a given pattern. If, for instance, carelessness and littering cause heavy losses, then appropriate measures would include plans for student and community involvement in the school's functioning; projects emphasizing beautification and school pride; contests; a responsibility-centered curriculum; and other measures designed to make the students care more about their school. If a school has a pattern showing heavy losses due to acts of thoughtlessness, consideration should be given to modification of facility design and to the development of a well-supervised recreation program. Finally, hostility-directed acts suggest traditional security measures, such as target-hardening.

If the Venn diagram is used to tabulate the types of acts occurring at different times, the manner in which those acts progress becomes clear. Figure 17-2 suggests what happens when destructive acts are performed without incurring consequences: over time, they change from those of carelessness to thoughtlessness to hostility-directed acts.

Use of the model helps prevent minor and routine acts from becoming hidden. Ignoring such behaviors does not deter them: they do not go away when they are ignored. If minor acts have no consequences, then those who wish to engage in risk-taking behavior will have to perform more serious acts.

Application of the "Preventable Property Damage" Approach

Only by shedding outmoded, limiting definitions of vandalism may we implement a positive approach to the problem. When the emphasis is on saving dollars from preventable destruction, everyone can accept ownership in the problem

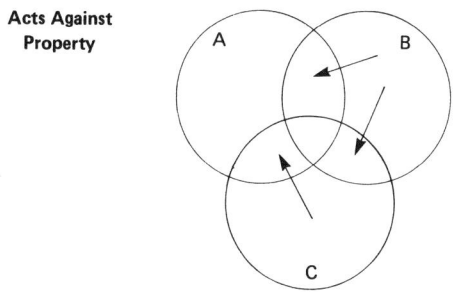

Figure 17-2. Progression of Destructive Acts

and participate in its alleviation. Likewise, instead of being afraid to report incidents, an administrator can receive gratification from discovering ways to save dollars. Reports to insurance companies can still be concerned with the singularly expensive and hostile events.

This approach is universally adaptable and applicable. It is through this approach—and only this approach—that reporting can be consistent in any school setting regardless of the ethnic and socioeconomic characteristics of students. Measures of seriousness generated by this model will remain valid and reliable over time, and will correctly reflect ways in which destruction occurs.

The use of the model allows early awareness of property destruction, as well as where and how such destruction is occurring. If problems are addressed while they remain minor, perhaps many of the larger and more expensive acts may be averted. Since apprehended student vandals and arsonists are seldom reported to have exhibited symptoms of mental illness, it must be concluded that their decisions to commit acts against property were rational ones—decisions based upon judgments about consequences of prior acts. Recall the tried and proven excuse that "Everybody does it!" Indeed, vandalism tends to go unnoticed until there is one act of proportions so great that it alarms everyone. When vandals wreak such enormous destruction that a school must be closed, it is often the students themselves who are most shocked.

The benefits of using the preventable property damage approach could not be more obvious. It dictates that students, staff, and community members gather and make a comprehensive, informed attempt to save dollars—rather than sit back and pay tribute in various security devices to an ill-defined malady. This approach offers a system organized to economize and to reward success as a replacement for one that is likely to punish those who point out existing flaws.

The economic plight of our nation's schools suggests that the public is concerned with efficient use of resources. The time is ripe for the educational community to take a good look at the often ignored cumulative dollar losses in public schools and to address the problem with a thoughtful, positive new course of action.

18 Understanding Vandalism

S.D. Vestermark, Jr. and *Peter D. Blauvelt*

Along with the other great school discipline problem—violence—vandalism has become the crucial concern of school security. While many school-security programs did, in fact, begin because of a need to respond to school vandalism, that phenomenon has been increasingly magnified. In recent years, public agencies have, with shock and dismay, discussed violence and vandalism as twin problems in American schools; public attention has become sharply focused on both. Thus, the skilled publicist who attempts to build support for a school-security program learns quickly that lurid stories of vandalism will draw as many irate demands for immediate action as will horror stories of school violence.

The net effect of much of the current concern over school vandalism has been to leave school officials in a quandary as to what to do about it. And their anxiety is compounded by endless suggestions which, like a shotgun blast, serve to scatter and diffuse coherent efforts to control vandalism in school settings. As a consequence of their confusion, officials have tended simply to develop lists of every vandalism-control program anyone has ever conceived, rather than to develop a logical strategy for dealing with vandalism.

Implicit in the fact that people are continually fascinated by recounting incidents of vandalism is another aspect of the difficulty of addressing the problem; as with other social problems (and more than many of us might want to admit), we have grown comfortably accustomed to being shocked and surprised by vandalism. In other words, vandalism has become a convenient target for those who want to be outraged by youth. Thus, we need to put aside the sensationalism associated with vandalism and begin to develop a rational approach for understanding and controlling the phenomenon.

Why Schools Are Targeted by Vandals

As targets for vandalism, schools share certain characteristics with other principal targets: public housing facilities, parks, and mass transportation vehicles. First, school is a *public place*, which means that it has no particular owner who can personally confront the vandal. Since it belongs to "everyone," it is

---

From *Controlling Crime in the School: A Complete Security Handbook for Administrators* by S.D. Vestermark, Jr., and Peter D. Blauvelt. Published by Parker Publishing Company, Inc., West Nyack, New York. Copyright © 1978 by Vestermark and Blauvelt. Reprinted by permission.

everyone's fair game. ("Public" need not always mean "publicly owned." Note that even in a residential private school, the classroom and nondormitory facilities are "common" areas where the students may have little direct sense of ownership.) Second, there are long periods when the school is *unoccupied*, or when *the human presence is reduced to negligible significance*. A janitor working in an obscure corner of a mammoth high school is just as helpless to stop vandals as is the worried mother spying graffiti artists at work from the tenth floor of her public flat. Third, the school is a *secular* place, which means that no religious and few moral scruples are involved in damaging or destroying it. In spite of a few dramatic incidents of defacement directed against minority churches and cemeteries, such places remain largely immune to vandals.

To sum up, schools are made-to-order arenas for the vandals. In many locales, they are in fact the only easily accessible public, secular, and frequently unoccupied places. The fact that they are schools—places of enforced learning, discipline, and socialization—only reinforces their attractiveness as targets for the vandals. For some young people will always view schools as places where they are forced to do things they do not want to do. Thus, the potential vandal can always rationalize vandalism against his school, or any school, as an act of revenge.

Why Schools Should Appear Occupied

The job of controlling vandalism begins with recognizing what can and cannot be done to change the basic characteristics of schools. While most schools must always remain public and secular, the third factor noted above can indeed be extensively modified; it is clearly possible to decrease the degree to which a school building is unoccupied and, therefore, vulnerable to vandalism. The practicable key to controlling vandalism is thus to make the school a place that, in some sense, is continuously occupied by some form of human or mechanical presence which will deter or respond to the vandal. The establishment of this presence, which defines the building as no longer an inert target, must be at the heart of any effective approach to dealing with vandalism.

The Concept of "Social Cost"

Most studies of vandalism emphasize those costs that can be measured in direct monetary terms. These costs are not only staggering and highly visible, but they also are relatively easy to assign. Vandalism has another critical dimension, however: its impact in social terms, on individuals and groups. It is very hard to put a price tag on this kind of cost, but in some cases it is far more important than the financial one, not only with regard to estimating the damage, but as well with regard to developing a strategy to cope with vandals.

How do you assign a dollar value to the total impact on an educational program when vandals destroy fifty microscopes? What price do you set when a child sees the carnage left by vandals who have mutilated pet hamsters in the classroom? How much money do you put in your budget to cover the disruption that results when one group's personal belongings are systematically vandalized by another group—and then a brawl begins? Although there is some monetary cost in each case, that does not constitute the real damage. Rather, that real damage is to the process of acquiring knowledge, to the individual and his or her capacities to feel and imagine, and to the abilities of people in groups to work together harmoniously in school.

Granted that defining the concept of the social cost of vandalism can be more difficult than assigning monetary values, we think that this cost has three major components. First, there is damage to the educational program, ranging from lost hours of instruction to the more subtle point that, because of the damage done, course content has had to be defined and educational opportunities lost. Second, there is the psychological impact on students and adults. And third, there is the disruptive influence on group and intergroup relations. Since the social costs of vandalism may be difficult to estimate and may have different effects on different segments of the school community, the school-security administrator and educator must be especially sensitive to how these costs may be expressed in behavior and attitudes—and they must be prepared to respond effectively to the needs that are so expressed.

Impacts upon the Education Program

By and large, most acts of vandalism that are serious in monetary terms will also have a great impact upon the educational program. Vandals who destroy a school's library, who throw paint on walls, floors, and equipment, who stop up sinks and flood a school, who destroy audiovisual equipment, who disable the school's heating plant in the winter, have all committed acts which have both high monetary costs and highly disruptive impacts on the planned educational program. As a consequence of such acts, schools must sometimes be closed for appreciable periods.

Psychological Impact

While these acts have some psychological impact upon students and teachers, other acts of vandalism have greater psychological impacts, even though their monetary costs are much less. Acts which fall into this category include mutilation of classroom pets or laboratory animals, systematic destruction of student projects, human excrement left in a teacher's desk drawer, and the repeated destruction of a teacher's personal belongings. The intent of these behaviors is often to frighten and intimidate younger students, and to cause anger and resentment among older students and teachers.

Group Impact

There are certain acts of vandalism which are directed toward identifiable groups of students in a school; such groups may be victimized because of their race, socioeconomic backgrounds, geographic location, social attitudes, or lifestyles. The vandals select as their targets property or school projects which are easily identified with one or more specific segments of the student population. For instance, the destructive youths might vandalize an American Indian art display, a display of Mexican-American crafts, or a project which depicts the contributions of blacks to American culture. Acts in this category also include vandalism to property of students who come from one geographic section of the community, or "trashing" the lockers of students who have lifestyles differing from the norm or who express certain unpopular social attitudes. While these types of incidents generally have a low monetary cost, their disruptive impact on a student body can be enormous. Fights, student protests, and even the carrying of weapons can be among the social effects of acts of vandalism directed toward specific groups of students.

Relationships Between Monetary Costs and Social Costs

An Approach to Managing the Vandalism Problem

Monetary costs and social costs are two broad variables which may be utilized in assessing the impact of vandalism. When they are properly examined in relation to each other, these variables give important insight into how to approach the vandalism problem as one of school-security management. Indeed, they point to a procedure for evaluating any act of vandalism and for setting priorities to prevent or respond to them.

When we reflect upon the whole range of possible acts of vandalism, we perceive a critical fact: vandalism can be high on one cost variable while it is low on another. For example, a school safe can be blown open or a cherry bomb dropped down a toilet. While the costs are high in monetary terms, life can continue to go on in school with relative ease—so that there is little social cost. However, the proportions of monetary and social costs may be completely reversed; a few cents worth of spray paint can be used to write "SCREW NIGGERS" across a school wall—and can start a mass disruption

Understanding Vandalism

which closes the whole school. And some acts of vandalism can be high on both cost variables; youngsters can wreck the school's central office area, ruining equipment and valuable records. In such a case, there would not only be serious monetary damage in terms of replacement costs and labor, but all educational functions which depend on the school's records would also have to be at least temporarily suspended or redirected. On the other hand, there are acts of vandalism which are low on both cost variables. These include the single broken window, whose tinkle maddens only the principal, and to the damage wrought by the drag racer who cuts across a wet lawn, leaving ugly tire tracks.

These relationships between monetary cost and social cost can be expressed more formally. Figure 18-1 presents a simple matrix in which monetary costs are arrayed against social costs, giving four basic types of vandalism: Type I is high on both cost variables; Type II is high on monetary cost but low on social cost; Type III is low on monetary cost but high on social cost; Type IV is low on both monetary and social cost. In passing, we should note that there is a certain apparent decrease in the severity of a given act of vandalism, from

	High	Low
High Monetary Cost	**Type I Vandalism** Incidents having a *high monetary* cost as well as a *high social* cost. **Examples** 1. Destruction of school media center. 2. Destruction of school records. 3. Vandalism which closes the school.	**Type II Vandalism** Incidents having a *high monetary* cost but a *low social* cost. **Examples** 1. Large number of broken windows. 2. Cherry bomb dropped in a toilet. 3. Vandalism to vending machines.
Low	**Type III Vandalism** Incidents having a *low monetary* cost but a *high social* cost. **Examples** 1. Racial graffiti. 2. Systematic vandalizing of minority-owned property. 3. Killing of classroom animals.	**Type IV Vandalism** Incidents having a *low monetary* cost as well as a *low social* cost. **Examples** 1. Tire tracks in the lawn. 2. Cutting of the flagpole rope. 3. Painting of names on the bleachers. 4. Single broken window.

Figure 18-1. Types of Vandalism: Social Cost

Type I, which is the most costly vandalism, to Type IV, which is the least costly. (Even this progression probably does not really hold, though, as we will suggest in a moment.) Beyond this, the Roman numeral values have no meaning. Our purpose is to provide a compact typing of the major effects vandalism can have, regardless of motive. For this is the real issue in managing vandalism— examining possible or actual effects, and seeing what deterrent or remedial actions can feasibly be taken.

Classifying Acts of Vandalism by Type

The typology presented here classifies an act of vandalism according to its effects; for this is the essential first step in learning how to manage the vandalism's consequences. Because monetary and social costs may vary independently of each other, reaching a final decision on how to classify a particular act of vandalism will often require lumping together different sorts of measures and estimates.

The process of classification could very quickly become very complicated. The methodologist could have a field day pointing out the different "incommensurables" in our matrix of types; but the immediate goal here is really quite modest. We think that by looking at all acts of school vandalism in terms of these four types, we can point the school-security manager toward some real priorities involved in how to respond to potential or actual effects of vandalism. These response priorities may, in fact, be quite different from the priorities that many administrators now have. A hard-pressed administrator is quite likely to put many valuable resources into the immediate repair of an act of vandalism which is obviously costly in monetary terms. Meanwhile, he will have ignored the cheap little act of racial graffiti which has started a gang fight in the cafeteria, resulting in the school's closing and in the loss of thousands of man-hours from education. Such an administrator's priorities will, then, have caused him to overlook what is ultimately the far more expensive act.

Before considering how the types point toward some new response priorities in dealing with vandalism, we must try to define those types as sharply as possible, through some concrete cases. Remember that classifying an act of vandalism may be complicated by certain questions of situation and magnitude. For instance, local values can be very important. In most settings, a single broken window is an act of Type IV vandalism. (Granted, some schools may be so "uptight" that this one window is a big issue—but the problem, then, really is not one of vandalism, but of dealing with the Captain Queeg who runs the principal's office.) Yet, fifty broken windows may be Type II vandalism—if the school's budget for repairs is tight. Five hundred broken windows may be Type I, so that the school might have to be closed.

Furthermore, it will always be hard to assess individual psychological costs against any other cost criterion. Is the emotional damage one child suffers at seeing a disfigured pet hamster less costly than a hole knocked in the side of the school when all the children were home in bed? Is the quickly erased Type IV graffiti which one youngster happened to see less costly, in the long run, than the graffiti which remained on the wall for some time and had Type III effects, triggering a riot or walkout? Obviously, then, we are not presenting a classification scheme which is free from serious questions of judgment. Used in the right way, however, it can certainly be helpful.

Developing Strategies for Controlling Vandalism: Basic Objectives

Setting Priorities

If a school administrator had unlimited material resources, then this discussion of types or a further discussion of strategies would be of little interest to him. He could simply buy whatever he needed to replace whatever was lost—even if the vandals were to bulldoze down the entire school! If children are emotionally damaged, then such an administrator could easily intervene with the therapeutic resources to help them adjust.

However, the typical administrator concerned with school security has a much different prospect. Pressures are mounting all across the school budget. Therefore, as vandalism increases, he must determine what kind of strategy will lead to maximum success in controlling the phenomenon and its effects. Is it possible, then, that one can establish such priorities that if a system were to experience many different types of vandalism, it could establish an approach which is capable of dealing with all of them? Can one find an approach which will focus primarily on the most serious type, and still be effective in dealing with others?

The notion that vandalism has a social cost suggests that finding the right strategy for handling this phenomenon involves much more than simply laying out money and material resources. Increasingly, vandalism-control strategies will need to consider very carefully the relationship between monetary and social costs. At first glance, those planning a vandalism-control program might conclude that their efforts ought to deal with all four types of vandalism according to the priorities noted in table 18-1. This list assumes, sometimes not incorrectly, that the greater the monetary cost, the greater the priority for control; for monetary costs are the real costs, or at least a good indicator of all costs of vandalism. (This issue could in fact be the subject of an interesting research study.)

We suspect that in most school systems today, the real priorities in a vandalism-control program cannot actually be easily ranked in order from I to IV.

Table 18-1
Apparent Priorities in a Vandalism-Control Program

Priority		
Type I	(Monetary Cost: High	Social Cost: High)
Type II	(Monetary Cost: High	Social Cost: Low)
Type III	(Monetary Cost: Low	Social Cost: High)
Type IV	(Monetary Cost: Low	Social Cost: Low)

In most systems experiencing rapid change and severe budgetary problems, we believe that the real priorities are probably as they are listed in table 18-2. The order of Types I and IV on this list does not require much discussion. Type I vandalism very likely closes a school, so that it must be repaired in order to reopen. Thus, its prevention is a high priority. Type IV is, at best, trivial, and too much time spent worrying about it wastes what resources are available for more urgent matters. Regarding the order of priorities in Table 18-2, then, the point in need of some discussion is the placement of Type II below Type III. It may well be that in a financially constrained system, some acts of Type II vandalism should only be patched. In the short run, repairing them may in fact be wasteful; for school goes on, in spite of some ugliness and inconvenience. In contrast, Type III vandalism can sometimes close a school, even if little monetary cost has been incurred. So, we are suggesting that the key to most vandalism-control programs today will be not whether monetary costs can be limited by prevention and detection systems, but rather whether the program will keep schools open and functioning, through controlling social costs, until such time as additional monetary resources become available.

Hopefully, the issue will seldom be quite so starkly presented. If an administrator develops a program to control Types I and III, he should have markedly increased the prospect of controlling Type II acts. But the day may well be coming when a system, faced both with limited resources and with disruptions flowing from Type III vandalism, must be prepared to divert part of its resources toward the explicit objective of limiting Type III's social costs through inhibiting Type III vandalism. For example, plans to install an alarm system in every

Table 18-2
Real Priorities in a Vandalism-Control Program

Priority		
Type I	(Monetary Cost: High	Social Cost: High)
Type II	(Monetary Cost: High	Social Cost: Low)
Type III	(Monetary Cost: Low	Social Cost: High)
Type IV	(Monetary Cost: Low	Social Cost: Low)

school may have to be deferred so that in certain selected, troubled schools there may be both alarms and specially trained patrols or school residents serving to prevent or quickly deal with socially costly vandalism. In choosing to take such action, the system may be deliberately deciding to accept a certain level of Type II losses.

Controlling Access and Time

By no means do we mean to imply that developing vandalism-control plans is so complex as to be impracticable for the average school administrator. Remember, to control any act of vandalism certain clearcut, constant things must be done. One must make the school a place that in some sense is continuously occupied by some form of human or mechanical presence which will deter or respond to the vandal. This is necessary because two basic variables control the ability of a vandal to commit his act of vandalism: one, access to the target; and two, time to commit the act. Thus, the best approach to controlling vandalism would be to limit both access and time for each of the four types.

To commit each type of vandalism, the vandal must have access and time. Therefore, a high payoff strategy for controlling vandalism would limit access and time across all types. In practice, such a strategy is nearly impossible to design. For example, a system for limiting access to school at night may not work during the daytime; while an effective burglar alarm will keep vandals from having sufficient time to commit one type of vandalism, they might find sufficient time to commit another type when the alarms are turned off.

Objectives of Effective Strategies

In general, then, strategies for controlling vandalism should have these objectives:

1. Ideally, they should limit the time and access required to commit all four types.
2. At a minimum, they should limit time and access in such a way as to control the more costly types which, depending upon the situation, may include Types II and III, as well as Type I.
3. When possible, they should limit both social and monetary costs.
4. In schools or systems where Type III social costs are potentially more critical than Type II costs, special resources should be directed to preventing and limiting Type III effects.

5. By and large, they should view attempts to control Type IV vandalism as ineffectual. Indeed, probably the only effective response to Type IV vandalism is quickly to repair the damage caused by it. If the school has the capacity to do so, and if Type IV vandalism is its main problem, then the administration might attempt to institute a program of peer-group rewards and punishments.

19 Vandalism in High Schools: An Exploratory Discussion

Michael H. Ducey

The dollar cost of the destruction of property on high-school premises currently runs into the millions in major metropolitan areas and into the tens of thousands in smaller cities and towns. Even where this loss represents a small percentage of a school system's total budget, it is still a symptom of serious inadequacy in the system.

The Youth in Illinois Project of the Institute for Juvenile Research spent three years (1971-74) gathering data on many aspects of juvenile behavior in and out of school. The ethnographic component of this project has compiled 10,000 pages of field notes and interview material documenting, in great detail, the thought and behavior patterns of teenagers. In order to use this information for an accurate diagnosis of the causes of vandalism in high schools, we must be able to identify certain aspects of the situation of youth which may contribute to the phenomenon.

Symbolic Versus Pragmatic Action

In the minds of its perpetrators, the destruction of high-school property can serve either a symbolic or a pragmatic purpose or both. We will argue that at the present time high-school vandalism is mostly symbolic action, very seldom conceived of by its perpetrators as an act of instrumental pragmatism.

Symbolic action is meaningful in itself. It is a form of communication in which the actors define the world and their places in it as an orderly whole which gives each participant a legitimate basis for a sense of personal worth. While the audience for symbolic action can be as wide as the whole of society or as narrow as oneself alone, the degree of sophistication involved in it can range from the complexity of traditional solemn rituals to the inarticulate groping of a disturbed individual. But in every case, symbolic action is a statement containing a message. This is its purpose, the source of its satisfaction for the performer, and the ground for correctly interpreting it.

A symbolic act of high-school vandalism could be on the material level; that is, it could be anything from littering to arson. On the level of motivation, intent, and purpose, however, a symbolic act of vandalism simply states a message. Such communications could signify a wide variety of specific things, including hatred for what the actor believes the school to stand for or personal valor displayed for a sympathetic crowd of peers.

On the other hand, pragmatic destruction of high-school property could be, for instance, the freezing of locks in order to achieve unobserved access for the purpose of theft or sabotage. As we consider it here, pragmatic action is a means to an end. It is not meaningful in itself, but only in the context of the goals to which it leads. Pragmatic arson could be conceived of as a paramilitary act designed to cripple the institution, weaken society, lead to revolution, and so forth.

When examining the vandalism committed in any institution over a given period of time, it is important to make this distinction between symbolic and pragmatic action, for the least costly and most effective responses to the two different kinds of vandalism are very different. In particular, the assumption that vandalism is pragmatic when it is, in fact, symbolic could easily lead not only to a vicious cycle of expensive and harsh security measures, but also to an increase in such behavior.

The Half-Culture of American Youth

Current interpretations of youthful misbehavior in America tend to oscillate between the poles of psychic pathology and counterculture conspiracy. The activities of gangs as well as of individuals are often seen as cases of motivational pathologies. Granted that some youthful misbehavior is produced by pathology and some by an articulated counterculture or dissenting ideology, these two sources of behavior can really be understood only against the background of youthful subculture itself. With regard to the current wave of vandalism in high schools, relying on theories of pathology and of conspiracy leads to an obvious absurdity: we have either widespread insanity or organized revolution.

Based on the data from the Youth in Illinois Project, we propose that many forms of youthful misbehavior (particularly vandalism in high schools) are rooted in the normal dynamics of culture among American youth. That is, as youth reflect on their situation of growing up in America, they establish various sets of concrete values so as to create what could be called youthful subcultures. Essentially, these values constitute reasonable grounds on which youngsters may build for themselves models of the world and for their own behavior. Because they are based on group experience, these values have a taken-for-granted consensual aspect. Although youthful subcultures vary in content according to locale, ethnicity, socioeconomic status, and other factors, they have a common structural characteristic which warrants our speaking of the half-culture of American youth.

The prima facie evidence supporting the use of this phrase is the inability of pathology and conspiracy theories to explain youthful misbehavior. To understand the persistence and wide distribution of vandalism, for example, it is intuitively sensible to look for its source in the normal course of youngsters' responses to their social situation. Such slim evidence is, of course, in itself not sufficient to support a full-blown theory. But once we open this line of inquiry, we find the data from the Youth in Illinois Project exactly the kind of evidence we need.

What we are calling a half-culture is best understood in comparison with a fully developed culture. The latter is an integral meaning system, based on group experience and formulated in articulated symbols which are socially understood and accepted. A fully developed culture takes time to mature, is not easily changed, and elicits great loyalty and requires great energy from its members. Likewise, culture is developed around the relationship between intuitions and symbols; we might describe the process of creating culture as one in which intuitions seek articulated symbols. The term half-culture, then, designates a group whose intuitions of values have found some legitimate articulation, but not enough to support a fully autonomous group project.

Clearly, then, the concept of a half-culture is not a mathematical one. The mathematical terminology is necessary, however, because the formation of intuitions into legitimate and socially articulated symbol systems is a process which has many stages. It is only in modern industrial society, with its patterns of cultural pluralism and rapid technological change, that we are faced with social systems that embody various stages of this process. If we regard the relationship between intuitions of value and the formation of symbols from this perspective, we are able to see that the distinction between youth as a cultural system and as a mere social group is false. Moreover, by simply replacing the notion of culture versus social group with that of half-culture, we may shed light on some adolescent behavior problems for which social scientists have not previously agreed on solutions.

The half-culture of American youth expresses deep convictions about some important issues and lays down rules and regulations for behavior which are widely accepted within the age group. The foundation for such formulations exists in group experiences which fortify personal feelings and intuitions. Because of their raw power, these feelings and intuitions have considerable impact on behavior, even in the absence of fully articulated symbols, so behavior which conforms to the dictates of the youthful half-culture leads to a sense of personal honor rather than to a sense of shame.

The Social Supports of Youthful Half-Culture

Youthful half-culture in America emerges from the common condition of subordination and marginality experienced by all American adolescents. However, this common condition is experienced differently by different segments of American youth, and youthful half-culture, therefore, has a variety of concrete forms. For example, the children of traditional wealth do not have the same complaints and convictions as the children of poor blacks. But, because of those shared aspects of the general situation of youth in America, continuities exist even among such diverse concrete forms of their subcultures. This is illustrated, for instance, by the fact that vandalism occurs in high schools in wealthy suburbs as well as in those of the inner city.

The subordination and marginality characterizing the experience of all American youth occur on account of three primary factors: (1) exclusion from full participation in the labor force; (2) the legal classification as minors, which excludes adolescents from free access to adult recreations; and (3) the statutory and customary obligation to remain in high school and be subject to the authority of teachers and administrators.

This structure position of adolescents is an adjunct of their process of transition, which Parsons defined in 1942 as being from "the family of orientation" to "the occupational world." Indeed, one focal point of the youthful half-culture is the strain, intrinsic to this transition, involved in changing the nature of interpersonal relationships from ones which are familial, personalistic, and particularistic to those which are formal, instrumental, and universal. This is an objective strain insofar as it is contained in social and cultural institutions; therefore, the actors in question are not necessarily conscious of it. In fact, it is partially because of this very lack of awareness that the youth culture is a half-culture: a central issue of the social situation is not the object of articulate symbolic focus. Yet this strain does cause a considerable portion of adolescents' psychic energy to be invested in experimenting with, testing of, ruminating about, and judging the balance between friendship and intimate relationships on the one hand, and utilitarian instrumental activities and relationships on the other.

Instrumental Moratorium, Cultural Activity

Defining this balance in legitimate symbol systems is a fundamental task of culture. To be viable, any culture must successfully address the relationship between the feelings of personal worth which are derived from domestic relationships—family and friendship; and those derived from societal relationships—chiefly work. In societies where this relationship is definitively established, the process of socialization chiefly involves that meditation necessary to internalize the established norms. The literature on youth in America of the 1940s and 1950s concluded that American youth was engaged in this kind of meditation. There appeared to be a psychosocial moratorium.

However, recent events have caused variety and pluralism to exist in adults' commitments to the demands of "the occupational system." There is no longer a clear definition of the relationship between the personal and domestic sphere of life on the one hand, and the occupational and societal aspect of individual connectedness on the other. This has, in turn, affected the meditation of youth, for adolescents have become aware of new alternatives. Thus, as our data from the Youth in Illinois Project clearly indicate, adolescence in America is now a time not only of instrumental moratorium, but also of intense cultural activity. Today, youngsters must pause to contemplate their options at a fundamental level; they no longer face the simple process of committing themselves to an occupation or role, but instead must define the relationship between the self of personal and intimate connectedness and the self of societal connectedness. Youth's problem is thus a full-fledged cultural one. Indeed, this issue affects adolescents most acutely, for at the core of their stage of socialization is the transition from childhood to the occupational system.

We must not, however, confuse intense cultural activity with high cultural achievement. Adolescents ask trenchant questions about meaning; they are not necessarily in a position to answer them adequately. Even when their questioning is latent and inarticulate, it is still a powerful force in directing their feelings about the people and institutions they encounter in everyday life. Moreover, in a culture as individualistic as ours, youngsters are not easily dissuaded from acting upon their intuitions about meaning. Such issues of meaning are organized into the partially legitimatized symbol system we call the half-culture of American youth.

This definition has some specific and serious implications for the problem of high-school vandalism. The first general implication is that the destruction of high-school property need not be due to individual craziness or to organized conspiracy, but to something else. Acts of vandalism occur because of inarticulate, socially supported, and partly legitimatized claims to virtue, wisdom, and truth on the part of adolescents.

The Variety of Youthful Half-Cultures

When we look at the full range of meanings which youthful half-cultures try to handle, we find that there are three ideal types of such systems. We can call them (1) the socie way of the middle class; (2) the greaser way of the working class; and (3) the way of the freak. There are important variations in the manner in which these types are manifested for the youth of different racial and ethnic groups and for youth who live in different communities. But as ideal types, these are valid aids to understanding the situation of youth in any concrete setting.

The socie cultural style places great value on skills and behavior which harmonize well with occupations requiring "a good impression," literacy, and mental proficiency. Thus, socies' dress is patterned after that of the upper-middle class, and they compete in things that largely involve verbal skills. The greaser cultural style places great value on skills and behavior that harmonize well with occupations requiring manual skills. Thus, greasers dress according to the style of skilled manual laborers, and they compete in areas that largely depend on physical excellence. Youth of both groups form friendships primarily within their own sphere.

Although both socies and greasers may be highly critical of adults, they accept the validity and importance of their connection to a particular stratum of the occupational world. The freak cultural style, however, is based on a suspension of this acceptance. Freaks greatly value behavior and skills that demonstrate this absence of commitment to occupational striving. Thus, their dress and behavior emphasize appearance and demeanor unacceptable in the occupational worlds of socies and greasers.

The socie/greaser/freak typology is very helpful for understanding the social organization of the peer-group world, and for understanding many decisions that adolescents make in daily life. But for understanding the relatively narrow issue of high-school vandalism, we can use another typology. This is fivefold and is based on only one aspect of youth half-cultures; belief in the legitimacy of adult authority. The types are: (1) the demonstratively deferential; (2) the quiescent; (3) the questioning; (4) the truculent; and (5) the militant.

This typology concerns only one aspect of youthful lifestyle and can be superimposed over the socie/greaser/freak typology (if one is not too literal). This system is valuable to the present discussion in that it allows us to make a useful set of hypotheses about the causes of high-school vandalism.

The first of these hypotheses is that the values of any individual teenager tend to range over any three contiguous styles in the typology; that is, each youth could be deferential/quiescent/questioning, or quiescent/questioning/truculent, and so forth. The second hypothesis is that the distribution of youths is skewed over these categories, with the mean being in the quiescent. According to the third, the truculent (youths who are either principally or temporarily characterized by that) account for the vast majority of acts of vandalism to high-school property. Finally, we hypothesize that the social support of vandalism is distributed in a linear fashion from low in category one to high in category five.

Let us describe these five types of youth more fully. Due to complex factors of their experience to date, teenagers come to school with a scalar like or dislike of adult authority. The demonstratively deferential are frequently regular churchgoers, not because they have to be, but because they find religion intrinsically meaningful. While they vary in intelligence, in style of dress, and in social background, they like to participate in activities organized by adults. The quiescent move through youth unobstrusively. They are not joiners, cause no trouble, and do average to excellent work in class. The questioners are outwardly very much like the quiescent, except they are more aware of the problems of others. They have not yet taken any position, and they see no wisdom in openly confronting authority. The truculent, by contrast, are by tradition or personal disposition more likely to engage in open confrontation. Although they have no clearly defined justification for their feelings, they are willing to act. An ideology confirms the militant in their truculence.

As far as the socie/greaser/freak typology is concerned, we encountered various combinations in our field work. The youth's common condition of being economically and politically subordinate makes possible many mixtures of occupational orientation and feelings about adult authority. The militant socie is an example: this is the straight-looking academic achiever, definitely headed for college, who could still spray-paint "off the pigs" on a school building. The deferential freak occurs frequently: denim-clad, loose, long-haired, ex-dope using Jesus enthusiast. Every other possible combination also exists. Neither socie nor greaser nor freak is limited to one style of thinking and action with regard to adult authority symbols.

High School: Symbol and Operation

The high school is a symbol as well as an operation. What it does in its day-to-day program is one thing; what it stands for in the minds of its students is another. Adults usually think of high school as a pragmatic program for acquiring the skills necessary for economic success and the social habits of mature citizenship. In the minds of the students, however, high school certainly has its instrumental side, but it is also a symbol of adult civil authority, power, and control.

Some high schools succeed in presenting themselves as familial communities in which the quality of personal relationships between adults and adolescents is as important as the instrumental effectiveness of role relationships between teachers and students. When this occurs, it is usually in the smaller private schools which charge tuition, not in the vast majority of American high schools, for the latter are civil institutions designed to serve purely instrumental purposes. The interactions between staff and pupils are based primarily on clear role definitions. While the quality of personal relationships between particular staff members and particular students is expected to conform to the minimum standards of politeness and decency, instrumental effectiveness overshadows interpersonal solidarity. Furthermore, to the extent that school personnel assume the maturity of the culture which determines their activities, they are not readily open to review issues of meaning. Their focus is pragmatic.

The staff of a high school has control over its students, and adult individuals and groups have control over the school premises. What to build and how to build it, when the buildings will be open or closed, what activities will be permitted in them, maintenance, and so forth—all these rights and responsibilities fall elsewhere than on the students in the school. Thus, there are manifold grounds on which high-school students may doubt that the facilities they use belong to them. Rather, they belong to such civil entities as the state, town, or community.

The treatment of high-school property can thus very easily become a focal point for youthful sentiments about their relationship to the civic whole. If we recognize that the potential for alienation is inherent to the status of adolescents, we have our first basis for considering vandalism as the logical outcome of the relationship between the half-culture of youth and the socialization agencies of society.

The Legitimization of Discontent

Dissent is an articulate cognitive stance in disagreement with established norms. Discontent, however, is an inarticulate feeling. In the half-culture of American youth, there is some legitimization of dissent, but this is not nearly so widespread as the legitimization of discontent. We do not need a catalogue of specific complaints to understand the general support in the half-cultures of youth for gestures which express feelings ranging from mere unconcern to positive hostility regarding high schools. Dissent is not necessary for the performance of vandalism; discontent is sufficient. In fact, because of the very inarticulateness of discontent, it is more likely to be a basis of vandalism than is dissent; the latter leads more easily to organized forms of protest. The vandalism we are witnessing today is characteristically disorganized.

The Distribution of Vandalism

The high schools which suffer least from vandalism appear to be smaller, private, expensive schools which provide academic training to the children of the affluent. High schools in small towns or communities which have preserved a familial atmosphere are also comparatively safe. But our ethnographic data show that even here the children of a town's "better families" no longer protect the school from acts of vandalism as well as they used to.

In both of these cases, what protects school property from vandalism is the connection of the students to the school, which is fostered by the connection of the students' parents to the school. In the small town, the parents' membership in the local community contributes to their sense of control over the school. In private schools, parents' monetary investment often brings with it a sense of personal investment. Since parents are generally welcome and frequent visitors and advisors in a private school, students there can feel that the institution is an extension of the family. This community solidarity or direct family investment constructs a social bond between domestic solidarities and values and the educational institution.

When we look at the large, complex school systems of big cities, we find greater geographic mobility of families and the phenomenon of large-scale, impersonal bureaucracies. In its own way, each of these phenomena breaks the personal connection between parents and school. Additionally, urban high schools are often integral parts of a civic whole which has failed to integrate and satisfy the needs of large segments of its population. High schools are only one vulnerable target for the anger of children of excluded minorities.

The Meanings of Vandalism

The high cost of vandalism is the result of many relatively small acts of destruction which accumulate over time to cause severe damage to high-school property. Although arson and even bombings do occur, they are rare and account for a small percentage of the total dollar cost of vandalism. What adds up to the immense cost we are speaking of is a graffito here, a smashed window there, now a forced lock, now a broken chair, and so forth.

Given that the high school symbolizes adult control over adolescent life, that in it there is a pervasive undercurrent of discontent, and that there is widespread distribution of truculence, we can see that these small acts of vandalism can arise from a variety of motives.

Some destruction occurs by accident or through misguided exuberance. Because of a playful shove or an angry argument, bodies move and something gets broken. This happens even in homes. But in school, everything belongs to the government and money is an issue; so nobody wants to get caught.

Another motive is selective carelessness. If the phenomenon of littering were investigated carefully, we would surely see that one causative factor is subliminal alienation. Teenagers do not throw beer cans on the kitchen floor of their own homes, nor do they put out cigarettes on the top of their family television set. But if they dislike high school, which they are forced to attend, they perceive many opportunities for extending the boundaries of normal wear and tear.

Narcissistic projection is another motive. Students have always carved their initials on their desks, but former generations lacked our indelible felt-tipped pens and our spray paint. Moreover, in an institution where individuals feel anonymous and lost, there also are many other ways to make one's mark so as to go down in history and gain the momentary respect of fellow sufferers. Acts so motivated can account for a lot of property damage. They do not require conspiracy, or even a lot of thought. Rather, they simply require a half-culture which gives tacit approval before, during, and after the fact.

If we add to these less articulated motives the organized truculence of some youth gangs, ideological protest, and property-oriented terrorism, we have a full range of motivations for vandalism. But these last three phenomena are much less important than those mentioned previously. Although this is only our own subjective impression which still must be subjected to empirical verification, we strongly believe that these three motives lead to only a small percentage of the current destruction of high-school property.

Furthermore, these last three phenomena cannot exist in isolation from the ones mentioned earlier, but those others can exist in isolation from these. This is true because extreme or organized forms of truculence are extensions of the central phenomenon: the passive and inarticulate forms of discontent permitted by the intuitions and feelings which are the basis of the half-culture of youth. Without this symbolic matrix of uncertainty and exploration, the truculent expressions of alienation would have no social support at all. This is a case of bandits being sheltered by the ethos of the poor and disenfranchised.

Responses to Vandalism

Four models for responses to high-school vandalism seem to address themselves to real facets of the situation.

Dominance/Antagonism Model

One is the dominance/antagonism model, currently being used in many institutions and counterinsurgency military operations. This involves, for example, electronic surveillance, police presence, indestructible partitions, undercover agents, and informers. Although sensitive officials already recognize that the use of these techniques turns schools into jails or armed camps, they are first attempts by amateurs in the fields of public safety and military tactics. It is clearly possible for such techniques to move away from reliance on crude technology, and for officials to develop strategies which draw on more sophisticated techniques of warfare.

There is, for example, the technique of blandishment and deceit; this involves calling for open discussion of the situation, getting the enemy to reveal itself, and then punishing severely. A less extreme program would be the detection and isolation of the truculent and militant segments of schools through special programs or special schools; maximum-security institutions. There are any number of rationalizations for such procedures. When the problem is seen purely as a behavioral one, and the correct relationship between school and students is seen as one of dominance in the face of antagonistic interests, this type of technique is not unthinkable.

Therefore, the main problem with using the techniques of penology and warfare has nothing to do with failure of technology or limited ingenuity of authorities. If officials really set their minds to it, they have the resources and the skills to win this war. Rather, the problem involves mistakenly defining the situation in terms of dominance and antagonistic interests. How can any society make war upon its own children?

Public-Relations Model

The logic underlying the public-relations model is that most vandalism is symbolic rather than pragmatic in nature, and that the response to vandalism should, therefore, be to manipulate symbols. A public-relations campaign would, then, address the symbolic deficiencies of high school. One tactic might be to change the vague definition of the high school as part of the civic whole and to present its real services to the students and to the local community. It would thus symbolically appear to be more of a local community institution, closer to its students, and less of an impersonal extension of distant powers. There are doubtless many other tactics which could be used according to this model. To the extent that a high school or a high-school system is the innocent victim of unjustified symbolic connections, a skillful ad campaign could prove helpful.

There are two important difficulties with this approach. One is that high-school students are acutely able to recognize symbolic glibness. When this fact is coupled with the frequently naive views of administrators and faculty toward their own institutions, the possibility of failure to do the job with insight becomes very real. The second major problem is that, in many cases, the adolescent and parental diagnosis of the high school's failings is painfully accurate. In cases where the school is oppressive, unprofessional, discriminating, self-righteous, and so forth, even the best of public-relations campaigns will fall flat.

The Student Connection: Negotiation Model

The peculiar nature of the half-culture of youth poses serious problems for any negotiation model based on traditional images of political process or labor contract negotiation. The central difficulty is the asymmetric articulation of the positions to be negotiated.

Adults have a culture; adolescents have a half-culture. Teenagers have strong feelings and intuitions about their situation, but, in their condition of marginality and subordination, they lack the material and symbolic resources adults have for articulating and defending their position. Second, the adults involved in high schools are organized, whereas the students are disorganized. Third, according to statute, custom, and tradition, adults in high schools have dominative power. High-school students have no power at all.

Because of this total asymmetry in the positions of the two parties presumed to have an interest in the problem, negotiations cannot follow any traditional two-party model or third-party arbitration model. In the first place, students cannot easily come to the bargaining table with defensible, articulated demands. Second, because of the variety of youthful half-cultures and the disorganization of youth, there is, at present, no solidarity of support for student demands. Third, if negotiations break down, the inequality of power places student leaders in an extremely vulnerable position. In order for high-school students to take part in progressive negotiation about the preservation of these institutions, they must have power, solidarity, and cultural assistance.

The Parental Connection: Community Process Model

We noted earlier that those high schools that have created a familial atmosphere and that operate with the serious investment and close concern of parents seem to be relatively free of vandalism. We also noted that such institutions are rare. One logical implication of the first of these observations is that a strong parental connection can result in decreased vandalism.

However, such a connection is a social relationship dependent on a fine web of informal interactions which take place over long periods of time. It is also a political relationship between civil authorities and local population groups. High schools which enjoy good social and political relations with their local communities are, in fact, open and accessible to parents. In school districts that encompass greatly diverse economic and ethnic groups, have high rates of geographic mobility, and are enmeshed in a large bureaucracy, openness and accessibility are notoriously difficult to achieve. In many cases, creating them appears to require complete reorganization of the social and political relationships between community and school.

It is not surprising that such reorganization may be necessary to effect a substantial decrease in high-school vandalism. For, if vandalism is related to the combination of youth's social and political marginality on the one hand and to the half-formed nature of youth culture on the other, then it must be a natural result of the lopsided distribution of power in the community/school complex. Indeed, the "naturalness" of vandalism is basic to the hypotheses advanced in this chapter. Admittedly, ours is a theory which must yet be tested empirically; but our data on the overall situation of youth indicates that our ideas must be taken seriously. Both the family and the school are institutions of great importance to the socialization of youth. Thus, the triangular nature of the linkages among family, school, and teenagers has to be the focal point for analysis and reform.

Conclusion

An empirical investigation into the sources of vandalism on high-school property would begin by surveying the distribution of the phenomenon in schools in different settings. This should lead to an analysis of the grievances on which the symbolic action is based. Such a study should in turn lead to an understanding of the conflicts which may divide the high-school—its personnel, policies, and programs—from its teenaged clients and their families. This set of conflicts could then be presented together in the form of an alienation profile of the high schools in question. The profile could provide a clue to the relative usefulness of the four models for responding to vandalism.

20 A Preparadigmatic Field: A Review of Research on School Vandalism

April Zweig and
Michael H. Ducey

The nature of research about school vandalism has changed in the past several years. While older research (1958-1969) follows normal science models for juvenile-delinquency studies, recent research (1970 to the present) is mostly administration oriented and features the tentative development of new theoretical approaches. The early research (Clinard and Wade 1958; Bates 1962; Bates and McJunkins 1962) produced a description of the youthful vandal as a working-class, minority male with possible personality disorders. His destructive behaviors were frequently attributed to his family life, rather than to dissatisfaction or frustration with school. Vandalism did not become a major concern until the 1970s when its clear prominence brought about changes in the style of research. There was a need for more practically oriented research which would provide educators with workable recommendations for reforms they could implement in school programs. Our literature search clearly shows these two distinct trends in research.

We initially surveyed the literature by reviewing abstracts from two Education Resources Information Center (ERIC) searches titled "School Vandalism" and "School Vandalism and Students' Attitudes Toward Authority." We also obtained bibliographies from a recently completed dissertation, from government research projects concerned with delinquency, and from the Stanford Research Institute's final report, which contained 255 references. Material was obtained from these sources until it began to overlap. This chapter will review the various approaches we discovered in the study of school vandalism and will attempt to define what is needed to prevent it now.

Incidence and Costs

Government agencies and school districts have worked together in conducting investigations to obtain estimates of the incidence and cost of vandalism in schools. The most voluminous of these investigations is Bayh's (1975) report to Congress, which estimated the annual cost of vandalism at $500 million. The U.S. Office of Education, however, estimates that damage to school property approaches $100 million annually.

In its attempts to determine the severity of this problem, research has not yet even overcome the difficulties involved in finding nonuniform accounting techniques and definitions of vandalism:

> In our review of the literature, and work with heavily vandalized schools and school systems, it has been evident that there is little general agreement on the meaning of terms much less on the effectiveness of specified measures. [The Council of the Great City Schools, 1976, p. 7]

Formerly, vandalism was viewed as a local phenomenon, and individual school districts defined their own problems and found their own solutions. But vandalism has now been recognized as a national problem, and those discrepancies in figures which result from the lack of agreement just noted increase the difficulty of finding solutions.

Three additional issues currently receiving research attention are: (1) identification of the perpetrators of vandalism; (2) causes of school vandalism; and (3) development of response programs that enable schools to reduce this behavior.

Identification of Student Vandals

Clinard and Wade's (1958) typological approach to juvenile delinquency depends almost entirely on demographic characteristics as independent variables. According to their statistics, more boys than girls are involved in vandalism. These vandals are preadolescents to adolescents, and they tend to outgrow the behavior in late adolescence. Clinard and Wade found that the empirical evidence concerning social class is contradictory, leading them to speculate that while vandalism serves a similar function for working-class and middle-class boys, it is instigated for different reasons. These authors describe studies on the group nature of vandalism; it often starts as random group play and, through continuation, becomes deliberate. This study represents an attempt to use standard but unrefined techniques to attack the problem. Bates' study (1962) similarly relies on demographic characteristics as measures. Both works reflect the position of sociologists in the 1960s. But vandalism is more complex than they would have it; if we are to find solutions, there must be more theoretical refinement.

Richards' recent research on vandalism (1976) explores sex and grade trends; relationships between attitudes and self-reported vandalism; interactions in family life which are related to vandalism; and school experiences which are related to this behavior. Her study contained self-report data from 3,000 middle-class children in the fifth through twelfth grades. Self-reports of damaging and defacing property peaked around the seventh grade and declined steadily through high school. Richards' data on sex differences contradict the usual assumption that vandalism is more frequent among boys than girls. For girls not only reported more vandalism than was expected, but in some instances (such as participation in school defacement), their rates even exceeded those of boys.

In tracing relationships between attitudes and self-reported vandalism, Richards found the strongest links to be those connected with students' expressions of anger toward parents or school officials. The target of this anger appeared to be important, for items related to daily interactions with authority figures showed associations with vandalism. This suggests that students' dependent situation and lack of autonomy may be connected to experiences and attitudes (for example, feeling ignored) which show some relationship to vandalism. Measures of psychological maladjustment show the weakest links with self-reported vandalism.

Richards suggests that it is students' responses to school experiences, rather than any specific school experience per se, which most influence the child's decision to vandalize. Again, her data indicate that the relationship between specific situations and self-reported vandalism is such that property destruction is more targeted than it is generally assumed to be.

An assumption of sociological research in the 1950s and 1960s—that working class, maladjusted boys commit most acts of vandalism—is not substantiated by current research (Goldmeier 1974; Bayh 1975; Richards 1976; McGuire 1976). Thus, in an analysis of causes and incidence, we move from issues of social class, gender, and personality characteristics toward a broader explanation that takes into account the influence of provoking situations and the youth culture in which they occur. The attempt to develop more sophisticated causal models is a recent phenomenon.

Causes of School Vandalism

As researchers continue their efforts to explain causes of school vandalism, Cohen's (1971) and Ward's (1973) distinction between conventional and ideological vandalism helps bring to the surface the perception of vandalism as a form of violence that must be considered apart from such other acts of violence as homicide, burglary, and rape. Of the two, Ward's analysis of types of vandalism has the greater focus on meanings, motives, and patterns. In addition to his delineation of conventional forms of vandalism (acquisitive, tactical, vindictive, play, malicious) and distinctions between rationales for conventional and for ideologically inspired vandalism, Ward recognized that the convergence in adult perceptions and responses of each is because "the overt behavioral characteristic of ideological vandalism is identical with that of conventional vandalism" (Ward 1973, p. 114).

Cohen recognized these convergences between conventional and ideologically inspired vandalism, but he questioned the effect society's interpretation of vandalism has on the behavior itself. He suggests that society's dramatization of the extent and costs of vandalism should tell us something about the community that places a "high degree of problem awareness" on such behavior.

Cohen's and Ward's studies mark the transition from traditional demographic approaches and current situational approaches. The former represent valuable theoretical efforts reflecting the position of sociologists in the 1960s and early 1970s, while the latter confront issues of social reform, social relationships, and the environment.

Some examples of situational factors are school architecture, adult and community responses, family relationships, and perceptions of school experiences (Ward 1973; Zeizel 1974; Zimbardo 1969). According to Zimbardo, symbols of social order are the targets of vandalism. For, in engaging in such behavior, students are expressing their dissatisfaction and frustration with their lives at home and at school, and with their role in the community. Indeed, much speculation and empirical research has attempted to identify the origin of this dissatisfaction.

Through examining variables such as school performance, parental expectations of a child's performance, family rule structure, and peer processes, Richards found some modest relationships between those variables and vandalism, but not enough to provide a basis for theorizing.

Hence, objective aspects of adolescents' lives do not appear to cause them to vandalize; rather, it would seem that the combination of feelings and experiences in daily life produce a sense of alienation from the adult world. The adolescent's role in society is not well-defined (Ducey 1978); he or she constantly encounters a world that does not trust his or her judgment as a youth. The youngster's difficulties and nonacceptance in school and in the community result in his or her feeling alienated. Beyond speculating, no one has yet explored what the measurable conditions are that create a sense of alienation, but it is to this very point that synthesizing previous research has led us.

Clearly, this body of research is moving toward causal models to define the problem of vandalism. Much of this has, in fact, been done in the area of juvenile delinquency, but the work there has not been systematically applied to school vandalism.

The importance of the physical environment of school as a determinant of behavior has been noted by Ward (1973), Zeizel (1974), Zimbardo (1969), and others. However, this concept has been applied primarily in responding to vandalism and will be dealt with in the following section.

Local Response Programs

Education journals are replete with articles on how to deal with vandalism in schools. For the most part, these articles report the initiatives taken by a particular school or district to reduce vandalism. Most of these programs tighten security through the use of alarm systems, closed-circuit television, increased lighting, and plainclothes police. Success is measured in dollars saved (Dukiet 1973; Miller and Beer 1974). Other approaches reported to reduce vandalism are behavioral-modification techniques (Haney 1973) and increasing community involvement in schools.

However, several issues arise when we attempt to evaluate the effectiveness of these local programs. First, there is the "Hawthorne Effect": what is the result of focusing the students' and community's attention on the problem?

> There may have been a cyclical dropoff having nothing whatever to do with the experiment itself. Perhaps the "Hawthorne Effect" may be an explanation, that is, the mere fact that some attention was being drawn to the schools' vandalism problems may have been sufficient to effect the glass breakage reduction. (Greenberg 1974, p. 14)

Another explanation which has not been considered previously is the "sleeper effect." If there is no further intervention, immediately perceived success at the behavioral level may disappear, for the stimuli (security measures) do not address root causes. A *Year One* vs. *Year Two* definition of success may be invalid.

We must also question what is meant by a "successful" program to reduce school vandalism. The literature reports that, at great expense, schools have created security systems to prevent window smashing, equipment theft, and defacement of property. Destructive behavior decreases, but the difference between the cost of it and that of security systems can be minimal (Greenberg 1974). Is it worth the effort and money required to install such devices, and how does such installation affect other behavior? As these systems work to decrease vandalism, what will happen with regard to the experiences that instigate vandalism? That is, if vandalism is caused by motivations such as anger and frustration, is it necessary for students to find other outlets for their expression?

Although the education literature is filled with reports on successful programs, Greenberg cites one instance of a costly failure. And current reports reveal that there are other similar cases. Such failures occur because the schools rely on using power rather than on restructuring social relationships. The security measures used in schools represent such power. The use of power should be a last resort in the resolution of social conflict. The vandalism problem is complex, and it has not been solved by government hearings, mail surveys to ascertain its extent, or literature reviews describing how school vandalism has been decreased at great expense. Studies have not yet produced less repressive and less costly solutions.

A review of the measures of success in local response programs shows the lack of well-grounded criteria for evaluating these programs. And, because of the lack of theoretically grounded measures, problem solving is difficult.

However, the current interest in prevention may indicate that concerned individuals are ready to balance the behavioral control outlook with an approach that deals with motivational aspects of the problem. More efficient, theoretically oriented evaluation techniques should present educators with information on the sources of vandalism.

A difficulty inherent in many prevention programs is that strategies to reduce vandalism are planned before the problem has been carefully diagnosed. The desire to stop vandalism at any expense has preceded and overshadowed consideration of that behavior's motives and meanings. Now, though, we must question whether just changing the behavior is what we want. If we are interested in so-called primary prevention (Ward 1973), then it is as important that we examine motivators as it is that we solve the overt behavioral problem itself.

Zimbardo (1969) has impressively shown the important relation of the physical environment to the behavior of individuals in the community. He suggests that modification of the physical environment to make it more harmonious with social needs is more effective than social coercion. This notion that the physical environment influences social behavior relocates the pathology from the individual to his surroundings (Ward 1973).

Ward (1973) and Zeizel (1974) have utilized this theory of "architectural determinism" in their prevention programs to reduce crime. They present two alternatives, the first of which is to design the school so that it is aesthetically pleasing and thereby to instill pride and care in its students. The second is to create a structurally crime-proof fortress with no windows, special paint to prevent defacement, and so forth.

The idea of restructuring the physical environment to lessen vandalism is legitimate for environments that invite the behavior. One example of such a physical change would be to construct a fence around the school. Obviously, the school is for children to use, but in this case, the presence of the fence to protect the school from these same children would create a paradox, for that would produce anger and alienation. The fence would be an encouragement, a challenge, so that structure, if not the school, would become a more likely target for vandals.

The recent orientation of research dealing with situational factors moves away from reliance on power as a means of social control and heads toward restructuring the social and physical environments. Thus, the apparently random failure of tight security systems has in fact begun to lead researchers toward a broader view of vandalism.

National Response Programs

Government agencies have been sponsoring major research efforts to help design programs to reduce school violence. For instance, in 1976, the Law

Enforcement Assistance Administration (LEAA) requested Research for Better Schools (RBS) to design a program which would establish a working relationship between LEAA and the educational community and which would provide information for LEAA to use in helping schools reduce crime. The specific tasks of RBS were: (1) to examine the nature and extent of school violence; (2) to find out what efforts are being made to reduce school violence; (3) to determine what schools need in order to reduce crime; and (4) to find out how other federally funded programs are helping schools.

With respect to this fourth task, however, RBS found that evaluations of school programs are few. This is due, in part, to the constantly changing techniques and goals of the programs. And, using available data from a earlier study in which school superintendents were asked what LEAA could do to improve delinquency prevention, RBS additionally notes that only 42 percent of the school districts responded to the questionnaire. This group also stated that, according to teachers, school administrators are not facing up to the problem of school crime. This has been an issue in contract negotiations.

RBS suggests, however, that the burden of problem definition be assigned to each school requesting assistance. This recommendation is problematic in the light of such lack of participation on the part of school administrators. Though regional and national LEAA staffs will be available to support local efforts, there is neither a systematic approach to evaluating an individual school's crime problem nor much coordination between the diagnosis of the problem and the organization of the responses. To achieve the desired changes, crime prevention programs must speak to the problems which exist in each specific school. A wider range of alternatives, in the areas of both problem definition and problem solving, must be presented to administrators, teachers, and agencies concerned with crime prevention.

RBS developed a technical assistance strategy having the following features: (1) provision of small grants to individual schools or districts to stimulate adoption of programs; (2) establishment of regional staffs to offer technical assistance; and (3) development of national programs to support local efforts. The strategy designed by RBS appears to provide lines of communication between government personnel and school officials and thus to establish a relationship between the two. However, specific objectives and evaluation criteria are still lacking, and this lack can cripple any efforts that are made.

The *Safe School Study*, conducted between 1977 and 1978 by the National Institute of Education at the request of Congress, was designed to provide two major types of information: (1) descriptions of the nature and extent of crime in schools and of current attempts at prevention; and (2) an explanation of why crime varies between schools and an indication of the effectiveness of crime-prevention strategies being used in the different schools. This study uses established theories derived from research in sociology, psychology, and criminology, and it is the first major attempt to apply delinquency theory to policy issues on vandalism.

The project's overall conception and its objectives are indicative of a new and positive trend in research in this area. For school vandalism cannot be isolated from other problems in the educational community; rather, it must be studied in a climate of openness, with a realistic view of the environment in which it occurs.

The final report of the Stanford Research Institute study (1975) documents the methodological approach for evaluating the problem of vandalism. Special data-collection forms were sent to schools in order to achieve a unified reporting scheme which would aid in the analysis of information concerned with cost and frequency of vandalism; methods used to combat vandalism; characteristics of the known vandal; and questioning of representatives of schools. However, this was the most difficult and time-consuming task of the study, and it was ultimately "far beyond the resources that were available to this project" (Stanford 1975, p. 15).

Interviews with members of the school community showed that there are differing opinions about the motivational factors involved in vandalism and that the level of concern over vandalism as a problem depends on the individual who is affected. For instance, students perceive locker vandalism as a greater problem than do school administrators, while the administrators are more concerned about graffiti.

The project of the Stanford Research Institute has shown that vandalism must be viewed as a multifaceted problem, no aspect of which can be ignored. Whether research focuses on motivational aspects of the problem or on overt behavioral characteristics, shortcuts taken simply to stop immediate manifestations will not necessarily serve as long-term preventive measures.

Concluding Remarks

The main contribution of early research on vandalism is its pointing out of an intellectual dead end. By themselves, conventional demographic approaches to the problem lead nowhere. Since 1970, five distinct research issues have been identified, the first being the absence of satisfactory reporting and measuring techniques to provide baseline data. The second is the development of causal models which include situational factors and motivational constructs. The third is the problematic relationship between school vandalism and larger social forces. The fourth is an outcome of the defensive stance which many schools take in response to research focused on vandalism as their problem. The fifth is the absence of any theoretical basis for well-grounded cost-benefit studies of security programs.

Clearly, the social-science community has not dealt adequately with the phenomenon of school vandalism. In this respect, researchers and administrators are in the same situation. The *Safe School Study* of the National Institute of Education is the most important of the many recent research efforts. But in terms of analysis, this is a preparadigmatic field, and we can expect still more failure before the emergence of a successful diagnosis.

Bibliography

Acock, A.C. and DeFleur, M.L. A configurational approach to contingent consistence in the attitude-behavior relationship. *American Sociological Review* 37 (1972):714-726.

Ahlstrom, W.M. and Havighurst, R.J. *400 Losers.* San Francisco: Jossey-Bass, 1971.

AIR. *Ex-students Pinpoint Wrongs in Nation's High Schools.* Palo Alto, CA: American Institutes for Research, 1976.

Allen, V.L., and Greenberger, D.B. Destruction and perceived control. Edited by A. Baum and J. Singer. In *Advances in Environmental Psychology* (vol. II). Hillsdale, N.J.: Erlbaum, 1980.

──── . An aesthetic theory of vandalism. *Crime and Delinquency* 24 (1978): 309-21.

Allen, V.L., and Spencer, D.R. Initial complexity and preference for destruction. Unpublished manuscript, University of Wisconsin, Madison, 1977.

Allen, V.L., and Sobel, S. Preference for destruction and size of stimulus object. Unpublished manuscript, University of Wisconsin, Madison, 1978.

Archer, R.L. *Secondary Education in the 19th Century.* Cambridge, England: Cambridge University Press, 1921.

Argyris, C. *Personality and Organization.* New York: Harper and Row, 1957.

Aries, P. *Centuries of Childhood.* New York: Alfred A. Knopf, 1962.

Arnold, D.O. A process model of subcultures. In *The Sociology of Subcultures.* Edited by D.O. Arnold. Berkeley: Glendessary Press, 1970.

Aronson, E. Some antecedents of interpersonal attraction. In *Nebraska Symposium on Motivation.* Edited by W.J. Arnold and L. Levine. 1969.

Aronson, E. and Mettee, D.R. Dishonest behavior as a function of differential levels of induced self-esteem. *Journal of Personality and Social Psychology* 9 (1968):121-127.

Ashley-Cooper, A., Seventh Earl of Shaftesbury. The ragged schools. *Quarterly Review* 79 (1847):127-41.

Atkinson, J.W., and Feather, N.T. (eds.). *A Theory of Achievement Motivation.* New York: John Wiley, 1966.

Ausubel, D.P. and Robinson, F.G. *School Learning.* New York: Holt, Rinehart, and Winston, 1969.

Backman, J.G. *The impact of family background and intelligence on tenth grade boys.* Vol. II of *Youth in Transition.* Ann Arbor: Institute for Social Research, 1970.

Backman, J.G.; Green, A.; and Wiranen, I.D. *Dropping out—problem or symptom.* Vol. III of *Youth in Transition.* Ann Arbor: University of Michigan, Braun-Brumfield, Ind., 1971.

Backman, J.G.; Kahan, R.L.; Mednick, M.T.; Davidson, T.; and Johnston, L.D. *Blueprint for a longitudinal study of adolescent boys.* Vol. I of *Youth in Transition.* Ann Arbor: Institute for Social Research, 1967.

Bailyn, B. *Education in the Forming of American Society.* Chapel Hill: University of North Carolina Press, 1960.

Balow, B. The emotionally and socially handicapped. *Review of Educational Research* 36 (1966):120-33.

Bandura, A. Self-efficacy: Toward a unifying theory of behavioral change. *Psychological Review* 84 (1977):191-215.

Bandura, A. and Walters, R.H. *Adolescent Aggression.* New York: Ronald Press, 1959.

Barker, R.G., et al. *Big School, Small School: Studies of the Effects of High School Size upon the Behavior and Experiences of Students.* Lawrence, Kans.: Midwest Psychological Field Station, University of Kansas, 1962.

Barker, R.G. and Gump, P.V. *Big School, Small School: High School Size and Student Behavior.* Palo Alto, Calif.: Stanford University Press, 1964.

Bates, W.C. Class and vandalism. *Social Problems* 9 (1962):349-53.

Bates, W. and McJunkins, T. Vandalism and status differences. *Pacific Sociological Review* 2 (1962):89-92.

Bayh, B. *Our Nation's Schools: A Report Card—'A' in School Violence and Vandalism.* Washington, D.C.: U.S. Government Printing Office, 1975.

Becker, H.S. *Outsiders.* New York: Free Press, 1963.

Begle, E. Time devoted to instruction and student achievement. *Educational Studies in Mathematics.* Holland: Reidel Publications, 1971.

Bellaby, P. The distribution of deviance among 13-14 year old students. In *Contemporary Research in the Sociology of Education.* Edited by John Eggleston. London: Methuen, 1974, pp. 167-68.

Bend, E. *The Impact of Athletic Participation on Academic and Career Aspiration and Achievement.* New Brunswick, N.J.: The National Football Foundation, 1968.

Bennett, V.D.C. An investigation of the relationships among child's self-concept, achievement, intelligence, body size, and the size of their figure drawing. Unpublished manuscript, n.d.

Berg, I. *Education and Jobs: The Great Training Robbery.* Boston: Beacon Press, 1971.

Berger, M. *Violence in the Schools: Causes and Remedies.* Bloomington, Ind.: The Phi Delta Kappa Educational Foundation, 1974.

Berkowitz, L. (ed.). *Roots of Aggression: A Reexamination of the Frustration Aggression Hypothesis.* New York: Atherton, 1969.

Berlyne, D.E. *Aesthetics and Psychobiology.* New York: Appleton-Century-Crofts, 1971.

_____. *Conflict, Arousal, and Curiosity.* New York: McGraw-Hill, 1960.

Bernard, J.L. and Eisenman, R. Verbal conditioning in sociopaths with social and monetary reinforcement. *Journal of Personality and Social Psychology* 6 (1967):203-206.

Bledsoe, J.C. Self-concepts of children and their intelligence, achievement, interests, and anxiety. *Journal of Individual Psychology* 20 (1964):55-58.
Bloch, A.M. The battered teacher. *Today's Education*, March-April 1977.
──. Combat neurosis in inner-city schools. *American Journal of Psychiatry* 135 (1978):1189-92.
Boocock, S.S. *An Introduction to the Sociology of Learning.* New York: Houghton Mifflin Company, 1972.
Bordua, D.J. Sociological perspectives. In *Social Deviancy among Youth, The Sixty-Fifth Yearbook of the National Society for Educators–Part I.* Edited by William W. Wattenberg. Chicago: The University of Chicago Press, 1966.
Borkovec, T.D. Autonomic reactivity in sensory stimulation in psychopathic, neurotic and normal delinquents. *Journal of Consulting and Clinical Psychology* 35 (1970):217-22.
Bourne, W.O. *History of the Public School Society of the City of New York.* New York, New York, 1870.
Bowles, S. Unequal education and the reproduction of the social division of labor. In *Schooling in a Corporate Society.* Edited by M. Carnoy. New York: David McKay Co., 1972.
Bowman, P.H. Effects of a revised school program on the potential delinquent. *Annals of the American Academy of Political and Social Science* 322 (1959):53-62.
Boyd, G.F. The level of aspirations of white and negro children in a non-segregated elementary school. *Journal of Social Psychology* 36 (1952):191-96.
Brameld, T. *Cultural Foundations of Education.* New York: Harper, 1957.
Brecher, E.M. *Licit and Illicit Drugs.* Boston: Little, Brown, 1972.
Brodow, R. *Reducing School Absenteeism: A Management Approach.* Ed. D. Dissertation, Teachers College, Columbia University, in progress.
Bronfenbrenner, U. The origins of alienation. *Scientific American* 231 (1973):41-53.
──. *Two Worlds of Childhood: U.S. and U.S.S.R.* New York: Russell Sage, 1973.
Brophy, J.E. and Good, T.L. *Teacher-Student Relationships: Causes and Consequences.* New York: Holt, Rinehart, and Winston, 1974.
Brown, R. *The Reform of Secondary Education.* New York: McGraw-Hill, 1973.
Brown, R.G. A comparison of vocational aspirations of paired sixth-grade white and negro children who attend segregated schools. *Journal of Education Research* 58 (1965):402-414.
Bryan, J.H. and Kapche, R. Psychopathy and verbal conditioning. *Journal of Abnormal Psychology* 72 (1967):71-73.
Buffalo, M.D. and Rogers, J.W. Behavioral norms, moral norms and attachment: problems of deviance and conformity. *Social Problems* 19 (1971):101-13.
Burgess, E.W. The economic factor in juvenile delinquency. *Journal of Criminal Law, Criminology, and Police Science* 43 (1952):29-42.
Butts, R.F. and Cremin, L.A. *A History of Education in American Culture.* New York: Henry Holt and Company, 1953.

Buxton, D.E. *Adolescents in School.* New Haven: Yale University Press, 1973.
Byrne, D. Attitudes and attraction. In *Advances in Experimental Psychology.* Edited by L. Berkowitz. New York: Academic Press, 1969.
_____. Interpersonal attraction and attitude similarity. *Journal of Abnormal and Social Psychology* 62 (1961):713-15.
California Commission for Reform of Intermediate and Secondary Education. *The RISE Report.* Sacramento, Calif.: California State Department of Education, 1975.
Calvin, J., *The Catechism on Manner to Teach Children the Christian Religion.* London: British Museum, 1556.
Caplan, R.D.; Cobb, S.; French, J.R.P., Jr.; Harrison, R.V.; and Pinneau, S.R., Jr. *Job Demands and Worker Health: Main Effects and Occupational Differences* (USGPO Catalog No. HE 20.7111:J57. USGPO Stock No. 1733-00083). Washington, D.C.: U.S. Government Printing Office, 1975.
Cardinelli, C.F. Relationship of interaction of selected personality characteristics of school principal and custodian with sociological variables to school vandalism. Unpublished doctoral dissertation, Michigan State University, 1969.
_____. Let's get at the causes of youthful vandalism. *American School Board Journal* 1 (1961):68-69.
Carnegie Council on Policy Studies in Higher Education. *Giving Youth a Better Chance.* San Francisco: Jossey-Bass, 1979.
Carnoy, M. and Levin, H. *The Limits of School Reform.* New York: David McKay Company, Inc., 1976.
Chao, T., and Allen, V.L. Characteristics of building materials as a factor in vandalism. Unpublished manuscript, University of Wisconsin, Madison, 1978.
Children's Defense Fund. *Children Out of School in America.* Washington, D.C.: Washington Research Project, 1974.
Clark, B.R. The 'cooling-out' function in higher education. *American Journal of Sociology* 65 (1960):569-576.
Clement, S.L. School vandalism—causes and cures. *NASSP Bulletin* 59 (1975):17-21.
Clifford, J. and Walster, E. The effect of physical attractiveness on teacher expectations. *Sociology of Education* 46 (1973):248-55.
Clinard, M.B. Criminological research. In *Sociology Today.* Edited by L. Broom and L.S. Cottrell. New York: Basic Books, 1959.
Clinard, M.B. and Wade, A.L. Toward the delineation of vandalism as a subtype in juvenile delinquency. *Journal of Criminal Law, Criminology and Police Science* 48 (1958):493-99.
Clore, G.L. and Byrne, D. A reinforcement-affect model of attraction. In *Foundations of Interpersonal Attraction.* Edited by T.L. Huston. New York: Academic Press, 1974.
Cloward, R.A. Illegitimate means, anomie, and deviant behavior. *American Sociological Review* 24 (1959):164-79.

Cloward, R.A. and Jones, J.A. *Social Class: Educational Attitudes and Participation.* New York: New York School of Social Work, Columbia University, 1962.
Cloward, R.A. and Ohlin, L.E. *Delinquency and Opportunity.* New York: Free Press, 1960.
Cobb, S.; Brooks, G.H.; Kasl, S.V.; and Connelly, W.E. The health of a longitudinal study. *American Journal of Public Health* 56 (1966):1476-81.
Cohen, A. The delinquent subculture. In *The Sociology of Crime and Delinquency.* Edited by M. Wolfgang, L. Savitz, and N. Johnston. 2nd ed. New York: Wiley, 1970.
_____. *Deviance and Control.* Englewood Cliffs, N.J.: Prentice-Hall, 1966.
_____. *Delinquent Boys: The Culture of the Gang.* New York: Free Press, 1955.
Cohen, S. "Property destruction: Motives and meanings. In *Vandalism.* Edited by C. Ward. London: Architectural Press, 1973.
_____. Direction for research on adolescent school violence and vandalism. *British Journal of Criminology* 11 (1971):319-40.
_____. The politics of vandalism. *The Nation* November 1968:497-500.
Cole, S. The growth of scientific knowledge: Theories of deviance as a case study. In *The Idea of Social Structure: Papers in Honor of Robert K. Merton.* Edited by L.A. Coser. New York: Harcourt, Brace, Jovanovich, 1975.
Cole, S. and Zuckerman, H. Inventory of empirical and theoretical studies of anomie. In *Anomie and Deviant Behavior.* Edited by M.B. Clinard. New York: The Free Press, 1964.
Coleman, J. et al. *Youth: Transition in Adulthood.* Chicago: University of Chicago Press, 1974.
_____. The children have outgrown the schools. *Psychology Today* 5 (1972): 72-75.
_____. *The Adolescent Society.* Glencoe, Ill.: Free Press, 1961.
Coleman, J.W. The myth of addiction. *Journal of Drug Issues* 6 (1976):135-41.
Conant, J.B. *The Education of American Teachers.* New York: McGraw-Hill, 1964.
Cops in, Robbers Out. *Nation's Schools and Colleges* 2 (June 1975):12-14.
Cortes, J.B. and Gatti, F.M. *Delinquency and Crime: A Biopsychosocial Approach.* New York: Seminar Press, 1972.
The Council of the Great City Schools. A prescriptive package proposal—vandalism in our schools. 1707 H Street, N.W., Washington, D.C., 1976.
Crime in our schools. *Parade Magazine* 15 June 1975, p. 4.
Csikszentimihalyi, M. Intrinsic rewards and emergent motivation. In *The Hidden Costs of Reward.* Edited by M.R. Lepper and D. Greene, New York: L. Erlbaum, 1978.
_____. What play says about behavior. *Ontario Psychologist* 8 (1976):5-11(a).
_____. The release of symbolic energy. Paper presented at the 1976 AATA Conference, Baltimore, October 1976(b).

_____. Play and intrinsic rewards. *Journal of Humanistic Psychology* 14 (1975): 41-63(a).

_____. *Beyond Boredom and Anxiety.* San Francisco: Jossey-Bass, 1975(b).

Csikszentimihalyi, M.; Larson, R.; and Prescott, S. The ecology of adolescent activities and experience. *Journal of Youth and Adolescence* 6 (1977): 281-94.

Cubberley, E.P. *Readings on Public Education in the United States: A Collection of Sources and Readings to Illustrate the History of Educational Practice and Progress in the United States.* Boston: Houghton Mifflin, 1934.

_____. *The History of Education.* Boston: Houghton Mifflin, 1920.

Cullen, F. and Tinto, V. A Mertonian analysis of school deviancy. Paper presented at the 1975 Annual Meeting of the American Educational Association, Washington, D.C.

Curley, T.J.; Griffin, C.L.; Sawyer, A.; and Savitsky, A.M. The social system: contributor or inhibitor of the school drop-out." Paper presented at the 1971 Meeting of the American Orthopsychiatric Association.

Cusick, P.A. *Inside High School.* New York: Holt, Rinehart, and Winston, 1973.

David, J. *Summer study: A two-part investigation on the impact of exposure to schooling on achievement growth.* Unpublished Ph.D. Dissertation, Harvard University, 1974.

Davies, J.G.V. and Maliphant, R. Autonomic response to male adolescents exhibiting refractory behavior in school. *Journal of Child Psychology and Psychiatry* 12 (1971):115-27.

Davis, J.A. The campus as frog pond: An application of the theory of relative deprivation to career decisions of college men. *American Journal of Sociology* 72 (1966):17-31.

Dawley, D. *A Nation of Lords.* Garden City: Doubleday Anchor, 1973.

Deal, T.E.; Intili, J.; Rosaler, J.A.; and Stackhouse, A. The early childhood education program: An assessment of its impact and implementation. Stanford: Stanford Center for Research and Development in Teaching, n.d.

Deal, T. and Nolan, R. *Alternative Schools: Ideologies, Realities, and Guidelines.* Chicago: Nelson-Hall, 1978.

DeCecco, J.P. and Richards, A.K. Civil War in the high schools. *Psychology Today* 9 (1975):51-56, 120.

de Charms, R. *Enhancing Motivation: Change in the Classroom.* New York: Irvington, 1976.

_____. *Personal Causation.* New York: Academic Press, 1968.

Deci, E.L. *Intrinsic Motivation.* New York: Plenum, 1975.

Della Fave, R.L. Success values: are they universal or class-differentiated? *American Journal of Sociology* 80 (1974):153-69.

DeMause, L. The evolution of childhood. *Journal of Psychohistory* 1 (1974): 403-575.

DeMyer-Gapin, S. and Scott, T.J. Effects of stimulus novelty on stimulation seeking in antisocial and neurotic children. *Journal of Abnormal Psychology* 86 (1977):96-98.

Dentler, R.A. Dropouts, automation, and the cities. *Teachers College Record* 65 (1964):479-83.

Devies, R.K. The use of the differential behavioral classification system of the juvenile offender to distinguish probation successes from probation failures. Unpublished Ph.D. dissertation, Kent State University, 1975.

Dewey, J. *How We Think.* Boston: D.C. Heath and Co., 1933.

―――. My pedagogic creed. *The School Journal* 54 (1897). Reprinted in *Teaching in American Culture.* Edited by K. Gezi and J. Meyers. New York: Holt, Rinehart, and Winston, 1968.

Dillman, C.M. *Southern rural culture: its effects on children's education.* Ph.D. Dissertation, Stanford University, 1979.

Dollard, J.; Doob, L.W.; Miller, N.E.; Mowrer, O.H.; and Sears, R.R. *Frustration and Aggression.* New Haven: Yale University Press, 1939.

Dornbusch, S.M. To try or not to try. *The Stanford Magazine* 2 (Fall/Winter, 1974):51-54; additional personal communications.

Douvan, E. and Adelson, J. *The Adolescent Experience.* New York: Wiley, 1966.

Douvan, E. and Gold, M. Model patterns in American adolescence. In *Review of Child Development Research.* Vol. II. Edited by M.L. Hoffman and L. Hoffman. New York: Russell Sage, 1966.

Dreikurs, R. and Grey, L. *Logical Consequences: A Handbook of Discipline.* New York: Meredith Press, 1968.

Drury, L.R. and Ray, K.C. *Essentials of School Law.* New York: Appleton, Century, Crofts, 1972.

Dubin, R. Deviant behavior and social structure: continuities in social theory. *American Sociological Review* 31 (1966):693-97.

Ducey, M.H. Vandalism in high schools: an exploratory discussion. In *Theoretical Perspectives on School Crime.* Washington, D.C.: National Technical Information Service, 1978.

Dudek, S.Z. and Lester, E.P. The good child facade in chronic underachievers. Unpublished manuscript, McGill University, Department of Psychiatry, n.d.

Duke, D. A high school studies its discipline problems. In press.

―――. Environmental influences on classroom management. In *Classroom Management, The Seventy-eighth Yearbook of the National Society for the Study of Education.* part II. Edited by Daniel L. Duke. Chicago: The University of Chicago Press, 1979, pp. 333-362.

―――. *The Management of Student Behavior Problems.* New York: Teachers College Press, 1979(b).

―――. Controlling student behavior problems—what are the alternatives? Paper presented at the American Educational Research Association, 1979(c).

―――. How administrators view the crisis in school discipline. *Phi Delta Kappan* 59 (January 1978):325-30(a).

―――. Looking at the school as a rule-governed organization. *Journal of Research and Development in Education* II/4 (Summer 1978):116-26(b).

―――. A systematic management plan for school discipline. *NASSP Bulletin* 61/415 (January 1977):1-10.

_____. Challenge of bureaucracy: The contemporary alternative school." *The Journal of Educational Thought* 10 (1976):34-48.

Duke, D.; Donmoyer, R.; and Farman, G. Emerging legal issues related to classroom management. *Phi Delta Kappan* 60/4 (December 1978):305-9.

Duke, D. and Perry, C. Can alternative schools succeed where Benjamin Spock, Spiro Agnew, and B.F. Skinner have failed? *Adolescence* 13 (Fall 1978): 375-392.

Dukiet, K.H. Spotlight on school security. *School Management* 17 (November-December 1973):16-18.

Dunn, C.F.W. *The Natural History of the Child.* New York: John Laul Co., 1920.

Edelman, M.W. Society's pushed-out children. *Psychology Today* 9 (1975):57-65.

Elder, G.H. Intergroup attitudes and social ascent among Negro boys. *American Journal of Sociology* 76 (1971):673-97.

_____. Socialization and ascent in a racial minority. *Youth and Society* 2 (1970):74-110.

Electronic surveillance proves effective. *American School and University* 46 (August 1974):16.

Elliott, D.S. Delinquency and perceived opportunity. *Sociological Inquiry* 32 (1962):216-27.

Elliott, D.S. and Voss, H.L. *Delinquency and Dropout.* Lexington, Mass.: Lexington Books, D.C. Heath, 1974.

Ellis, M. *Why People Play.* Englewood Cliffs, N.J.: Prentice-Hall, 1973.

Empey, L. and Lubeck, S.G. Conformity and deviance in the situation of company. *American Sociological Review* 33 (1968):760-73.

_____. *Explaining delinquency.* Lexington, Mass.: Lexington Books, D.C. Heath, 1971.

Emrich, R. Personal communication, 1978a.

_____. The safe school study report to the congress: evaluation and recommendations. *Crime and Delinquency* 24 (1978b):266-76.

Epps, E.G. *Family and Achievement: A Study of the Relations of Family Background to Achievement Orientation and Performance among Urban Negro High School Students.* Ann Arbor, Mich.: Institute for Social Research, 1969.

Erickson, K. *The Wayward Puritans.* New York: John Wiley & Sons, 1966.

Erickson, M.L. The group contest of delinquent behavior. *Social Problems* (1971):114-129.

Erickson, M.L. and Empey, L.T. Class position, peers and delinquency. *Sociology and Social Research* 49(1965):268-82.

Erickson, M.L.; Scott, M.L.; and Empey, L.T. *School Experience and Delinquency.* Provo, Utah: Brigham Young University, 1964.

Ernst, K. *Games Students Play.* Millbrae, Calif.: Celestial Arts Publishing, 1975.

Ertukel, D. School security: a student point of view. *NASSP Bulletin* 58 (1974):44-49.
Etzioni, A. Organizational control structure. In *Handbook of Organizations.* Edited by James G. March. Chicago: Rand McNally & Co., 1965.
Everhart, R. From universalism to usurpation: An essay on the antecedents to compulsory school attendance legislation. *Review of Educational Research* 47 (Summer 1977):499-530.
"Ex-Students Pinpoint Wrongs in Nation's High Schools." *Phi Delta Kappan* 57 (March 1976):484-85.
Falk, H.A. *Corporal Punishment: A Social Interpretation of its Theory and Practice in the Schools of the United States.* New York: Columbia Teachers College, 1941.
Farley, F.H. and Rosnow, J.M. Student analyses of motivation and school learning. *The Journal of Experimental Education* 43 (Spring 1975):51-54.
Faulkner, T.A. *The History of Legal Action in Corporal Punishment Cases in New York State, 1812-1965.* Ann Arbor, Mich.: University Microfilms, 1967.
Feather, N.T. *Values in Education and Society.* New York: The Free Press, 1975.
Feldhusen, J.F.; Denny, T.; and Condon, C.F. Anxiety, divergent thinking, and achievement. *Journal of Educational Psychology* 56 (1965):40-45.
Feldhusen, J.F., Thurston, J.R., and Benning, J.J. *A longitudinal study of the correlates of children's social behavior.* Paper presented at the annual meeting of the American Educational Research Association, 1973.
——. Prediction of academic achievement of children who display aggressive-disruptive classroom behavior. Paper presented at the annual meeting of the American Educational Research Association, New York, 1971.
——. Aggressive classroom behavior and school adjustment. *Journal of Special Education* 4 (1970):431-39.
——. Classroom behavior, intelligence, and achievement. *Journal of Experimental Education* 36 (1967):82-87.
Feldman, D. Psychoanalysis and crime. In *Delinquency, Crime and Social Process.* Edited by D.R. Cressey and D. Ward. New York: Harper and Row, 1969.
Ferracutti, F. and Dinitz, S. Cross-cultural aspects of delinquent and criminal behavior. In *Aggression.* Edited by S.H. Frazier. Baltimore: Williams and Williams, 1974.
Festinger, L. A theory of social comparison processes. *Human Relations* 7 (1954):117-40.
Feuer, L.S. *The Conflict of Generations: The Character and Significance of Student Movements.* New York: Basic Books, 1969.
Fish, K.L. *Conflict and Dissent in the High School.* New York: Bruce, 1970.
Flacks, R. Adaptations of deviants in a college community. Unpublished doctoral dissertation, University of Michigan, 1963.

Frease, D. The schools, self-concept, and delinquency. Unpublished doctoral dissertation, University of Oregon, 1969.

French, J.R.P., Jr.; Rodgers, W.; and Cobb, S. Adjustment as person-environment fit. In *Coping and Adaptation*. Edited by G.V. Coelho, D.A. Hamburg, and J.E. Adams. New York: Basic Books, 1974.

Freud, A. *The Ego and Mechanisms of Defense*. New York: International Universities Press, 1946.

Fuller, F.F. and Brown, O.H. Becoming a teacher. In *Teacher Education. The seventy-fourth yearbook of the National Society for the Study of Education*. Edited by Kevin Ryan. Chicago: The University of Chicago Press, 1975.

Galaskiewicz, J. *Exchange Networks and Community Politics*. Beverly Hills: Sage Publications, 1979.

Gallup, G.H. Seventh annual Gallup poll of public attitudes toward education. *Phi Delta Kappan* 57 (December 1975):228.

Gans, H.J. *The Urban Villagers*. New York: Free Press, 1962.

Garner, W. Personnel communication. 20 February 1978.

Gath, D.; Tennent, G.; Pidduck, R. Educational characteristics of bright delinquents. *British Journal of Educational Psychology* 40 (June 1970):216-19.

Geertz, C. *The Interpretation of Cultures*. New York: Basic Books, 1973.

Gersten, J.C.; Langner, T.S.; Eisenberg, J.G.; Simcha-Fagan, O.; and McCarthy, E.D. Stability in change in types of behavioral disturbance of children and adolescents. *Journal of Abnormal Child Psychology* 4 (1976):111-27.

Getzels, J.W. The social psychology of education. In *The Handbook of Social Psychology*. 2d ed., vol. 5. Edited by L. Garner and A. Elliot. Reading, Mass.: Addison-Wesley, 1969.

Gil, D.G. *Violence against Children: Physical Child Abuse in the United States*. Cambridge, Mass.: Harvard University Press, 1970.

Gist, N.P. and Bennett, W.S. Aspirations of Negro and white students. *Social Forces* 42 (1963):40-48.

Glaser, D. *Strategic Criminal Justice Planning*. Washington, D.C.: U.S. Government Printing Office, 1975.

Glasser, W. *Schools Without Failure*. New York: Harper and Row, 1969.

Glavin, J.P. and DeGirolamo, G. Spelling errors of withdrawn and conduct problem children. *The Journal of Special Education* 4 (1970):119-204.

Glavin, J.P.; Quay, H.C.; Annesley, F.R.; and Werry, J.S. An experimental resource room for behavior problem children. *Exceptional Children* 38 (1971):131-37.

Glidewell, J.C. Organization, adjustment, and classroom achievement. *Teachers College Record* 62 (1961):274-81.

Glueck, S. Glueck, E. *Unraveling Juvenile Delinquency*. Cambridge, Mass.: Harvard University Press, 1950.

Gnagey, W.J. *The Psychology of Discipline in the Classroom*. London: The MacMillan Company, 1970.

Gold, M. Scholastic experiences, self-esteem, and delinquent behavior: a theory for alternative schools. *Crime and Delinquency* 24 (1978):290-307.
——. *Delinquent Behavior in an American City*. Belmont, Calif.: Brooks-Cole, 1970.
——. *Status Forces in Delinquent Boys*. Ann Arbor, Mich.: The Institute for Social Research, 1963.
Gold, M. and Mann, D.W. Delinquency as defense. *American Journal of Orthopsychiatry* 42 (1972):463-79.
Gold, M. and Reimer, D.J. *Changing Pattern of Delinquent Behavior Among American 13-16 Years Old: 1967-72*. Rockville, Md.: National Institute of Mental Health, 1972.
Goldman, N. A socio-psychological study of school vandalism. *Crime and Delinquency* 7 (1961):221-30.
Goldmeier, H. Vandalism: The effects of unmanageable confrontations. *Adolescence* 9 (1974):49-56.
Goldstein, S. The scope and sources of school board authority to regulate student conduct and status: A nonconstitutional analysis. 117 *U.Pa. L. Rev.* 373, 1969.
Good, T.L. and Brophy, J.E. *Looking in Classrooms*. New York: Harper & Row, 1973.
Goode, E. *Drugs in American Society*. New York: Knopf, 1972.
Goodman, P. *Compulsory Mis-Education*. New York: Horizon Press, 1964.
Gordon, C.W. *The Social System of the High School*. Glencoe, Ill.: Free Press, 1957.
Gordon, M.M. The concept of the sub-culture and its application. *Social Forces* 26 (1947):40-42.
Gordon, T. *T.E.T.: Teacher Effectiveness Training*. New York: Peter H. Wyden, 1974.
Gove, W.R. The labeling perspective: an overview. In *The Labeling of Deviance*. Edited by W.R. Gove. New York: Wiley, 1975.
Granovetter, M.S. The strength of weak ties. In *A Developing Paradigm*. Edited by Samuel Leinhardt. New York: Academic Press, 1977.
Greene, D. and Lepper, M.R. (eds.). *The Hidden Costs of Reward*. New York: L. Erlbaum Associates, in press.
Greenberg, B. School vandalism: its effects and paradoxical solutions. *Crime Prevention Review* 1 (January 1974):11-18.
Grinker, R.R. and Spiegel, J.P. *The Neurotic Reactions to Severe Combat Stress in Men under Stress*. Philadelphia: Blakinston, 1945.
Grossbard, H.S. Ego deficiency in delinquents. *Social Casework* 43 (1962):71-78.
Grund, F. *The Americans in their moral, social and political relations*. 1837. Cited in L.A. Cremin, *The American Common School: An Historic Conception*. New York: Columbia University Press, 1951.
Hall, G.S. *Educational Problems, I*. New York: D. Appleton and Company, 1911.

Halprin, E. Applied mathematics as a flow activity. Unpublished manuscript, The University of Chicago, in progress.

Haney, S. School district reduces vandalism 65%. *American School and University*, December 1973.

Hangstrom, W.D. and Gardner, L.L. *Characteristics of Disruptive High School Students.* Washington, D.C.: Office of Education, HEW, 1968.

Harary, F. Merton revisited: a new classification for deviant behavior. *American Sociological Review* 31 (1966):693-97.

Hargreaves, D.H. *Social Relations in a Secondary School.* London: Routledge and Kegan Paul, 1967.

Harrison, R.V. *Person-environment fit and job stress.* In *Stress at Work.* Edited by C.L. Cooper, and R. Payne. New York: John Wiley, 1978.

Harvey, J.H. and Kelley, D.R. Effects of attitude similarity and success-failure upon attitude toward other persons. *Journal of Social Psychology* 90 (1973):105-14.

Hauberle, H., 1830. Cited in Falk, 1941:54.

Hauser, G.S. Student adaptation to high school academics and activities. Unpublished Masters Thesis, University of Oregon, 1965.

Havighurst, R.J. Youth in crisis. *School Review* 83 (November 1974):6.

_____. *A Profile of the Large-City High School.* Washington, D.C.: National Association of Secondary School Principals, 1970.

Havighurst, R.J.; Bowman, P.H.; Liddle, G.P.; Matthews, C.V.; and Pierce, J.V. *Growing Up in River City.* New York: John Wiley, 1962.

Havighurst, R.J. and Neugarten, B. *Society and Education.* Boston: Allyn and Bacon, 1967.

Havighurst, R.J. and Taba, H. *Adolescent Character and Personality.* New York: John Wiley, 1949.

Healy, W. and Bronner, A.F. *New Light on Delinquency and Its Treatment.* New Haven: Yale University Press, 1963.

Heath, L.G. *Portrait of the High School Rebel.* Washington, D.C.: Office of Education, HEW, 1970.

Heaton, R.C.; Safer, D.J.; Allen, R.P.; Spinnato, N.C.; and Prumo, F. A motivational environment for behaviorally deviant junior high school students. *Journal of Abnormal Child Psychology* 4 (1976):263-75.

Hebb, D.O. Drive and the CNS. *Psychological Review* 62 (1965):243-52.

Heider, F. *The Psychology of Interpersonal Relations.* New York: John Wiley, 1958.

Henry, J. *Culture against Man.* New York: Vintage Books, 1963.

Hetherington, E.M.; Stouwie, R.J.; and Ridberg, E.H. Patterns of family interaction and child-rearing attitudes related to three dimensions of juvenile delinquency. *Journal of Abnormal Psychology* 78 (1971):160-76.

Heussenstamm, F.N. and Hoepfner, R. Black, white and brown adolescent alienation. Paper presented at the annual meeting of the National Council on Measurement of Education, 1971.

Hewett, F.M.; Taylor, F.C.; and Artuso, A.A. The Santa Monica project: evaluation of an engineered classroom design with emotionally disturbed children. *Exceptional Children* 35 (1969):523-29.

Hewitt, L.E. and Jenkins, R.L. *Fundamental Patterns of Maladjustment: The Dynamics of Their Origins*. Springfield, Ill.: State of Illinois, 1946.

Heyns, B. Social selection and stratification within schools. *American Journal of Sociology* 79 (1974):1434-51.

Hezel, J.D. Some personality correlates of dimensions of delinquency. Unpublished Ph.D. Dissertation, St. Louis University, 1968.

Hicks, G.R. *Appalachian Valley*. New York: Holt, Rinehart, and Winston, 1976.

Hill, R.B. *Parent and Peer Group Pressures toward Deviant Behavior*. New York: The Free Press, 1951.

Hindelang, M.J. Causes of delinquency: a partial replication and extension. *Social Problems* 20 (1973):471-87.

──────. The commitment of delinquents to their misdeeds: do delinquents drift? *Social Problems* 17 (1970):502-9.

Hirschi, T. *Causes of Delinquency*. Berkeley: University of California Press, 1969.

Hollingshead, A.B. Behavior systems as a field of study. *American Sociological Review* 4 (1939):816-22.

Hollingsworth, E.J. Exploring remedies from within. *Education and Urban Society* 4 (1979):11.

Holloway, R.G. and Berreman, J. The educational and occupational aspirations and plans of Negro and white male elementary school students. *Pacific Sociological Review* 2 (1959):56-60.

Holt, J. *The Underachieving School*. New York: Putnam, 1969.

Hovland, C.I.; Lumsdaine, A.A.; and Sheffield, E.D. *Experiments in Mass Communication Studies in Social Psychology in World War II*. vol. 3. Princeton, N.J.: Princeton University Press, 1949.

Hoy, W.K. Dimensions of alienation and characteristics of public high schools. *Interchange* 3 (1972):38-50.

Huff, T. and Schnelle, J.F. Discrimination between appropriate and inappropriate classroom behaviors by well-behaved and poorly-behaved students. *Perceptual and Motor Skills* (1974):39.

Hunt, J. McV. Intrinsic motivation and its role in psychological development. *Nebraska Symposium on Motivation*. Edited by D. Levine. Lincoln, Neb.: University of Nebraska Press, 1965.

Hutt, C. Specific and diversive exploration. In *Advances in Child Development and Behavior*. Vol. 5. Edited by H.W. Reese and L.P. Lipsitt. New York: Academic Press, 1970.

Illich, I. *Deschooling Society*. New York: Harper, 1971.

Insel, P.M. and Moos, R.H. Psychological environments: expanding the scope of human ecology. *American Psychologist* 29 (1974):179-188.

Jablonsky, A. *The School Dropout: A Review of the ERIC Literature*. Washton, D.C.: HEW, 1970.

Jacobson, E. Denial and repression. *Journal of the American Psychoanalytic Association* 5 (1957):61-92.

Jackson, P.W. *Life in Classrooms*. New York: Holt, Rinehart, and Winston, 1968.

Jellison, J.M. and Arkin, R.M. Social comparison of abilities: A self-presentational approach to decision making in groups. In *Social Comparison Processes* pp. 235-237. Edited by J.M. Suls and R.L. Miller. New York: Halstead Press, 1977.

Jenkins, R.L. Deprivation of parental care as a contribution to juvenile delinquency. In *Childhood Deprivation*. Edited by A.R. Roberts. Springfield, Ill.: Thomas, 1974.

Jensen, G.F. Parents, peers and delinquent action: A test of the differential association perspective. *American Journal of Sociology* 78 (1972):562-75.

Johns, J.H. and Quay, H.C. The effect of social reward on verbal conditioning in psychopathic and neurotic military offenders. *Journal of Counsulting Psychology* 26 (1962):217-20.

Jordon, D.C. *Delinquency*. Amherst, Mass.: University of Massachusetts Press, 1970.

Jorgenson, G.W. Relationship of classroom behavior to the accuracy of the match between material difficulty and student ability. *Journal of Educational Psychology* 69 (1977):24-32.

Juillerat, E.E., Jr. For worried school districts: Here's lots of sensible advice for lasting ways to cut down school vandalism. *American School Board Journal* (January 1974):64-69.

Kahana, E. A congruence model of person-environment interaction. In *Theory Development in Environments and Aging*. Edited by M.D. Lawton. New York: John Wiley, 1978.

Kaplan, H.B. Sequelae of self-derogation: predicting from a general theory of deviant behavior. *Youth and Society* 7 (1975):171-97.

Karweit, N. A reanalysis of the effect of quantity of schooling on achievement. *Sociology of Education* 49 (July 1976):236-46.

Katz, D. and Kahn, R.L. *The Social Psychology of Organizations*. New York: John Wiley and Sons, 1978.

Keiser, R.L. *The Vice Lords*. New York: Holt, Rinehart and Winston, 1969.

Kelly, D.H. Status origins, track position, and delinquent involvement: a self-report analysis. *Sociological Quarterly* 16 (1975):264-71.

──────. Track position and delinquent involvement: a preliminary analysis. *Sociology and Social Research* 58 (1974):380-86.

Kelly, D.H. and Balch, R.W. Social origins and school failure: a re-examination of Cohen's theory of working-class delinquency. *Pacific Sociological Review* 14 (1971):413-430.

Kelly, D.H. and Pink, W.T. Social origins, school status and the learning experience. *Pacific Sociological Review* 16 (1973):121-34.

Kelly, J.G. (ed.). *Adolescent Boys in High School: A Psychological Study of Coping and Adaptation*. Somerset, N.J.: Lawrence Erlbaum, 1979.

Kennedy, J.; Mitchell, J.R.; Klerman, L.V.; and Murray, A. A day school approach to aggressive adolescents. *Child Welfare* 55 (1976):712-24.

Kent, R.N. and O'Leary, K.D. A controlled evaluation of behavior modification with conduct problem children. *Journal of Consulting and Clinical Psychology* 44 (1976):586-96.

Kiely, W. Stress and somatic disease. *JAMA* 224 (1973):521-23.

Kimmel, Mrs. W.G. Statement prepared by the National Congress of Parents and Teachers for inclusion in *Violence in Schools*. Edited by James M. McPartland and Edward L. Dill. Lexington, Mass.: Lexington Books, D.C. Heath and Company, 1977.

Kingston, A.J. and Gentry, H.W. Discipline problems and practices in the secondary schools of a southern state. *National Association of Secondary School Principals Bulletin* 45 (1961):34-44.

Kirkham, J.F.; Levy, S.G.; and Grotty, W.J. *Assassination and Political Violence*. Staff report to the National Commission on Causes and Prevention of Violence. Washington, D.C.: U.S. Government Printing Office, 1970.

Klein, M. Issues in police diversion of juvenile offenders: a guide for discussion. In *Juvenile Justice Management*. Edited by G. Adams et al. Springfield, Ill.: Charles Wiley, 1973.

Klingel, D.M. Person-environment fit and aggressive behavior in boys attending two suburban high schools. In *The Dynamics of Person-Environment Fit in the High School*. Symposium of the American Psychological Association, New Orleans, 1974.

Koerner, J.D. *The Miseducation of American Teachers*. Baltimore: Penguin Books, 1965.

Kohn, M.L. Social class and parent-child relationships: an interpretation. *American Journal of Sociology* 68 (1963):471-80.

──. Social class and parental values. In *The Family, Its Structures and Functions*. Edited by Rose L. Coser. New York: St. Martin's Press, 1974.

Korbin, S. The conflict of values in delinquency areas. *American Sociological Review* 16 (1951):653-61.

Kozol, H. *Death at an Early Age*. Boston: Houghton-Mifflin, 1967.

Kruglanski, A.W. The endogenous-exogenous partition in attribution theory. *Psychological Review* 82 (1975):387-406.

Kulka, R.A. Adjustment to high school: B=f (P,E)? In *The Dynamics of Person-Environment Fit in the High School*. Symposium of the American Psychological Association, New Orleans, 1974.

──. Interaction as person-environment fit. In *New Directions for Methodology of Behavioral Science: Methods for Studying Person-Situation Interactions*. no. 2. Edited by L.R. Kahle. San Francisco: Jossey-Bass, in press.

──. Person-environment fit in the high school: A validation study. 2 vols. Ph.D. Dissertation, The University of Michigan, 1975. Dissertation Abstracts International 36 (1976):5352B. University Microfilms No. 76-9438.

Kulka, R.A.; Klingel, D.M.; and Kahle, L.R. Antecedents and consequences of alienation and involvement in high school. In *Commitment, Rebellion, and Crime in the Public Schools*. Symposium of the American Psychological Association, September 1979.

Kulka, R.A.; Klingel, D.M.; and Mann, D.W. Dimensions of student-school fit as predictors of school crime and disruption. Paper presented at the meeting of the Society for Study of Social Problems, San Francisco, September 1978.

Kvaraceus, W.C. Preventing and treating juvenile delinquency—some basic approaches. *The School Review* 63 (1955):477-79.

———. *Juvenile Delinquency and the School*. New York: World Book Co., 1945.

———. Programs of early identification and prevention of delinquency. In *Social Deviancy Among Youth*. Edited by William W. Wattenberg. Chicago: University of Chicago Press, 1966.

Lambert, E.C. An attitudinal study of Missouri state leaders toward the public schools. *Phi Delta Kappan* 57 (December 1975):279.

Larson, K. *School Discipline in an Age of Rebellion*. New York: Parker Publishing Co., Inc., 1972.

Larson, K.G. and Karpas, M.R. *Effective Secondary School Discipline*. Englewood Cliffs, N.J.: Prentice-Hall, 1964.

Lawler, E.E., III. *Motivation in Work Organizations*. Belmont, Calif.: Wadsworth Publishing Co., 1973.

Leinhardt, S. (ed.). *Social Networks: A Developing System*. New York: Academic Press, 1977.

Lepper, M. and Green, D. (eds.). *Hidden Cost of Reward*. New York: L. Erlbaum, 1978.

———. Turning play into work: effects of adult surveillance and extrinsic rewards on children's intrinsic motivation. *Journal of Personality and Social Psychology* 31 (1975):479-86.

Lerman, P. Individual values, peer values, and subcultural delinquency. *American Sociological Review* 33 (1968):219-35.

———. Argot, symbolic deviance and subcultural delinquency. *American Sociological Review* 32 (1967):209-44.

Leveque, K.L. and Walker, R.E. Correlates of high school cheating behavior. *Psychology in the Schools* 7 (1970):159-64.

Levin, G.R. and Simmons, J.J. Response to praise by emotionally disturbed boys. *Psychological Reports* 11 (1962):10.

Levine, S. Speaking out. *National Elementary Principal* 52 (September 1972):67.

Lewin, K. *A Dynamic Theory of Personality*. New York: McGraw-Hill, 1935.

Lewis, O. *The Children of Sanchez*. New York: Vintage Books, 1961.

Liddle, G.P. Existing and projected research on reading in relationship to delinquency. In *Role of the School in Prevention of Juvenile Delinquency*. Edited by W.R. Carriker. Washington, D.C.: U.S. Government Printing Office, 1963.

Lippitt, R. The socialization community. In *Sociology of Education: An Anthology of Issues and Problems.* Edited by W. Cave and W. Chesler. New York: Macmillan, 1969.

Locke, E.A. What is job satisfaction? *Organizational Behavior and Human Performance* 4 (1969):309-36.

Lofland, J. *Deviance and Identity.* Englewood Cliffs, N.J.: Prentice-Hall, 1969.

Loft, R.D. Academic achievement and deviant behavior. Unpublished masters thesis, University of Oregon, 1969.

Lorber, N.M. Inadequate social acceptance and disruptive classroom behavior. *The Journal of Educational Research* 59 (April 1966):360-62.

Mack, J.L. Behavior ratings on recidivist and non-recidivist delinquent males. *Psychological Reports* 25 (1969):260.

Madison, A. *Vandalism: The Not-So-Senseless Crime.* New York: Seabury Press, 1970.

Madsen, W. *The Mexican-Americans of South Texas.* New York: Holt, Rinehart, and Winston, 1973.

Mann, D. When delinquency is defensive: self-esteem and deviant behavior. Unpublished Ph.D. dissertation, University of Michigan, 1976.

Mann, H. *Seventh annual report to the Massachusetts State Board of Education,* 1843.

Mann, H. and Smith, Rev. M.H. Sequel to the so-called correspondence between the Rev. M.H. Smith and Horace Mann. Boston: W.B. Fowle, 1847.

Martin, J. *National Panel on High Schools and Adolescent Education Report: The Education of Adolescents.* Washington, D.C.: U.S. Office of Education, HEW, March 1974.

──── . *Juvenile Vandalism.* Springfield, Ill.: Charles C. Thomas, 1961.

Martin, J.M. and Fitzpatrick, J.P. *Delinquent Behavior: A Redefinition of the Problem.* New York: Random House, 1964.

Marvin, M.; McCann, R.; Connolly, S.; Temkin, S.; and Henning, P. *Planning Assistance Programs to Reduce School Violence.* Philadelphia: Research for Better Schools, Inc., 1976.

Marwell, G. Adolescent powerlessness and delinquent behavior. *Social Problems* 14 (1966):35-47.

Maslow, A. and Honigmann, J.J. Synergy: some notes of Ruth Benedict. *American Anthropologist* 72 (1970):320-33.

Massimo, J. and Shore, M. The effectiveness of a comprehensive vocationally oriented psychotherapeutic program for adolescent delinquent boys. *American Journal of Orthopsychiatry* 33 (1963):634-42.

Matthews, V.M. Differential identification: an empirical note. *Social Problems* 15 (1968):376-83.

Matza, D. *Delinquency and Drift.* New York: Wiley, 1964.

──── . Subterranean traditions of youth. *The Annals* 338 (1961):102-18.

Mayers, P. The relation between structural elements and the experience of enjoyment in high school classes. Unpublished manuscript, The University of Chicago, 1977.

McDermott, R.P. Achieving school failure: an anthropological approach to social stratification. In *Education and Cultural Process*. Edited by George D. Spindler. New York: Holt, Rinehart, and Winston, 1969.

McGuire, W. Violence in the schools. *NEA Reporter* 15 (February 1976):3.

McKay, H. The neighborhood and child conduct. *Annals of the American Academy of Political and Social Science* 261 (1949):32-41.

McKeen, J. Annual report of Joseph McKeen, Superintendent of Common Schools for City and County of New York. In *Annual Report of the Superintendent of Common Schools*. Albany, N.Y.: Charles Van Benthnysen, 1851.

McKenney, J.W. The revolt of youth. *CTA Journal* 65 (January 1969):5.

McPartland, J.M. and McDill, E.L. Research on crime in schools. In *Violence in Schools: Perspectives, Programs, and Positions*. Edited by J.M. McPartland and E.L. McDill. Lexington, Mass.: D.C. Heath, 1977.

_____. *High School Rules and Decision-Making Procedures as Sources of School Stability* (Report No. 169). Baltimore: Johns Hopkins University, Center for Social Organization of Schools, 1974.

Meacham, M.L. and Wiesen, A.E. *Changing Classroom Behavior*. New York: Intext Educational Publishers, 1974.

Megargee, E.I. and Golden, R.E. Parental attitudes of psychopathic and subcultural delinquents. *Criminology* (February 1973):427-39.

Merton, R.K. Continuities in the theory of social structure and anomie. In *Social Theories of Social Culture*. Edited by M.B. Clinard. New York: The Free Press, 1968(a).

_____. Social structure and anomie. In Clinard, M.G. (ed.). Anomie and deviant behavior. New York: The Free Press, 1968(b).

_____. Anomie, anomia, and social interaction: contexts of deviant behavior. In *Anomie and Deviant Behavior*. Edited by M.B. Clinard. New York: The Free Press, 1964.

_____. Social conformity, deviation, and opportunity structures: a comment on the contributions of Dubin and Cloward. *American Sociological Review* 24 (1959):177-89.

_____. *Social Theory and Social Structure*. Glencoe, Ill.: Free Press, 1957.

_____. Social structure and anomie. *American Sociological Review* 3 (1938):672-82.

Meyer, J.; Chase-Dunn, C.; and Inverarity, J. *The expansion of autonomy of youth: responses of the secondary school to the problems of order in the 1960s*. Stanford, Calif.: The Laboratory for Social Research, Stanford University, 1971.

Miller and Beer. Security system pays off. *American School and University* 46 (April 1974):39-40.

Miller, L.C. Dimensions of psychopathology in middle childhood. *Psychological Reports* 21 (1967):897-903.

Mohl, R.A. Schools, policies and riots: the gang plan in New York City, 1914-1917. *Paedagogica Historica* 15 (1975):39-72.

Moore, B.M. The schools and the problems of delinquency: research studies and findings. In *Readings in Juvenile Delinquency.* Edited by R.S. Cavan. Philadelphia: Lippincott, 1964.

Moore, K. *Old saints and young sinners: a study of student discipline at Harvard College, 1636-1724.* Ann Arbor, Mich.: University Microfilms, 1972.

Moos, R. *Evaluating Treatment Environments: A Social Ecological Approach.* New York: Wiley, 1974.

Morgan, R. An exploratory study of three procedures to encourage school attendance. *Psychology in the Schools* 12 (April 1975):209-15.

Morison, S.E. *Three Centuries of Harvard, 1636-1936.* Cambridge, Mass.: Harvard University Press, 1937.

Mueller, K.H. Programs for deviant girls. In *Social Deviancy among Youth.* Edited by William W. Wattenberg. Chicago: University of Chicago Press, 1966.

Mullin, M. Personal and situational factors associated with perfect attendance. *Personnel and Guidance Journal* 33 (1955):438-43.

Murray, H.A. *Explorations in Personality.* New York: Oxford University Press, 1938.

Murrell, S.A. Relationships of ordinal position and family size to psychosocial measures of delinquents. *Journal of Abnormal Child Psychology* 2 (1974):39-46.

Narr, R. An attempt to differentiate delinquents from non-delinquents on the basis of projective drawings. *Journal of Criminal Law, Criminology, and Police Science* 55 (1964):107-10.

National Commission on Resources for Youth. *New York Newsletter.* Vol. IV. 1975.

National Education Association. *School Dropouts.* Washington, D.C.: NEA, 1963.

National Institute of Education. *Violent Schools—Safe Schools: The Safe School Study Report to the Congress.* Washington, D.C.: U.S. Government Printing Office, 1978.

National School Public Relations Association. *Discipline Crisis in Schools: The Problems, Causes, and Search for Solutions.* Education, U.S.A. Special Report. Arlington, Va: NSPRA, 1973.

NEA. Major problems of teachers. *NEA Research Bulletin* 49 (December 1971):103.

Neill, G. Control spectre hovers as HEW requests detailed reports on discipline measures. *Phi Delta Kappan* 56 (1975):286-87.

Newcomb, T.M. An approach to the study of communicative acts. *Psychological Review* 50 (1953):393-404.

———. *The Acquaintance Process.* New York: Holt, Rinehart, and Winston, 1961.

Newell, P. (ed.). *A Last Resort: Corporal Punishment in Schools.* Middlesex, England: Penguin Books, 1972.

New Jersey Department of Education. *Report of the Commissioner's Task Force on Adolescent Education.* Trenton, N.J.: New Jersey State Department of Education, 1977.

Newsweek 27 Aug. 1979:44.

Nisbett, R.E. and Valins, S. *Perceiving the Causes of One's Own Behavior.* New York: General Learning Press, 1971.

North Carolina State Superintendent's Task Force on Secondary Education. *Channels for Changing Secondary Schools.* Raleigh, N.C.: North Carolina Department of Public Instruction, 1974.

O'Leary, K.D. and Becker, W.C. Behavior modification of an adjustment class: a token reinforcement program. *Exceptional Children* 33 (1967):637-42.

O'Leary, K.D.; Becker, W.C.; Evans, M.C.; and Saudargas, R.A. A token reinforcement program in a public school: a replication and systematic analysis. *Journal of Applied Behavior Analysis* 2 (1969):3-13.

Oliver, D. *Education and Community: A Radical Critique of Innovation Schooling.* Berkeley: McCutchen, 1976.

Orris, J.B. Visual monitoring performance in three subgroups of male delinquents. *Journal of Abnormal Psychology* 74 (1969):227-29.

Ouchi, W.G. The relationship between organizational structure and organizational control. *Administrative Science Quarterly* 22 (March 1977):95-113.

Painter, S. *William Marshall: Knight-Errant, Baron, and Regent of England.* Baltimore: Johns Hopkins Press, 1933.

Palmore, E.B. Factors associated with school dropouts and juvenile delinquency among lower-class children. In *Society and Education.* Edited by R.J. Havighurst, B.L. Neugarten, and J.M. Falls. Boston: Allyn and Bacon, 1967.

Palmore, E.B. and Hammond, P.E. Interacting factors in juvenile delinquency. *American Sociological Review*, 29 (1964):848-854.

Palonsky, S. Hempies and squeaks, truckers and cruisers—A participant observer study in a city high school. *Educational Administration Quarterly* 11 (Spring 1975):98-99.

Parmer, O.E. Psychological services in twenty-eight elementary schools of Columbus, Ohio. *Journal of Experimental Education* 29 (2).

Parsons, T. The Social System. In Hill, R.B., ed., *Parent and peer group pressures toward deviant behavior.* New York: The Free Press, 1951.

_____. Age and sex in the social structure of the United States. *American Sociological Review* 7 (1942):604-16.

Patterson, G.R. A learning theory approach to the treatment of the school phobic child. In *Case Studies in Behavior Modification.* Edited by L. Ulman and L. Krasner. New York: Holt, Rinehart, and Winston, 1965.

Patterson, G.R. An empirical approach to the classification of distrubed children. *Journal of Clinical Psychology* 20 (1964):326-37.

Patterson, G.R.; Jones, R.; Whittier, J.; and Wright, M. A behavior modification technique for the hyperactive child. *Behavior Research and Therapy* 2 (1965):217-26.

Pelavin, S. and David, J. *Evaluating long-term achievement: an analysis of longitudinal data from compensatory education programs.* Menlo Park, Calif.: SRI International, March 1977.

Persons, R.W. Psychological and behavioral change in delinquents following psychotherapy. *Journal of Clinical Psychology* 22 (1966):337-40.

———. The relationship between psychotherapy with institutionalized boys and subsequent community adjustment. *Journal of Consulting Psychology* 31 (1967):137-41.

Persons, R.W. and Pepinsky, H.B. Convergence in psychotherapy with delinquent boys. *Journal of Counseling Psychology* 13 (1966):329-34.

Pervin, L.A. Performance and satisfaction as a function of individual-environment fit. *Psychological Bulletin* 69 (1968):56-68.

Peterson, D.R. Behavior problems of middle childhood. *Journal of Consulting Psychology* 25 (1961):205-9.

Peterson, D.R.; Quay, H.C.; and Tiffany, T.L. Personality factors related to juvenile delinquency. *Child Development* 32 (1961):355-72.

Philbrick, J.D. *Twenty-ninth semi-annual report of the superintendent of public schools in the City of Boston.* September 1874.

Phillips, B.N. Problem behavior in the elementary school. *Child Development* 39 (1972a):895-903.

———. School-related aspirations of children with different socio-cultural backgrounds. *Journal of Negro Education* 41 (1972b):48-52.

Phillips, J.C. The creation of deviant behavior in high schools: an examination of Cohen's general theory of subcultures. Unpublished doctoral dissertation. University of Oregon, 1974.

Phillips, J.C. and Schafer, W.E. *The athletic subculture: a preliminary study.* Paper presented at the annual meeting of the American Sociological Association, Washington, D.C., 1970.

Piaget, J. *The Origins of Intelligence in Children.* Cook, M., trans. New York: International University Press, 1952.

Polk, K. and Halferty, D.S. Adolescence, commitment and delinquency. *Journal of Research in Crime and Delinquency* 3 (1966):82-96.

Polk, K. and Pink, W. Youth culture and the school: a replication. *British Journal of Sociology* 22 (1971):160-71.

Polk, K. and Richmond, F.L. Those who fail. In *Schools and Delinquency.* Edited by K. Polk and W.E. Schafer. Englewood Cliffs, N.J.: Prentice-Hall, 1972.

Polk, K. and Schafer, W.E. (eds.). *Schools and Delinquency.* Englewood Cliffs, N.J.: Prentice-Hall, 1972.

Porter, J. *The Adolescent, Other Citizens and Their High Schools.* New York: McGraw-Hill, 1974.

Powell, M. and Bergem, J. An investigation of the differences between tenth-, eleventh-, and twelfth-grade 'conforming' and 'nonconforming' boys. *The Journal of Educational Research* 56 (December 1962):184-90.

Prendergast, M.A. and Binder, D. Relationships of selected self-concept and academic achievement measures. *Measurement and Evaluation in Guidance* (July 1975):92-95.

Prentice, N.M. and Jurkovic, G.J. The relationship of moral and cognitive development to dimensions of juvenile delinquency. Paper presented at the meeting of the Western Psychological Association, Los Angeles, April 1976.

Prewer, R.R. Some observations on window-smashing. *British Journal of Delinquency* 9-10 (1958-60):104-13.

Pritchett, W. and Willower, D.J. Student perceptions of teacher-pupil control behavior and student attitudes toward high schools. *The Alberta Journal of Educational Research* 21 (June 1975):110-15.

Ptaschnick, I.J. A comparison of the relevance of education in three city high schools: black, white, and integrated. Paper presented at the annual meeting of the American Educational Research Association, 1973.

Pucinski, R.C. Results of a survey of students' unrest in the nation's high schools. *Congressional Record,* 23 February 1970.

Quay, H.C. Psychopathic behavior: reflections on its nature, origins, and treatment. In *The Structuring of Experience.* Edited by F. Weizmann, and I. Uzgiris. New York: Plenum, 1977.

_____. Personality patterns in preadolescent delinquent boys. *Educational and Psychological Measurement* 16 (1966):99-110.

_____. Psychopathic personality as pathological stimulation seeking. *American Journal of Psychiatry* 122 (1965):180-83.

_____. Personality dimensions in delinquent males as inferred from the factor analysis of behavior ratings. *Journal of Research in Crime and Delinquency* 1 (1964):33-37.

Quay, H.C.; Glavin, J.P.; Annesley, F.R.; and Werry, J.S. The modification of problem behavior and academic achievement in a resource room. *Journal of School Psychology* 10 (1972):187-98.

Quay, H.C. and Levinson, R.B. The prediction of the institutional adjustment of four subgroups of delinquent boys. Unpublished manuscript, 1967.

Quay, H.C.; Morse, W.C; and Cutler, R.L. Personality patterns of pupils in special classes for the emotionally disturbed. *Exceptional Children* 32 (1966):297-301.

Quay, H.C.; Peterson, D.R.; and Consalvi, C. The interpretation of three personality factors in juvenile delinquency. *Journal of Consulting Psychology* 24 (1960):555.

Quay, H.C. and Quay, L.C. Behavior problems in early adolescence. *Child Development* 36 (1965):215-20.

Quay, H.C.; Sprague, R.L.; Werry, J.S.; and McQueen, M.M. Conditioning visual orientation of conduct problem children in the classroom. *Journal of Experimental Child Psychology* 5 (1967):412-517.

Quay, H.C.; Werry, J.S.; McQueen, M.; and Sprague, R.L. Remediation of the conduct problem child in a special class setting. *Exceptional Children* 32 (1966):509-15.

Radar, H. The child as terrorist: seven cases. *School Review* 84 (November 1975):31.

Redl, F. and Wineman, D. *Children Who Hate.* New York: Free Press, 1951.
Reiss, A.J., Jr. Social correlates of psychological types of delinquency. *American Sociological Review* 17 (1952):710-18.
Reiss, A.J., Jr. and Rhodes, A.L. An empirical test of differential association theory. *Journal of Research in Crime and Delinquency* 1 (1964):5-18.
──── . Status deprivation and delinquent behavior. *Sociological Quarterly* 4 (1963):135-49.
──── . Are educational norms and goals of conforming, truant and delinquent adolescents influenced by group position in American society? *Journal of Negro Education* 28 (1959):252-67.
Research for Better Schools, Inc. *Planning assistance programs to reduce school violence and vandalism and disruption.* Unpublished report, LEAA, 1976.
Resnick, J. Antisocial behavior: whose fault. In *Improving School Discipline.* Edited by Leslie J. Chamberlin and Joseph B. Carnot. Springfield, Ill.: Charles C. Thomas, 1974.
Reutter, E. Edmund, Jr. *Legal Aspects of Control of Student Activities by Public School Authorities.* Topeka, Kans.: National Organization on Legal Problems of Education, 1970.
Rhodes, A.L. and Reiss, A.J., Jr. Apathy, truancy, and delinquency as adaptations to school failure. *Social Forces* 48 (1969):12-22.
Richards, P. Patterns of middle class vandalism: a case study of suburban adolescence. Unpublished doctoral dissertation, Northwestern University, 1976.
Riggle, W.H. The white, the black and the gray: a study of student subcultures in a suburban California high school. Unpublished doctoral dissertation, University of California, 1965.
Rist, R.C. Student social class and teacher expectations: the self-fulfilling prophecy. *Harvard Education Review* 40 (1970):411-51.
Robins, L.N. Follow-up studies of behavior disorders in children. In *Psychopathological Disorders of Childhood.* Edited by H.C. Quay and J.S. Werry. New York: John Wiley, 1972.
──── . *Deviant Children Grown Up.* Baltimore: The Williams and Wilkens Company, 1966.
Robinson, W.P. Boredom at school. *British Journal of Educational Psychology* June 1975:p. 45.
Rosenbaum, J.E. The stratification of socialization processes. *American Sociological Review* 40 (1975):48-54.
Rosenberg, J. *The Logic of Survey Analysis.* New York: Basic Books, 1968.
Rosenberg, M. *Society and the Adolescent Self-Image.* Princeton, N.J.: Princeton University Press, 1965.
Rosenthal, C.F. *Social Conflict and Collective Violence in American Institutions of Higher Learning.* Vol. 1. Washington, D.C.: U.S. Department of Commerce, 1971.
Rosenthal, R. and Jacobson, L. *Pygmalion in the Classroom.* New York: Holt, Rinehart, and Winston, 1968.

Rothman, D. and Walker, G. Continuity of care between the psychiatric hospital and public schools. In *Tomorrow's Track: Experiments with Learning to Change*. Edited by P. Franklin and R. Franklin. Columbia, Md.: New Community Press, 1976.

Rotter, J.B. Generalized expectancies for internal versus external control of reinforcement. *Psychological Monographs* 80 (1966).

Rouman, J. School children's problems as related to parental factors. *Journal of Education Research* 50 (1956):105-12.

Rubel, R.J. *The Unruly School*. Lexington, Mass.: Lexington Books, D.C. Heath and Company, 1976.

Ryan, C. *The Open Partnership: Equality in Running the Schools*. New York: McGraw-Hill, 1976.

Sagan, E. *Cannibalism: Human Aggression and Cultural Form*. New York: Harper, 1974.

Sanders, W.B. *Juvenile Offenders for a Thousand Years*. Chapel Hill, N.C.: University of North Carolina Press, 1970.

Sanders, W.B. *Juvenile Delinquency*. New York: Praeger, 1976.

Sarason, S. *The Culture of the School and the Problem of Change*. Boston: Allyn and Bacon, 1971.

Sarason, S.B.; Davidson, K.S.; Lighthall, F.F.; Waite, R.R.; and Ruebush, B.K. *Anxiety in Elementary School Children*. New York: John Wiley, 1960.

Sarata, B.P.V. Alienation-education as a paradigm for delinquency reduction. *Journal of Criminal Justice* 4 (1976):123-32.

Sarbin, T.R. and Allen, V.L. Role theory. In *The Handbook of Social Psychology* 2d ed. vol. 1. Edited by G. Lindzey and E. Aronson. Reading, Mass: Addison-Wesley, 1968.

Schab, F. Cheating in high school: differences between the sexes. *Journal of the National Association of Women Deans and Counselors* 33 (1969):39-42.

Schafer, W.E. Participation in interscholastic athletics and delinquency: a preliminary study. *Social Problems* 17 (1969):40-47.

Schafer, W.E. and Olexa, C. *Tracking and Opportunity: The Locking-Out Process and Beyond*. Scranton: Chandler, 1971.

Schafer, W.E. and Polk, K. Delinquency and the schools. In President's Commission on Law Enforcement and Administration of Justice, *Task Force Report: Juvenile Delinquency and Youth Crime*. Washington, D.C.: Government Printing Office, 1967.

Schmidt, W.E. and Tyler, V.O. The 'pinpointing effect' vs. the 'diffusion effect' of peer influence. *Psychology in the Schools* 12 (October 1975):485.

Schwartz, S. A new way to fight school vandalism. *American School and University* 45 (June 1973):54-55.

Seeman, M. On the meaning of alienation. *American Sociological Review* 24 (1959):783-91.

Serbin, L.A. and O'Leary, K.D. How nursery schools teach girls to shut up. *Psychology Today* 9 (December 1975):57.

Sexton, P.C. *American School: A Sociological Analysis.* Englewood Cliffs, N.J.: Prentice-Hall, 1967.
Shaw, C. and McKay, H.D. *Juvenile Delinquency in Urban Areas.* Chicago: University of Chicago Press, 1942.
Sherif, M. Integrating field work and laboratory in small group research. *American Sociological Review* 11 (1954):759-71.
Shibutani, T. Reference groups as perspectives. *American Journal of Sociology* 60 (1955):562-69.
Shore, M. Psychological theories of the causes of antisocial behavior. *Crime and Delinquency* 17 (1971):456-68.
Shore, M.F. and Massimo, J.L. Comprehensive vocationally oriented psychotherapy for adolescent delinquent boys: a follow-up study. *American Journal of Orthopsychiatry* 36 (1966):609-15.
―――. Five years later: a follow-up study of comprehensive vocationally oriented psychotherapy. *American Journal of Orthopsychiatry* 39 (1969): 769-73.
Shore, M.F.; Massimo, J.L.; Mack, R.; and Malasky, C. Studies of psychotherapeutic change in adolescent delinquent boys: the role of guilt. *Psychotherapy: Theory, Research and Practice* 5 (1968):85-88.
Short, J.F., Jr. *Gang Delinquency and Deviant Subcultures.* New York: Harper and Row, 1968.
―――. Gang delinquency and anomie. In *Anomie and Deviant Behavior.* Edited by M.B. Clinard. New York: Free Press, 1964.
Short, J.F., Jr. Differential association with delinquent friends and delinquent behavior. *Pacific Sociological Review* 1 (1958):20-25.
Short, J.F., Jr. Differential association and delinquency. *Social Problems* 4 (1957):233-39.
Short, J.F. and Nye, F.I. The extent of unrecorded juvenile delinquency: tentative conclusions. *Journal of Criminal Law, Criminology and Police Science.* (1958), p. 49.
Short, J.F. and Strodtbeck, F.L. *Group Process and Gang Delinquency.* Chicago: University of Chicago Press, 1965.
Siegman, A.W. Personality variables associated with admitted criminal behavior. *Journal of Consulting Psychology* 26 (1962):199.
Silberberg, N.E. and Silberberg, M.C. School achievement and delinquency. *Review of Educational Research* 41 (1971):17-31.
Silberman, C.E. *Crisis in the Classroom.* New York: Vintage Books, 1970.
Silberman, M.L. (ed.). *The Experience of Schooling.* New York: Holt, Rinehart, and Winston, 1971.
Silverman, M. and Blount, W.R. *Alienation, Achievement Motivation, and Attitudes Toward School in Economically Disadvantaged Boys.* Tampa: University of Southern Florida, 1970.
Singer, J.L. Fantasy, the foundation of serenity. *Psychology Today* 10 (1976):32-37.

Skinner, B.F. *The Technology of Teaching.* New York: Appleton-Century-Crofts, 1968.

Skrzypek, G.J. Effect of perceptual isolation and arousal on anxiety, complexity preference and novelty preference in psychopathic and neurotic delinquents. *Journal of Abnormal Psychology* 74 (1969):321-29.

Smith, D.C. Vandalism in selected southern California school districts: nature, extent and preventive measures. Unpublished Ph.D. Dissertation, University of Southern California, 1966.

Sorrentino, J.N. *The Concrete Cradle: An Exploration of Juvenile Crime—Its Causes and Cures.* Los Angeles: Wollstonecraft, 1975.

Spady, W.G. Lament for the letterman: effects of peer status and extracurricular activities on goals and achievement. *American Journal of Sociology* 75 (1970):680-702.

Speck, R. and Attneave, C. *Family Networks.* New York: Random House, 1973.

Spergel, I. *Street Gang Worker: Theory and Practice.* Reading, Mass.: Addison-Wesley, 1966.

──── . *Racketville, Slumtown, Haulburg.* Chicago: University of Chicago Press, 1964.

St. John, N. The elementary classroom as a frog pond: self-concept, sense of control and social context. *Social Forces* 49 (June 1971):581-95.

Stanfield, R. The interaction of family variables and gang variables in the aetiology of delinquency. *Social Problems* 13 (1966):411-12.

Stanford Research Institute. *Program for the prevention and control of school vandalism and related burglaries.* Final report, Menlo Park, Calif., June 1975.

Stern, G.G. *People in Context: Measuring Person-Environment Congruence in Education and Industry.* New York: John Wiley, 1970.

Stevens, D.H. *Annual report of the superintendent of common schools, 1844.* Albany: Carroll and Cook, 1845.

Stewart, D.J. Effects of social reinforcement on dependency and aggressive responses of psychopathic, neurotic and subcultural delinquents. *Journal of Abnormal Psychology* 79 (1972):76-83.

Stinchcombe, A. *Rebellion in a High School.* Chicago: Quadrangle, 1964.

Stoops, E. and King-Stoops, J. *Discipline or Disaster?* Bloomington, Ind.: The Phi Delta Kappa Educational Foundation, 1972.

Stott, D.H. Sociological and psychological explanations of delinquency. *International Journal of Social Psychiatry,* Congress Edition, 1964, pp. 35-43.

Stratton, J.R. Differential identification and attitudes toward the law. *Social Forces* 46 (1967):256-62.

Strauss, G.H. School as power structure: student attitudes toward high school policies, student power position, and student rights. *Education and Urban Society* 7 (1974):3-27.

Strodtbeck, F. and Short, J. Aleatory risks versus short-run hedonism in explanation of gang action. *Social Problems* 12 (1964):127-40.

Bibliography

Stuart, R.V.; Tripodi, T.; Jayaratne, S.; and Camburn, D. An experiment in social engineering in serving the families of predelinquents. *Journal of Abnormal Child Psychology* 4 (1976):243-61.

Stulken, E.H. Education prevents delinquency. *The Phi Delta Kappan* 15 (April 1933):49.

Subcommittee on Economic Opportunity. *Oversight Hearing on Safe School Study*. Washington, D.C.: Committee on Education and Labor, 95th Congress, 2d Session), 1978.

Subcommittee to Investigate Juvenile Delinquency. School violence and vandalism: the nature, extent, and cost of violence and vandalism in our nation's schools. Washington, D.C.: Committee on Judiciary, 94th Congress, 1st Session, 1975.

Subcommittee to Investigate Juvenile Delinquency of the Committee on the Judiciary, U.S. Senate. *Challenge for the Third Century: Education in a Safe Environment—Final Report on the Nature and Prevention of School Violence and Vandalism*. Washington, D.C.: U.S. Government Printing Office, 1977.

Sugarman, B. Involvement in youth culture, academic achievement and conformity in school. *British Journal of Sociology* 18 (1967):151-64.

Sutherland, E.H. and Cressey, D.R. *Criminology*, 10th. ed. Philadelphia: Lippincott, 1978.

Sutherland, E.H. and Cressey, D.R. *Criminology*. 9th ed. Philadelphia: Lippincott, 1974.

Tappan, P. *Juvenile Delinquency*. New York: McGraw-Hill, 1949.

Task Force 1974. *The Adolescent, Other Citizens, and Their High Schools*. New York: McGraw-Hill, 1975.

Teacher 91 (January 1974):25.

The terror in the schools. *New York Post* 17 June 1975, pp. 4, 61.

Thaw, R.F. An acts against property model: a case study. An extension of the traditional vandalism model. Unpublished Doctoral Dissertation, United States International University (San Diego), 1976.

Thomas, D.R.; Becker, W.C.; and Armstrong, M. Production and elimination of disruptive classroom behavior by systematically varying teacher's behavior. In *Learning in Social Settings*. Edited by Matthew W. Miles and W.W. Charters, Jr. Boston: Allyn and Bacon, Inc., 1970.

Thomas C. W.; Kreps, G.A.; and Cage, R.J. An application of compliance theory to the study of juvenile delinquency. *Sociology and Social Research* 61 (1977):156-75.

Thomas, P. *Down These Mean Streets*. New York: Knopf, 1967.

Thibaut, J.W. and Kelly, H.H. *The Social Psychology of Groups*. New York: John Wiley, 1959.

Thrasher, F. *The Gang*. Chicago: University of Chicago Press, 1936.

Thurston, J.R. *Classroom Behavior: Background Factors Psycho-Social Correlates*. Madison, Wis.: Wisconsin State Department of Public Welfare, 1964.

Time 14 Nov. 1977:62-75.
Time 22 March 1976.
Timpane, M., et al. *Youth Policy in Transition*. Santa Monica, Calif.: RAND Corporation, 1976.
Tittle, C.R.; Villemez, W.J.; and Smith, D.R. The myth of social class and criminality. *American Sociological Review* 43 (1978):643-56.
Tobias, J. The affluent suburban male delinquent. *Crime and Delinquency* 16 (1970):273-79.
To catch a thief, try microwaves. *American School and University* 43 (July 1971):47-9.
Trent, J.W., et al. Technology, education, and human development. *The Educational Record* 67 (Spring 1965):87-93.
Turner, J.H. *The Structure of Sociological Theory*. Homewood, Ill.: The Dorsey Press, 1978.
Turner, R. *The Social Context of Ambition*. San Francisco: Chandler, 1964.
Turner, R.H. Sponsored and contest mobility and the school system. *American Sociological Review* 25 (1960):855-67.
Tyack, C. and Berkowitz, M. The man nobody liked: toward a social history of the truant officer, 1840-1940. *American Quarterly* 29 (Spring 1977):31-54.
Tyack, D. Ways of seeing: an essay on the history of compulsory schooling. *Harvard Educational Review* 46 (Summer 1976):355-89.
_____. *The One Best System*. Cambridge, Mass.: Harvard University Press, 1974.
Uniform Crime Reports. *Crime in the United States 1975*. Washington, D.C.: Department of Justice, 1975.
U.S. Senate Subcommittee on the Judiciary. *Our Nation's Schools—A Report Card: "A" in School Violence and Vandalism*. Preliminary Report of the Subcommittee to Investigate Juvenile Delinquency, Committee Print, 94th Congress, 1st Session. Washington, D.C.: Government Printing Office, 1975.
Vandalism. *Nation's Schools* 92 (December 1973):31-37.
VandenBerg, S. Student alienation: orientation toward and perceptions of aspects of educational social structure. *Urban Education*, 10 (1975):262-78.
Varner, S.E. *School Dropouts*. Washington, D.C.: National Education Association, 1967.
Veld Huisen, J. Insiders and outsiders in an urban high school. Unpublished Doctoral Dissertation, University of Oregon, 1972.
Velten, E. A laboratory task for induction of mood states. *Behavioral Research and Therapy* 6 (1968):473-82.
Veroff, J. and Feld, S. *Marriage and Work in America*. New York: Van Nostrand Reinhold, 1970.
Victor, J.B. and Halverson, C.F. Behavior problems in elementary school children: a follow-up study. *Journal of Abnormal Child Psychology* 4 (1976):17-29.

Victor, J.B.; Halverson, C.F., Jr.; Inoff, G.; and Buczkowski, H.J. Objective behavior measures of first- and second-grade boys' free play and teacher's rating on a behavior problem checklist. *Psychology in the Schools* 10 (1973):439-43.

Vinter, R.D. and Sarri, R.C. Malperformance in the public school: a groupwork approach. *Social Work* 10 (1965):3-13.

Violence in Evanston. *Time* 2 June 1975, p. 29.

Violence in the schools: everybody has solutions. *American School Board Journal* 162 (January 1975):27-37.

Violence in schools now seen as norm across the nation. *New York Times* 14 June 1975.

Violent Schools—Safe Schools: The Safe School Study Report to Congress. U.S. Department of Health, Education, and Welfare, Washington, D.C.: U.S. Government Printing Office, 1977.

VonBrock, R.C. Coping with suspensions and the Supreme Court. *National Association of Secondary School Principals Bulletin* 61, no. 407 March (1977):68-76.

Voss, H.L. Differential association and delinquent behavior. *Social Problems* 12 (1964):78-85.

Wade, A.L. Social processes in the act of juvenile vandalism. In *Criminal Behavior Systems*. Edited by M. Clinard and R. Quinney. New York: Holt, Rinehart, and Winston, 1973.

Walberg, H.J. Urban schooling and delinquency: toward and integrative theory. *American Educational Research Journal* 9 (1972):285-300.

Wallerstein, I. *University in Turmoil: The Politics of Change.* New York: Atheneum, 1969.

Ward, C. (ed.). *Vandalism.* London: The Architectural Press, 1973.

Warren, D. Neighborhood and community contexts in help seeking: problem coping and mental health. Data Analysis Monograph. Ann Arbor, Mich.: Program in Community Effectiveness, University of Michigan, 1976.

Warren, D. and Clifford, D. The decision to seek help: a pathways approach to mental health services delivery. Ann Arbor, Mich.: Program on Community Effectiveness, University of Michigan, 1973.

Warren, R.; Rose, S.; and Bergunder, A. *The Structure of Urban Reform: Community Decision Organizations on Stability and Change.* Lexington, Mass.: Lexington Books, D.C. Heath, 1974.

Washington State Department of Social and Health Services. Overview of House Bill 371. Olympia, Wash.: 1977.

Watternberg, W.W. Deviancy and the disadvantaged. In *Education and the Disadvantaged.* Edited by N. Goldman. Milwaukee: Proceedings of a Conference on the Disadvantaged at the University of Wisconsin (Milwaukee), 1967.

Webb, T.E. and Oski, F.A. Behavioral status of young adolescents with iron deficiency anemia. *Journal of Special Education* 8 (1974):153-56.

Weinberg, C. Achievement and school attitudes of adolescent boys as related to behavior and occupational status of families. *Social Forces* 42 (1964): 462-66.

Weinstein, R. and Morover, J. A comparative analysis of health and welfare organizations. *Pacific Sociological Review* (1977) pp. 79-103.

Weiner, R.; Frieze, I., Kukla, A.; Reed, L.; Rest, S.; and Rosenbaum, R.M. *Perceiving the Causes of Success and Failure*. New York: General Learning Press, 1968.

Weiss, J.N. Vandalism: an environmental concern. *NASSP Bulletin* 58 (1974):6-9.

Wenk, E. Schools and the community: a model for participatory problem solving. In *Delinquency Prevention and the Schools: Emerging Perspectives*. Edited by E. Wenk. Beverly Hills, Calif.: Sage Publications, 1976.

———. Schools and delinquency prevention. *Crime and Delinquency Literature* 6 (1974):236-58.

Werry, J.S. and Quay, H.C. Observing the classroom behavior of elementary school children. *Exceptional Children* 35 (1969):461-70.

Werts, C.E. and Watley, D.J. A student's dilemma: big fish—little pond or little fish—big pond. *Journal of Counseling Psychology* 16 (1969):14-19.

West, D.J. *Present Conduct and Future Delinquency*. New York: International Universities Press, 1969.

West, W.G. Adolescent deviance and the school. *Interchange* 6 (1975):49-55.

Westin, Jeane. Let's end family warfare. *The PTA Magazine* 68 (November 1973):14.

Wheeler, C.A. The relationship between psychopathy and the weak automatization cognitive style. *FCI Research Reports* 6 (1974).

Wheeler, K. and Wheeler, M. School phobia. *Instructor* 83 (May 1974):16.

White, M.A. *School Disorder, Intelligence and Social Class*. New York: Teachers College Press, 1966.

White, R. Motivation reconsidered: the concept of competence. *Psychological Review* 66 (1959):297-333.

Whitehill, M.; DeMyer-Gapin, S.; and Scott, T.J. Stimulation-seeking in antisocial preadolescent children. *Journal of Abnormal Psychology* 85 (1976):101-4.

White House Fact Sheet: Youth education and employment initiative. Washington, D.C.: The White House, 10 Jan. 1980.

Wicker, A.W. Undermanning, performances, and students' subjective experiences in behavior settings of large and small high schools. *Journal of Personality and Social Psychology* 10 (1968):255-61.

Wiley, D. Another hour, another day: quantity of schooling—A potent path for policy. *Studies of Educational Processes* July 1973.

Wiley, D. and Harnischfeger, A. Explosion of a myth: quantity of schooling and exposure to instruction, major educational vehicles. *Educational Researcher* 3 (1974):7-12.

Williams, R.L. and Cole, S. Self-concept and school adjustment. *Personnel and Guidance Journal* 46 (1968):478-81.

Wilson, J.Q. Crime in society and schools. *Educational Researcher* 5 (May 1976):4.

Winter, S.K.; Griffith, J.C.; and Kolb, D.A. Capacity for self-direction. In *Learning in Social Settings*. Edited by Matthew W. Miles and W.W. Charters, Jr. Boston: Allyn and Bacon, Inc., 1970.

Wirtz, W. (as interviewed by H. Shane). The academic test score decline: are facts the enemy of truth? *Phi Delta Kappan* 59 (October 1977):83-86.

Wittes, S. *Power and People: High Schools in Crisis*. Ann Arbor, Mich.: Institute for Social Research, The University of Michigan, 1970.

Wolfgang, M.E. The culture of youth. *Juvenile Delinquency and Youth Crime*. President's Commission on Law Enforcement and Administration of Justice. Washington, D.C.: U.S. Government Printing Office, 1967.

Worcester, E.; Ashbaugh, C.; Clarkson, F.E.; and Hayden, B.S. The relationship of family background factors and neurological status to hyperactivity in a normal class setting. Paper presented at the annual meeting of the American Psychological Association, 1972.

Wright, J.S. Student attendance: what relates where? *NASSP Bulletin* 62 (February 1978):115-17.

('Yes') to a self-directive day. *Phi Delta Kappan* 53 (October 1971):111-12.

Yinger, J.M. *Toward a Field Theory of Behavior*. New York: McGraw-Hill, 1965.

Yudin, L.W., et al. School dropout of college bound: study in contrast. *The Journal of Educational Research* 67 (October 1973):87-93.

Zaleznik, A. Interpersonal relations in organizations. In *Handbook of Organizations*. Edited by James G. March. Chicago: Rand McNally and Co., 1965.

Zeitlin, H. Phoenix reports on high school misbehavior. *Personnel and Guidance Journal* 35 (1957):384-87.

Zeizel, J. *Schoolhouse*. Newsletter from Educational Facilities Laboratory, New York, March 1974, pp. 1-7

Ziller, R.C. *The Social Self*. New York: Pergamon Press, 1973.

Ziller, R.; Hagey, J.; Smith, M.; and Long, B. Self-esteem: a self-social construct. *Journal of Consulting and Clinical Psychology* 33 (1969):84-95.

Zimbardo, P.G. A field experiment in auto shaping. *Time* 28 February 1969, pp. 62-65.

Zimmerman, E.H. and Zimmerman, J. The alteration of behavior in a special classroom situation. *Journal of the Experimental Analysis of Behavior* 5 (1962):59-60.

Index

Absenteeism, 55, 167–178; causes of, 170–175; during nineteenth century, 55; increasing rates of, 167–169; prevention of, 175–177; problems caused by, 169

Alienation, 53, 145, 176, 241, 246. *See also* Mental health

American Institutes for Research, 42

Anxiety, 53; among teachers, 81. *See also* Mental health

Appalachian children, 91–97.

Alternative education and schools, 146–49; lack of violence in, 59. *See also* Teaching methods.

Authority and power: and absenteeism, 171; effect of on schools, 145, 164, 171, 237; loss of respect for, 26; respect for, 93; students' lack of, 236, 239; students' opportunity and motivations for, 55, 59; youthful dislike of, 234

Baker v. *Owen,* 74
Bannister v. *Paradis,* 76
Behavior modification techniques, 134
Behaviorism, 33
Berkeley's Center for the Study of Higher Education, 35
Bishop v. *Cermenaro,* 76
Board of Curators of the University of Missouri v. *Horowitz,* 74
Burnside v. *Byers,* 72

Cary v. *Piphus,* 74
Civil Rights. *See* Constitutional Rights; Court decisions
Cognitive Balance Theory, 116–118
Compulsory education laws, 9
Conduct disorder, 130, 131–138. *See also* Mental health
Constitutional rights, 3, 72, 74, 75–79, 104, 147
Corporal punishment, 74; throughout history, 5, 6, 7–8, 10–11, 14, 15

Costs of crime, 18, 19, 212, 220, 222–24, 229, 237, 243. *See also* Vandalism

Counseling: children under treatment in guidance clinics, 129; inadequacy of vocational guidance, 42; peer counseling centers, 65; problem diagnosis and counseling, 105

Court decisions, 23–24, 71–79, 103. *See also* Constitutional Rights; Supreme Court; and individual cases

Crime: categories of, 32; as challenge by antisystem students, 189; confusion over definition of criminal acts, 18, 210; group crime, prevalence of, 140; motivation for, 188–89

Crimes against property. *See* Vandalism

Crossen v. *Fatsi,* 75

Curriculum: ability tracking, 58, 125; compensatory education for disadvantaged youth, 146; shortcomings of, 187, 191–192; special programs for disruptive youth, 134–137. *See also* Teaching methods

Davis v. *Firment,* 75

Definitions: confusion over, 18, 210; of criminal behavior, 19; of deviant behavior, 151–52, 166; of juvenile crime, 139; of types of crimes, 19; of vandalism, 210

Deviant or disruptive behavior, 152–166; a quest for challenge, 188; rebellion, 160; retreatism, 159; ritualistic behavior, 157–158; sequence of, 163; and socioeconomic status, 157

Discipline: connection between in school and family, 4; "Crisis of disciplinary roles of educators, 101–115; doctrine of "in loco parentis" and, 4, 14, 103; historical,

4-7; need for effective, 88, 147; role conflict in relation to, 103-104, 110; special classes for discipline problems, 147-48.
Dixon v. *Alabama State Board of Education,* 73
Dropping out, 55
Drug use, 74, 141, 143, 144
Due process, 18, 73, 106

Educational Resources Education Center (ERIC), 243
English schools, 11-12; 42
Employment, theory of, 183-186
Environment: objective, 50; subjective, 50
Expulsion, 64, 148

Family background, 34-36, 43; and absenteeism, 171; and discipline, 4; and vandalism, 240
Fear: and absenteeism, 173; among students, 20, 24-25; among teachers, 85
Flow state, 184-85

Gallup Poll of Public Attitudes Toward Education, 17, 32
Goals, 181-82, 186. *See also* Grading system, rewards; scholastic achievement
Goss v. *Lopez,* 73, 78
Government programs, reports, and studies: Bayh report, 243; Department of Health, Education and Welfare (HEW), 22; Justice Department, 22; Law Enforcement Assistance Administration (LEAA), 249; National Commission on Resources for Youth, 66; Office of Juvenile Justice and Delinquency Prevention (OJJDP), 22, 77; Research for Better Schools (RBS), 249; Safe School Study, 19-20, 24, 173, 249, 250; Senate Subcommittee to Investigate Juvenile Delinquency, 17, 21.

Grading system, 58, 119-20. *See also* Rewards; Scholastic achievement

Hasson v. *Boothby,* 72

Immaturity, 129-130. *See also* Counseling; Mental health
"In loco parentis," doctrine of, 4, 14, 103
In re Gault, 73
Ingraham v. *Wright,* 74, 78

Juvenile delinquency. *See* Teenage gangs

Kettering Foundation's Task Force, 1974, 47

Law Enforcement Assistance Administration (LEAA): and Research for Better Schools (RBS), 249
Legislation, federal, 21-22
Leonard v. *School Committee in Attleboro,* 75

Mental health, 51, 53, 56-57, 67, 145, 176, 241, 246; conduct disorder, 130, 131-138; immaturity as cause of behavior problems, 129-30; personality disorder, 130; special classes for emotionally disturbed, 129-30; of teachers ("combat neurosis"), 81-89
Misbehaviors, cause of, 33-47
Motivation theory, 181-192

National Commission on Resources for Youth, 66
National Educational Association, 32

Objective person, 50
Office of Juvenile Justice and Delinquency Prevention (OJJDP), 22, 77
O'Rourke v. *Walleer,* 72

Peer group: as cause of misbehavior, 36, 43; peer counseling centers, 65;

Index

popularity and delinquent's behavior, 58; reinforcement of deviancy, 154, 161; and vandalism, 205–06. *See also* Subcultures; Teenage gangs
Person-environment congruence or fit, 49–57
Person growth, 58
Poverty: and criminal or disruptive act, 92, 97
Procunier v. *Navarette,* 79
Pig Sky v. *Sellmeyer,* 76

Recreation, 67
Regional codes of conduct, 92
Religion: freedom of, 75; influence of education, 7
Reporting of data, 3; on absenteeism rates, 178; misconceptions because of changes in, 3–4; need for adequate, 107; on vandalism, 209–10, 213, 244
Research for Better Schools (RBS), 249
Research, recommended, 47
Rewards, 181, 186. *See also* Grades
Richards v. *Thurston,* 76
Riots, 78
Roger v. *Board of Education of C.R. Coblentz* School, 76
Rules: rule adjudication, 104; rule development, 104; rule-breaking, tolerance of, 26, 45, 71

Safe School Study (HEW), 19–20, 24, 173, 249, 250
Scholastic ability and achievement, 53, 57, 59, 131, 144–45, 181, 186; and absenteeism, 173; and deviant behavior, 153, 154–57; structural change to improve, 146; and violent behavior, 119–21, 125. *See also* Grading system; Rewards
School administrator: lack of support for teachers, 84; need to face problem of school crime, 249; role of, 20, 85–86; and solutions to absenteeism, 169; and vandalism, 249

School buildings: historical, 9, 10; need for occupation of, 227; recommended modifications of, 207, 248; utilization of space for community socialization organizations, 65
School community relations, 61–70
School personnel: need for reciprocal role relations between, 108; role-related problems, 108–113. *See also* School administrator; Teaching method; Teachers
School violence: geographic distribution of, 20
Scott v. *Board of Education,* 76
Security systems: financing for, 3, 18; need for, 190; patrolling parts of school, 104; student response to, 164; and vandalism, 219, 238, 247
Senate Subcommittee to Investigate Juvenile Delinquency, 17, 21
Size of schools, 18, 59; and absenteeism, 173
Socialization, youthful, 61–70, 191, 240; social network, 61–63; youth advocates, 68
Society: as cause of misbehavior, 42–45
Socioeconomic status of and deviancy, 92, 97, 157
Soviet schools, 110–111
Standards of institutional behavior, 57
Stanford Research Institute Study on Vandalism, 243, 250
Stromberg v. *French,* 76
Student advocacy, 107
Student revolts, historically: 6, 12. *See also* Violence
Subcultures, deviant or youthful, 115–18, 130, 139–149, 182–183; drug culture, 141, 143, 144; teenage gangs, 37, 49, 84, 122, 129, 141–142, 172, 237–238; "theft subculture," 142; and vandalism, 142, 230–235, 237–239; varieties of, 233–235

Supreme Court, 14, 18, 73, 74, 75. *See also* Court decisions; Individual court cases

Suspensions: as response to misbehavior, 64; in-school suspension centers, 105, 176

Teacher Effectiveness Training Program, 39

Teachers: as victims of violence, 81–89; blamed for student misbehavior, 37–40; disciplinary roles of, 101–115; interest in students. *See also* School personnel; Teaching methods

Teaching methods: compensatory education for disadvantaged youth, 146; crime prevention programs and, 146; crisis teaching, 105–106; historical, 8, 12; special programs for disruptive youth, 134–37; team teaching, 106. *See also* Alternative education and schools; Curriculum; Teachers

Teaching, quality of, 25, 38, 42

Teenage gangs and juvenile delinquency, 37, 49, 84, 122, 129, 141–142; and absenteeism, 172; historical, 9, 37, 49; and vandalism, 237–238. *See also* Peer group; Subcultures

Tinker v. *Des Moines Independent School District No. 281*, 73

Uniform Crime Reports, 139–140
Universities, 8, 12

Vandalism, 19, 24, 139, 193–209, 209–218, 219–228, 243–251; aesthetics of, 193–198; Bayh report on, 243; confusion over definition of, 209–210; consequences of, 245–246, 248; conventional v. ideological, 245; and deviancy, 210; Educational Resources Information Center (ERIC) searches on, 243; impact of, 221; increases in, 209; motives for, 193–209, 237–238, 245–246; as national problem, 244; prevention of, 209–218, 225–228, 238–240, 246–250; reporting of, 209–210, 213, 244; and risk, 205–206; sex trends and, 244–245; Stanford Research Institute report on, 243, 250; and subcultures, 142, 230–235; as symbolic action, 229, 239; types of, 214–215, 224–225, 245

Victims: "society of," 31; teachers as, 81–89

Violence: apparent or perceived increases in, 17–18; and failure in school, 119–121, 125; and flow state, 185–186; as a form of deviancy, 160; historical perspective on, 3–15; non-ideological v. ideological, 12; reported increases in, 103; school responses to, 161. *See also* Student revolts

West Virginia State Board of Education v. *Barnette*, 75
Wood v. *Strickland*, 74, 79

Yoo v. *Moynihan*, 75
Youth advocates, 68
Youth in Illinois Project of the Institute for Juvenile Research, 229

About the Contributors

Vernon L. Allen is professor of psychology at the University of Wisconsin, Madison. He received the Ph.D. in social psychology from the University of California, Berkeley, and was a postdoctoral Fellow of Wolfson College, Oxford, and a Fellow at the Netherlands Institute for Advanced Study in the Humanities and Social Sciences. He is editor of *Psychological Factors in Poverty, Children as Teachers*, and (with J. Levin) *Cognitive Learning in Children*.

Beatrice F. Birman is currently a policy analyst in the Department of Education's Office of Planning and Budget. Dr. Birman completed undergraduate work in sociology at Barnard College and graduate work in sociology of education, sociology, and counseling psychology at Stanford University. In addition to writing about high-school absenteeism, her publications and papers have focused on problems in the local implementation of federal education programs and different patterns of interaction between high-school students and their counselors. Her current work addresses finance implications of the delivery of educational services to handicapped children.

Peter D. Blauvelt is chief of security services for the Prince George's County, Maryland, public schools. He designed, implemented, and now supervises his school district's security system. A former police officer and special agent for the Naval Investigative Service, Mr. Blauvelt is a graduate of the University of Maryland and has served as lecturer in school security to numerous professional associations, including the National Association of Secondary School Principals, the National Academy for School Executives, and the American Association of School Administrators. He is the author of many practical training materials for school security personnel and is president of the Institute for Reduction of Crime, a firm that provides specialized security training and other services to school districts and to state departments of education. He is coauthor of *Controlling Crime in the School*.

Alfred M. Bloch, M.D., is an assistant clinical professor of psychiatry at UCLA's School of Medicine. Dr. Bloch is a psychiatrist, psychologist, and psychoanalyst. He has written extensively on stress, especially as it pertains to teaching. He has consulted with government agencies at every level, including the U.S. Senate, the California Legislature, and various school boards. Dr. Bloch serves as the director of the Bloch Medical Clinic, which has been involved in the evaluation and treatment of more than 1,000 teachers who have experienced severely disturbing problems while working in classrooms. Currently, he is president of the Psychiatry Section of the Los Angeles County Medical Association.

Ruth Reinhardt Bloch received the B.A. in English from UCLA, where she also served as an editor in the Department of Orthopedic Surgery and senior writer in the Department of Surgery. She has done extensive research and writing in the fields of psychiatry, psychology, cardiology, ophthalmology, orthopedic surgery, and genetics. In addition to serving as a research assistant in the area of teacher stress, she has prepared a number of grant proposals in the fields of stress and suicidology.

James W. Coleman received the Ph.D. from the University of California at Santa Barbara. He is currently an associate professor in the Department of Social Sciences at California Polytechnic State University, San Luis Obispo. He has served as a lecturer at Chapman College at Vandenberg Air Force Base and as an instructor at Ventura College.

Mihaly Csikszentmihalyi is professor and chair, Committee on Human Development, Department of Behavioral Sciences, at the University of Chicago. He received the Ph.D. in human development from the University of Chicago in 1965. His research interests include the study of creativity and optimal psychological functioning. He is the author of *Beyond Boredom and Anxiety* and coauthor of *The Creative Vision.*

Michael H. Ducey wrote his chapters for this book while working on the Youth in Illinois Project of the Institute for Juvenile Research. He received the Ph.D. in sociology from the University of Chicago in 1974. His dissertation was published as the book *Sunday Morning: Aspects of Urban Ritual* (1977). Before studying sociology, Dr. Ducey was a Jesuit and worked and studied in India and the United States for fourteen years. Since 1978, he has been working in Wisconsin as a planner for the state mental health agency and is actively involved in political organizing around the energy issue.

Daniel L. Duke is a professor of education at Stanford University. He has conducted research on various aspects of youth behavior problems, including the etiology of student misconduct and the effectiveness of alternative schools for troubled students. He has written many articles on classroom management, restructuring school organization to reduce behavior problems, and policy implications of student behavior. In addition he is the author of *Managing Student Behavior Problems* (1980) and the editor of the 1979 volume of the National Society for the Study of Education, *Classroom Management.*

Arthur H. Goldsmith is a partner in the Boston law firm Goldsmith, Little & Guisbond; he is a member of the Massachusetts, New Jersey, and Pennsylvania Bars. Mr. Goldsmith has previously served as associate counsel and research assistant at Boston University, has worked for the Pennsylvania Department of Education, helping to recodify their school laws, and has worked for the New Jersey Attorney General's Office. He also served on the Massachusetts Legislature's Equal Rights Amendment Commission Task Force on Education. Mr. Goldsmith specializes in constitutional, employment, and educational law and has spoken and published widely on these subjects. Mr. Goldsmith received the A.B. from Lafayette College in 1971 and the J.D. from Temple University School of Law in 1974.

David B. Greenberger is a graduate student in the social psychology program at the University of Wisconsin, Madison. His research focuses on changes made to the physical environment, particularly those involving destruction and vandalism.

David M. Klingel studied clinical psychology at the University of Michigan and worked for several years as an assistant study director on a longitudinal study of adaptation to high school at the University of Michigan's Institute for Social Research. He is currently employed as a research associate in the Survey Research Center of the Institute for Social Research. He has recently coauthored papers on the antecedents and consequences of alienation and involvement in high school and on the impact of low adolescent self-esteem on interpersonal problems. His long-term research interests include the development and modification of aggressive behavior and negative attitudes toward school and strategies for resolving methodological problems encountered in research on deviant behavior.

Richard A. Kulka received the Ph.D. in social psychology from the University of Michigan in 1975. Since that time he has worked as an assistant research scientist in the Survey Research Center at the University of Michigan's Institute for Social Research. His current research interests include social roles and mental health, survey methodology, and person-environment congruence or fit. His other contributions to research on person-environment fit include a methodological critique, "Interaction as Person-Environment Fit," published in a recent issue of *New Directions for Methodology of Behavioral Science*, and an empirical test of the theoretical model presented in this volume (coauthored with David Klingel and David Mann) to be published in the *Journal of Youth and Adolescence.*

Reed Larson is one of a group of researchers at the University of Chicago who are developing the experiential sampling method. With Mihaly Csikszentmihalyi he has used the new method to study peer and family relationships, mood variability, aloneness in daily life, and the classroom experience, as well as juvenile delinquency. He received the Ph.D. from the University of Chicago. Currently he is research director of a Spencer Foundation grant to study intrinsic motivation in education and is a postdoctoral Fellow in the Adolescent

Clinical Research Program at Michael Reese Hospital and the University of Chicago. He has also served as research consultant to the Minnesota Governor's Crime Commission and the Minnesota Department of Corrections.

David W. Mann received the Ph.D. in personality psychology from the University of Michigan in 1975. He has been assistant research scientist and study director in the Research Center for Group Dynamics at the University of Michigan's Institute for Social Research. He currently directs research on alternative secondary-school programs for failing, disruptive students. His published work includes articles on the defensive nature of delinquent behavior in the *American Journal of Orthopsychiatry* (with Martin Gold) and an empirical test of the theoretical model of person-environment fit that appears in this book (coauthored with Richard Kulka and David Klingel) to be published in the *Journal of Youth and Adolescence*.

Adrienne M. Meckel is an advanced doctoral student at Stanford and coauthor of numerous articles with Daniel Duke. Currently she is working with him on a text for beginning teachers, *Teachers' Guide to Classroom Management*. Ms. Meckel is director of the Stanford Secondary Teacher Education Program and has served as a research assistant with the Stanford Teacher Corps.

Gary Natriello is an assistant professor in the Graduate Institute of Education at Washington University in St. Louis. He received the A.B. in English from Princeton University and the A.M. in sociology and the Ph.D. in education from Stanford University. His previous work focused on evaluation systems in educational organizations, patterns in teachers' handling of classroom problems, and the influence of students' perceptions of their likely adult roles on their high-school performance. He is currently conducting a study of the effects of evaluation systems on teacher motivation and a study of the effects of school organization on student behavior problems.

Graeme Newman was educated in Australia, where he was an elementary school teacher and school psychologist. He received the Ph.D. in sociology from the University of Pennsylvania and subsequently worked as a research expert for the United Nations in the area of criminal justice. He is currently professor and associate dean at the School of Criminal Justice, the State University of New York at Albany. Among his published works are *Comparative Deviance, The Punishment Response*, and *Understanding Violence*.

Joan Newman was educated in Australia, where she was an elementary school teacher and school psychologist. She received the M.A. in psychology from the University of Melbourne and the Ph.D. in social psychology from the State University of New York at Albany. Her current position combines teaching developmental psychology in the School of Education at SUNYA and doing clinical work at the University-affiliated Center for Learning Disabilities. Her research has been in the fields of maintaining intrinsic motivation, place in the family, and sibling influences upon personality development.

John C. Phillips received the Ph.D. from the University of Oregon in 1974. He has published several articles on the sociology of sport, concerning academic consequences of participation in school sport and racial discrimination in sport. Dr. Phillips is head of the criminology program at the University of the Pacific and teaches courses in criminology, corrections, social psychology, and sociology of sport. He recently completed a large study of drug abuse, "Poly Drug Use among Youth in San Joaquin County" (with G.H. Lewis).

Herbert C. Quay received the Ph.D. in clinical psychology from the University of Illinois in 1958. He taught at Vanderbilt, Northwestern, Illinois, and Temple before assuming his present position at the University of Miami in 1974. He is the author of more than seventy-five articles and books, including the second edition of *Psychopathological Disorders of Childhood* (with John S. Werry, 1979).

Sarah J. Snider received the B.S., M.A., and Ed.D. from the University of Tennessee. She taught in secondary schools in Virginia and Georgia and at the college level at Carson Newman College and the University of Tennessee. She has published a number of articles related to teaching techniques and classroom management and discipline, including: "Discipline—What Can It Teach?" *Elementary School Journal* (February 1975) and "Classroom Conduct Theory into Practice System," *Action in Teacher Education* (Fall/Winter 1978).

Jacqueline R. Scherer is associate professor of sociology and director of the Center for Community and Human Development at Oakland University (Rochester, Michigan). Dr. Scherer has taught at the University of London, Oakland University, and several community colleges. Her publications include *Contemporary Community: Sociological Illusion or Reality?* (1972); *Annual Editions in Sociology* (editor, 1975-1980); and articles in community studies, education, and religion. She is currently principal investigator in a two-and-one-half-year National Institute of Education grant, "School-Community Social Networks: A Decade of Desegregation."

Richard F. Thaw II is president of Vandalism Prevention Inc., Morgan Hill, California. He has taught at the elementary, secondary, community-college and university levels in California. He has degrees in journalism, public relations, and administration from San Jose State University and received the Ph.D. in leadership and human behavior from United States International University in San Diego.

Vincent Tinto is an associate professor of education and sociology at Syracuse University. He received the Ph.D from the University of Chicago. Dr. Tinto's research has focused on issues of social inequality in higher education in the United States and abroad, especially in Turkey, where he taught for two years as a visiting professor at the Middle East Technical University, Ankara. Currently he is directing a two-year study, funded by the National Institute of Education, on the effect of college and graduate school characteristics upon career attainments of male and female college graduates. He has frequently served as a research consultant for the U.S. Office of Education and for private research firms in the evaluation of national educational levels. His publications include numerous research articles in the *Review of Educational Research, The American Educational Research Journal, Research in Higher Education, The Annual Review of Research in Education,* and *Education and Urban Society.* He was also coauthor of a book for the Carnegie Commission on Higher Education, *Where Colleges Are and Who Attends: Effects of Accessibility on College Attendance* (1971).

Seymour D. Vestermark, Jr., is a university lecturer on the public and private issues of contemporary security practice. He is also a security consultant to government and industry. Mr. Vestermark was graduated from Swarthmore College and Harvard University. He served in the Executive Office of the President of the United States as staff member of a task force charged with developing policies to deal with the aftermath of political assassinations and collective violence. He directed one of the first studies of violence in the public schools and, as a consultant to the U.S. Office of Education, prepared one of that agency's first statements of research needs on problems of school violence and disruption. Mr. Vestermark is an advisory editor of *Assets Protection,* an international security journal, and coauthor of *Controlling Crime in the School.*

April Zweig received the B.A. in psychology from Pitzer College and the M.A.T. and Ph.D. from Northwestern University. She is currently a law student at DePaul University College of Law.

About the Editors

Keith Baker is a social-science analyst in the Office of the Assistant Secretary for Planning and Evaluation, Department of Education. He received the B.A. from Miami University and the M.A. and Ph.D. in sociology from the University of Wisconsin. Dr. Baker has worked on the evaluation staff at the Office of Economic Opportunity and has taught at The Pennsylvania State University. In addition to publishing articles in several journals, he is coauthor of *Prison Education, Comprehensive Services to Rural Poor Familes,* and *Year-Round Schools.*

Robert J. Rubel is assistant director of the Institute of Criminal Justice Studies at Southwest Texas State University in San Marcos. His special area of concern is in the study of crime and violence in public schools. He received the doctorate in urban educational policy studies in 1977 from the University of Wisconsin, Madison. He served as deputy staff director to the Interdepartmental Council to Coordinate All Federal Juvenile Delinquency Programs (U.S. Department of Justice) and as a Visiting Fellow to the Office of Juvenile Justice and Delinquency Prevention (studying school-based violence). Dr. Rubel cofounded the Center for Improved Learning Environments in College Park, Maryland, a nonprofit organization dedicated to providing technical assistance and training to school systems beset by severe violence problems. Dr. Rubel has published extensively in the area of school-based violence; his other book in this area is *The Unruly School* (Lexington Books).